Carl,

Thank you so much
for your constant
encouragment & support!

In Christ,

Allison

12-6-15

A Highway Will Be There

AND THOSE THE LORD HAS RESCUED WILL RETURN

by
Allison Hodges

A Highway Will Be There
Copyright © 2015 by Allison Hodges
Published by CreateSpace, an Amazon company
November 2015

Edited by Laura Armistead

ISBN-13:
978-1517627126

ISBN-10:
1517627125

In memory of my Grandy
(1917-2012)

Thank you for my first laptop. . .
Your gift allowed me to find my passion.

TABLE OF CONTENTS

Introduction | A Letter from the Author   1

Prologue | The Joy of the Redeemed   4

Chapter 1 | Until It Overflows: My Story   11

Chapter 2 | She is My Sister: Angamita Susan   28

Chapter 3 | He Lifted Us Up: A Marriage on The Brink   50

Chapter 4 | The Story in My Heart: The Morrow Crew   64

Chapter 5 | Three Growing Families: The First Trip   81

Chapter 6 | I Will Fight for You: The Doyle Family   113

Chapter 7 | "Dees Ees Af-free-kah": The Second Trip   145

Chapter 8 | The Display of His Splendor:
                 The Children of Family Spirit   170

Chapter 9 | The Road Traveled by The King: The Third Trip   186

Chapter 10 | A Son: Nyakoojo Isaac   211

Epilogue | The Future of Family Spirit and The Masindi Project   232

Notes | A Bibliography   254

Acknowledgements   266

Bonus Material | A 14-Day Devotional   271

About the Author   286

Foreword

"I have something for you to pray about... boy and girl twins born in Masindi to a mother dying of AIDS." This email came in the late summer of 2010, and it may have been the first any of us heard about Masindi — a district in Northern Uganda. It was from a dear friend who had moved to Jinja with a one-way ticket to start a special needs ministry there.

Remarkably, that one-way ticket was on a flight less than a year earlier that included Mandy Gallagher and Anne Morrow — who were taking their first trip to Africa — and Drew and Tara Maddux, who were adopting two boys from Amani Baby Cottage. Also traveling with this group was Josiah Thiesen, a young filmmaker who was beautifully capturing all that was unfolding.

The twins in Masindi had been left at Family Spirit, a school in Masindi that has taken in numerous orphans. Their birthmother, Irene, loved them, but was dying and could no longer care for them. The boy had HIV, and the girl was thought to have cerebral palsy because of her disfigured hands and arms. Family Spirit was overwhelmed at the time, having very little resources and trying to provide care and education for as many as 200 children, many with HIV. So the twins' health was getting worse. Besides HIV, the boy had malaria, pneumonia, and was starving, and the girl had no strength. Their condition was very serious when they were first seen by a medical team from a nearby medical mission.

Two young American nurses, Abigail and Leah, were on this medical team. Of the many kids they saw that day, they were especially concerned about the twins. They returned to Family Spirit many times to check on them in the days ahead, and ultimately Abigail and Leah knew these babies wouldn't make it if they didn't personally take them in. So they took a simple, caring step in faith. They filed for a formal Care Order and welcomed the twins into their home. This saved the twins' lives, and it began more than any of us could have asked for or imagined in all of our lives.

For our family, these twins would ultimately become our beloved son and daughter. Our journey to adopt them would cross our paths with another dear family as they adopted two older Ugandan girls. When we returned home to Nashville, the paths of the Morrow and Doyle families crossed with two other orphaned girls Abigail and Leah had rescued. Both were adopted.

Many other families and communities have gone on to "adopt" Masindi and Family Spirit in their hearts and their missions. Magnificent testimonies, films, photos, and ongoing ministries have since come, bearing witness to this humble place of great beauty and great need.

In all of it, we see simple, caring steps of faith moving mountains of fear and transforming lives. We see our Father in Heaven, orchestrating it all in His great love for the people of Masindi, and His great love for those He sends there. And we see the life-changing, nitty-gritty, redeeming grace of Jesus, perfecting all of our faith one step at a time.

Mike & Mandy Gallagher
Co-Founders
The Chosen & Dearly Loved Foundation

Introduction | A Letter from the Author

January 22, 2013

As I write this introduction, the white keyboard of my laptop has the dust, the remnants, of the red Ugandan dirt on it. I can feel it gritty on my fingers and fresh in my heart. I'm at a loss. But here I am. Available to tell the story that God has made of my life – thus far – and the stories of others that God has brought into my life. All whom God has woven into this magnificent larger story… this story that goes far beyond even the ones mentioned here. I can't make a good word come out, unless it pours from Your mouth into mine, Spirit. Speak Lord, for your servant is listening. (I Sam. 3: 9-10)

This is a story of God's heart for adventure. Of His amazing grace. Of His mind-boggling miracles. Of His mighty, relentless and reckless love. Of the precious orphans He loves, *Oh how He loves.* And of this orphan… born with parents, but waiting for purpose. Born into material blessings, but into spiritual bankruptcy. Never a day without bodily nourishment, but many years without manna, without soul food.

Taste and see that the Lord is good; blessed is the one who takes refuge in him. Fear the Lord, you his holy people, for those who fear him lack nothing. The lions may grow weak and hungry, but those who seek the Lord lack no good thing. Come, my children, listen to me; I will teach you fear of the Lord.

Psalm 34: 8-11

This is a story about adventure, a real life story. Because I believe we serve a God of adventure, a real and living God who has created each of us with a very specific purpose... with a very unique story. Each of us has a part to play that is ours, and ours alone.[1]

So many times in the writing of this book, and in the space between trips, I lost sight of the end goal. I forgot about the finish line. This book is a microcosmic picture of my faith walk, on which I also tend to forget the final destination. Like Scotty Smith has said, "We are Cinderellas with amnesia."[2] We know that there is a fairy-tale to be told, for we are living in the echoes of it, but many times we simply lose all sight and all vision... all faith - that there truly is a happy ending for us in Christ, even in the worst pain and suffering.

Lord, give me the strength to persevere and finish this part of the story. I have counted the cost – it is physical, spiritual, emotional, and eternal. It spans two continents, two countries, two communities and beyond. It is life and death, both now and forever. I will not be able to cross the finish line without you, but may I, through Your power, be able to say in the end, "I did not run or labor in vain" (Phil. 2: 16).

Which of you intending to build a tower, does not sit down first and count the cost, whether he has enough to finish it…

Luke 14: 28

As I was writing this *Introduction*, I accidentally misspelled the first word I ever typed: "Intorduction." Fitting. So it should be known from the onset that this is not a perfect story, and much less is it a perfect telling. But I pray that His perfection is seen through it.

Though I am less than the least of all the Lord's people (Eph. 3: 8), and though I speak with fumbling lips (Ex. 6: 12, 30), God's glory is not limited by my shortcomings and deficiencies. I know that full well. He uses me not in spite of them, but because of them. So where I am weak, I will boast all the more! (2 Cor. 12)

Lord, I love you "personally, passionately, and with great devotion."[3] I pray what is sown in weakness will be raised in power. (1 Cor. 15: 43) ...and I pray, Lord, that it is You who speaks, not I.

The one who calls you is faithful, and he will do it.

I Thessalonians 5: 24

Soli Deo Gloria,

Allison

Prologue | The Joy of the Redeemed

The desert and the parched land will be glad;
the wilderness will rejoice and blossom.
Like the crocus, it will burst into bloom;
it will rejoice greatly and shout for joy.
The glory of Lebanon will be given to it,
the splendor of Carmel and Sharon;
they will see the glory of the Lord, the splendor of our God.
Strengthen the feeble hands, steady the knees that give way;
say to those with fearful hearts,
"Be strong, do not fear;
your God will come, he will come with a vengeance;
with divine retribution he will come to save you."
Then will the eyes of the blind be opened
and the ears of the deaf unstopped.
Then will the lame leap like a deer,
and the mute tongue shout for joy.
Water will gush forth in the wilderness and streams in the desert.
The burning sand will become a pool,
the thirsty ground bubbling springs.
In the haunts where jackals once lay,
grass and reeds and papyrus will grow.
And a highway will be there;
it will be called the Way of Holiness;
it will be for those who walk on that Way.
The unclean will not journey on it;
wicked fools will not go about on it.
No lion will be there, nor any ravenous beast;
they will not be found there.
But only the redeemed will walk there,
and those the Lord has rescued will return.
They will enter Zion with singing;
everlasting joy will crown their heads.
Gladness and joy will overtake them,
and sorrow and sighing will flee away.

Isaiah 35

The Lord laid this passage of scripture on my heart very early in my journeying to Africa. I have returned to it time and again, searching for its endless truth, probing continually for new promise, and holding constantly onto the hope offered within.

I pray these verses for the children, and for Susan and Isaac, mother and father to the 200 plus. What is God writing in their redemption stories today? What things are bursting into bloom along their journeys? And when will I return to see it for myself again? For surely then, we will sing together and praise God hand-in-hand. Gladness and joy will overtake us all, and sorrow and sighing will flee away, even if only briefly.

I always long to see new life, renewed health, new stores of food in the kitchen and new clothing on the children at Family Spirit. New stories of healing, new stories of redemption and rescue. In Isaiah 43:19, as in Isaiah 35, the prophet speaks, "See I am doing a new thing! Now it springs up; do you not perceive it? I am making a way in the wilderness and streams in the wasteland..."

I long for ever-increasing development of the physical structures and facilities... at this writing the boys' dormitory is coming along, and the girls' dormitory and latrines have been completed (real bathrooms with tile on the floor, as opposed to the "pit latrines:" large holes in the dirt). The dining hall is in progress, and changes are happening faster and faster these days. I long for more progress, as I know they do, because we long for more children to find safe haven... and the sweet ones already there, to find the heart of a home. In the physical structures erected there, but also in the Heart of Jesus.

I long for Jesus, more and more, to breathe His Spirit over their farmland, for new workers to find employment, for new crops to grow up, for self-sustainability to take root, slowly, as each new acre is slowly opened to farming. Even more, I long for His Spirit to dance over the children, crowning their heads, raising each precious one up in His Royal Family and for His Royal Purposes.

Each time I have come home from Uganda, I have longed for the next time I would return, longed to see what thing God will do next there on my own journey with Him, too. How will God strengthen my own feeble hands, steady my own weak knees? Water gushes forth in the wilderness there, for me. I never cease, in Uganda, to see glory and splendor in the parched places of my heart. My eyes are opened in new ways and my ears unstopped.

It's not just that I fell in love with Africa or the children or a sister there, it is that I also fall deeper in love with God, every time I go.

And as I began to tell the story of Family Spirit in Masindi, Uganda, the stories of Susan and Isaac, the stories of the children, and much of my own story, before and after Africa, God began to show me the importance of the "highways" in my life. The bridges linking the "befores" and "afters," and the journeys in between, travelling down the varied roads and paths of my life.

The passage in Isaiah 35 speaks, I think, both to God's coming Kingdom (future) and his Kingdom coming (present). There is a heavenly home that awaits us, finally and eternally, *one* day. We also have a glimpse of that glorious inheritance – right now, in our hearts and lives *this* day.
My journeys have given me a small foreshadowing of Heaven. I pray this book gives you a similar window into the heart of our God, who is the same yesterday and today and forever (Heb. 13: 8). And I pray it increases your longing for a final home with Him.

For those who have fully surrendered to Christ and placed their faith in Him alone, our eternal journey is marked. A fixed and secure destination awaits the believer who is still here under Heaven – our salvation has been purchased. However, the process of our sanctification is a continual pilgrimage on this earth. Our faith-walk is a lifelong journey, a series of different roads (mini-journeys, if you will), mapped out and woven together, leading us to Christ at every turn.

I am thankful that my journey intersects with yours, if only for a moment, in the pages between these covers.

In the last months of writing this book, which is itself a collection of journeys that intersect at various crossroads, Adam and I, together with our kids, attended Young Life Family Camp at Windy Gap in Asheville, NC. Dustin Swinehardt was the speaker to the adults that weekend. During each of his talks, he focused on John 4: 43-54 – one man's journey to Jesus.[1]

The theme of Dustin's four talks at Family Camp was very similar to the theme of my writing for the past two years - our journeys to Jesus… the bridges and byways of our adventures with Jesus on this Earth, and the highways we travel and traverse from here to heaven… how Jesus uses journeys to bring us closer to Himself, and ultimately, to bring us home.

Through Dustin, God lavished me with sweet confirmation and encouragement to finish this book, to walk the last mile, to complete just another small leg of my own journey on this earth. As if God weren't good enough, clear enough, or speaking to me loudly enough during his first three talks, Dustin's final message to us that weekend was about his own journeys to Africa.

That is just like our God! He not only gives us a gift, but seals it with a beautiful bow – every time. Not just the cake, but always the icing. Not just meeting our expectations – but always blowing the roof off of them.

I so badly needed this message from The Lord, not only because I constantly desired renewed motivation in writing (a stick-to-it-ness that always comes only from God), but also because I needed reassurance with Africa in general. After having been three times in a year and a half (Fall 2011, Summer 2012 and Christmas 2012), I found myself in the late spring of 2014, with no certain return visits on the horizon. I missed Susan and the kids, I missed Mustafa and Joel and George; I even longed to pay a visit to church friends who had become missionaries to Uganda – Brooke and

Steven Edging, who moved to Kampala from Nashville in the summer of 2013.

I missed the places: Nakumat and Café Java, Adonai Missionary Guest House, and the Masindi Hotel, where Ernest Hemingway used to stay as last point of civilization on safari expeditions. It was Hemingway who said, in *Green Hills of Africa*, "Where a man feels at home, outside of where he's born, is where he's meant to go."[2]

I longed to be in the place, outside Tennessee, that had come to feel like a second home to me. I longed to go...

I missed suicidal boda rides, bumpy bus rides with wind whipping through all the open windows, and miles and miles of lush hills and red clay roads. I missed the incredible mangoes and pineapple. I even missed the Starbucks Via sleeves.

I could fix myself one anytime at home, to be sure, but of course, it wasn't the same without the raw Kakira sugar...[3] the one with "Aslan" on the yellow package. I looked often at the one tiny package perched on my kitchen shelf, carried many miles home from my last trip, and I bolstered myself on so many occasions, "But courage, child: you are between the paws of the TRUE Aslan..." (emphasis mine)[4] even in America.

And almost daily I had to remind myself that God had plans for me to return, "In His perfect timing... In His perfect timing." I would preach patience to myself, and quote Isaiah 55:9, "As the heavens are higher than the earth, so are my ways higher than your ways, and my thoughts higher than your thoughts."

The problem was, the longer time wore on, the more I saw the enemy attacking, the more I heard the accuser lying, the more I doubted God's perfect plans. I doubted His "higher ways," and I doubted even His "highways" (especially the one between Nashville International Airport and the airport in Entebbe!). I missed Masindi more and more– like a reverse-homesickness. I left a piece of my heart in Uganda, and I was missing that part of myself that took root there, as well.

In Dustin Swinehardt's journey, God was using Africa profoundly. God is certainly doing the same in my own life and in our marriage. And even in the lives of my children, God is using Africa as a part of their stories, too, shaping their futures and molding their character and slowly unfolding the plans He has for them.

I pray that you will allow Him, if only through reading this book, to use Africa as a part of your journey with Him, as well.

I pray that He will use this story, this collection of stories, to touch your life. Perhaps He is writing you into the story that He has authored in Masindi, elsewhere in Africa, or anywhere near or far in His vast world beyond. I pray He convinces you that you have a part to play in His Larger Story – through your calling, your church, your children, your community, your city, or in countries abroad.

I pray He encourages you in your purpose and in the plans He has for your life. And I pray He opens your eyes to the many journeys you have travelled in life, how they have led to where you are now and where you are going. And I pray that your ultimate destination is Home to His Heart, both now and in Heaven.

May the journeys of your wilderness wandering spill over with purpose and redemption as God draws you closer to Himself and shines His glory on even your darkest hours. May your seasons of dry, desert wasteland bubble up like springs of water with the splendor of God. Though weeping may endure for the night, may joy come in the morning. (Ps. 30:5)
May God, through this book, strengthen feeble hands and steady knees that give way, my own among them. May He open eyes and ears... Come, Lord Jesus!

May this prologue, like this entire book, remind you of the future promised in the last book of the Bible, of the end that is really the true beginning, which shouts to us all – on every journey – drawing us closer to Jesus and closer to home:

The Spirit and the bride say, "Come!" And let the one who hears say, "Come!" Let the one who is thirsty come; and let the one wishes take the free gift of the water of life… He who testifies to these things says, "Yes, I am coming soon." Amen. Come, Lord Jesus.

Revelation 22: 17, 20

Chapter 1 | Until It Overflows: My Story

I was born in August of 1976. Not two seasons passed before I was baptized. I was raised in a church-going home. We went to church and Sunday school most Sundays, and I was an acolyte there. I was confirmed in the church when I was in middle school. I actively attended Young Life in high school.

It never occurred to me that I was not a Christian.

...Not even when I started drinking in high school. Not even when I became sexually promiscuous. I say "promiscuous," because I didn't actually have sex until college. (Am I sounding like Bill Clinton yet? I hope so, because I am sure this is how I sounded to God when I rationalized my behavior.)

I desired intimacy and romance, fun, adventure and popularity far more than I thought about right or wrong... far more than I thought about what God might want. Far more than I thought about God. Period. Strange that I didn't give a thought in the world to The God of The Universe, seeing as how I was a "Christian." I didn't care about what God wanted. It never even occurred to me to care. I cared about what Allison wanted.

I desired many things, in fact, far more than God: good grades, appearing good to my parents and teachers, doing the "right things" around some, while doing exactly what I wanted around other people. I desired an outward moral appearance, to look motivated and bright. I studied a lot and partook in all the right extra-curricular activities to pursue that goal. I also desired an outward physical appearance: to be thin and to be beautiful.

I ran track for seven years to chase that goal. I ran in other ways, too. I ran from my parents. I ran from life.

…You are like whitewashed tombs, which look beautiful on the outside but on the inside are full of the bones of the dead…

Matthew 23: 27b

We moved to a new city when I was a freshman in high school. To this day, I can still say it was one of the most difficult times in my entire life. (I was my own brand of displaced: a stranger in a strange land.) I left behind my friends, my boyfriend, my home, and my childhood - all in one fell swoop. I spent those next four years running. And searching.

Running from one thing. Searching for the next. Searching for things and people that would fill the gaping hole that was left in me by the things and people that I left back home. High school for me was a strange bridge, a largely empty waiting period - from the life I missed, to the life I desired. It was a no-man's land, forged much alone, as I waited for the day when I left for college… when I left the place that was never my home … and moved to the new place that I would call home for four years.

Don't hear me entirely wrong: I certainly made friends in high school and got involved in extra-curricular activities. And high school held more of my heroes than any other time period, I suppose: the teachers who not only taught me, but shaped and molded me, who simultaneously inspired and anchored me. Heroes to me then, and heroes now, especially as my life's calling has returned to the path laid for me *in large part* by those same teachers… teachers of English, literature, writing, and editing.

My love for writing was planted in elementary and middle school,; it was nourished and sown in high school. Thank you, Mr. Henegar, Mr. Reyelt, Mr. Revelle, Mrs. Steimer, and Nat Worley – a friend with whom I am still in touch! (And who would be so proud that I do not leave prepositions dangling at the end of my sentences, mostly.)[1]

And there were those who planted the eternal seeds, far beyond any school subject, that would encapsulate my passions. My Young Life friends and leaders sowed seeds of faith in me, which would shape literally everything about me, inside and out. (Thank you most especially to Robin and Jonathan).

But only in looking back, can I see that my high school season in Charlotte was one of many highways in my life. To get me from my hometown of Knoxville, my home and my heart, not just to my new life in college, but to my new life in Christ. To my new being and new start.

Therefore, if anyone is in Christ, the new creation has come: The old has gone, the new is here!

2 Corinthians 5: 17

The day I arrived on my college campus, I instantly welcomed the clean slate and fresh start I had so long desired. To be on the same page, again, as everyone else around me. To make my own decisions, chart my own course, to be "free" from (many of) the people and places that had dictated the hardest four years of my young life. The reality of it washed over me, in a mix of hopes and dreams, anticipation and expectation. The certainty of it too, as I was finally closing a chapter in my life that was largely filled with longing. The end, and then the beginning, had finally arrived.

I was in charge. This all sounded about right to my newly-minted, albeit narcissistic, "adult" self. I turned 18 and started college the same week. I attended the university of my choosing. I moved into the dorm that had been my first choice, with my best friend from high school, top choice for a roommate. The first week of school, I approached a guy whom I had chosen out of a crowd, and we dated for the next three years. I took classes, all of which I had chosen, carefully mapping out my life. My new life, captain and chief commander: Me. It all looked, as par for the course of my life, very good on the outside.

And in an interesting twist, I joined a sorority that fall (my top choice, of course) because it was (among other things) across the street from the most beautiful church of my denominational upbringing. I attended that church fairly regularly for the next four years.[2] Rector to students, Stephen Stanley, and the leaders and friends there, played an irreplaceable role in my faith journey. God used them, like my high school Young Life leaders, as seed-planters in my life. But it was through the sorority "I" chose that GOD chose to bring me to Himself. It was through Kappa Delta (and *Greek Life*) that God finally made me new.

I had great plans for my life, my relationships and my social status. God had other plans – greater plans. He had been directing my feet all along, though I had not yet chosen to give Him credit, let alone acknowledge Him. I knew Jesus was Lord, but my heart served only one functional god: Me.

The only problem was that my fresh-start, college-clean-slate scrubbed me outside shiny-clean to where I appeared amazingly refreshed, but it did nothing to resuscitate my heart which continued to wither and die. I needed a resurrection, not just a passing refreshment.

Jesus answered, "Everyone who drinks this water will be thirsty again, but whoever drinks the water I give them will never thirst. Indeed, the water I give them will become in them a spring of water welling up to eternal life."

The woman said to him, "Sir, give me this water so that I won't get thirsty and have to keep coming here to draw water."

…Then Jesus declared, "I who speak to you am he."

John 4: 13-15, 26

My self-charted course didn't sail into smooth seas. If anything, I felt more and more like I was drowning. And not in an ocean. More like a tar pit. I was covered in slime and paralyzed from the muck I had chosen, and from which I could not escape, as all of my searching always led me further down another dead end road. My life had become anything but smooth sailing; I had navigated myself straight into a hurricane, with my bow facing certain destruction.

And I stopped caring as much about how great the outside appeared and started to care about the empty inside.

I waited patiently for the Lord, he inclined unto me, and heard my cry. He brought me up also out of a horrible pit, out of the miry clay and set my feet upon a rock, and established my goings.

Psalm 40: 1-2 KJV

The second semester of my junior year in college, said boyfriend was away on semester abroad. I was pining away for his return, but otherwise behaving in my usual manner. Our sorority formal had just occurred, and I was in rare form, drinking heavily and being completely, off-my-rocker crazy.

I was very familiar with the party scene, but I did my fair share of studying too. Rarely, however, did I study in a library. Libraries were for introverted nerds. (Kudos to you, if you were one of them, because I am sure you made better grades than I did!) I was extroverted and couldn't be de-sensitized and distracted by the dull colors, strange smells and deafening silence in the library.

The week after my formal it was back to the books, and I cut a deal with a sorority sister of mine: She would go with me to study at a coffeehouse, if I would first go with her to a Greek Life meeting (of the former Campus Crusade for Christ, now known as Cru). One of our Christian sorority sisters, Angela Stem (Mills), was sharing her "testimony," and my study pal had promised Angela that she would go. My friend didn't want to go to the meeting alone, and I didn't want to study alone. Deal made.

I went with much hesitation to hear Angela, wanting to get it over and move on as quickly as possible. Please remember, I already thought I was a

Christian. It was *those other types* of Christians at whom I rolled my eyes. (And there were a lot of them in my sorority, so I did a lot of eye rolling.)

Words like "testimony" made me cringe, along with words like "salvation and saved, born-again and believer." I usually thought of other more appropriate and acrimonious words like "Bible-beater and holy-roller." But what I heard when Angela spoke, was not a judgmental and perfect girl, who insulated herself with meaningless words from the Bible. What I heard was an imperfect, struggling, authentic and approachable girl, who was very much, in fact, like me.

What I heard... changed my life. I heard a girl who searched for meaning in many other things (although not necessarily in the same ways I had) and always came up empty when she searched for anything or anyone but Christ, first and foremost.

For the first time in my life, I heard scripture that came alive. These Words offered more than good sense to me at best, and more than antiquated and outdated, meaningless words on a page, at worst... They offered Life. Meaning. Purpose. Hope. Love. Healing. Intimacy. Romance. Adventure. Beauty. I sensed that night that my deepest desires were far from changing – they were actually about to be met and realized! Fulfilled – in and through the person of Jesus. The giver of hope. Of all good things.

Praise the Lord, my soul, and forget not all his benefits – who forgives all your sins and heals all your diseases, who redeems your life from the pit and crowns you with love and compassion, who satisfies your desires with good things so that your youth is renewed like the eagle's.

Psalm 103: 2-5

I remember I wanted to stay and talk to Angela, but I also remember that I did eventually go study that night. Still, my mind was swirling unstoppable with questions. The next day I ran down the hall to Angela's room in our sorority house. I do not remember what was said... but at that moment I am sure, I forged a mentoring relationship with Angela in the spring of 1997... and a life-altering relationship with Jesus Christ.

I had spent a lifetime running after things and people and experiences that promised to fill the gaping hole in my heart, things and people and experiences that overpromised and under-delivered. Things and people and experiences that always left me worse off than before – left me longing still. Longing for more. I had always thought, each time, that I was running for life, but I was instead hurling myself headlong into death's door. Until I met Jesus – *the* way, *the* truth, and *the* life.

The short remainder of my junior year, I ceased running to good things, to worthless things, to periphery things, to *all* things... And I started running towards life, as I ran to Angela's room almost daily. I asked many questions, about anything and everything. I finally sensed I had met someone who *did* have all the answers to life.

Only later, did I realize it wasn't *she* who had all the answers, but the Person whom she knew - *He* had all the answers. It wasn't she who offered life, but her Savior.

My Savior.

Jesus answered, "I am the way and the truth and the life. No one comes to the Father except through me."

John 14: 6

I would ask Angela things, and she would often say, to start or to finish a conversation on a particular topic, "Let's pray about that."
She didn't claim to have all the answers, but she spent countless hours praying with me, in short little snippets of prayer here and there. Her prayers sounded vastly different than the liturgical prayers I had known. She introduced me to a new way to pray to the Heavenly King of Kings, which sounded very much like talking to an earthly best friend.

Though I have grown in many ways as a believer in Christ, my early life with Jesus looked very much like it still does today. It is still much like the way He made me as a person... spastic and spontaneous. Full of life and desperation, brimming with love and passion. Drama and comedy, tears from the core of my soul, and laughter, too, from the center of my being. And I think that is the way He wants it, because that is precisely the way *He* made me.

When I need something, I go to Jesus. Have a question: Go to Jesus. Want to cry, cuss, cheer or celebrate: Go to Jesus. He knows my thoughts before I think them; there are no pretenses. I just go to Jesus!

You have searched me, Lord, and you know me. You know when I sit and when I rise; you perceive my thoughts from afar. You discern my going out and my lying down; you are familiar with all my ways. Before a word is on my tongue you, Lord, know it completely. You hem me in behind and before, and you lay your hand upon me. Such knowledge is too wonderful for me, too lofty for me to attain. Where can I go from your Spirit? Where can I flee from your presence? If I go up to the heavens, you are there; if I make my bed in the depths, you are there. If I rise on the wings of the dawn, if I settle on the far side of the sea, even there your hand will guide me, your right hand will hold me fast. If I say, "Surely, the darkness will hide me and the light become night around me," even the darkness will not be dark to you; the night will shine like the day, for darkness is as light to you. For you created my inmost being; you knit me together in my mother's womb. I praise you because I am fearfully and wonderfully made; your works are wonderful, I know that full well.

Psalm 139: 1-14

I vividly remember one morning that ended in prayer in Angela's room. I was walking across the quad, returning from class to the sorority house. It was a glorious spring day, and I remember the sun casting light prisms through the canopy of ancient trees overhead. Looking back, I know beyond the shadow of a doubt that it was the first time I experienced the Holy Spirit in a tangible and sensory way.

I kept "thinking" about my boyfriend of three years, whose return was getting closer by the day. (I soon realized, however, it was God Himself who had perfectly timed those thoughts and ushered them into my head.) I thought about how I had changed and what would become of the two of us, as a couple.

I remembered thinking that I wanted God to change and impact him, just like He had done for me. That would be the easiest, most obvious answer, after all. Wouldn't it? Wouldn't it be the most evident solution to any impending difficulties that might come from our time apart?

I remembered carrying on imaginary conversations, prior to his return, that I would have with him to try to describe the indescribable… to try to explain the unexplainable… so that he could fathom the unfathomable. Of *what* exactly *had* happened to me while he had been gone for the semester.

I wound up back in Angela's room, feeling very intuitive and adept. I told her what had just happened in my brain and in my heart, while crossing the quad. I exclaimed naively, "Angela, I think I have given everything in my life to the Lord, but it dawned on me this morning, that I have not given Him this relationship."

She replied, as she often did, "Let's pray about it," and pray, we did.

And a little over 12 hours later, in the middle of the North Carolina night, my boyfriend called me from India, on the other side of the world, and broke up with me "out of the blue." I was sad and broken, even shocked, when I considered how our relationship had been heading, up until that point, toward marriage. And *everyone* knew *that*.

However, I was getting to know a God who knew far better than *"everyone."* It was the first time I learned about peace that passes all understanding. I spent days crying, but I knew in my "inmost being" that God had orchestrated his perfect will and timing in my life. He *had* answered *my* prayers, after all.

And so, it also was the first time I wrote scripture on my heart, committing it to memory. It was *not*, however, the first time (or the last) that He saved me. Not the first time or the last, that his plans were better than my plans, that his ways were higher than my ways.

Do not be anxious about anything, but in every situation, by prayer and petition, with thanksgiving, present your requests to God. And the peace of God which transcends all understanding, will guard your hearts and your minds in Christ Jesus.

Philippians 4: 6-7

My baby Christian self was really growing quite smitten with God. He continued to perform other miracles to impress and woo me, doing things in my life that I have held near to my heart to this day. And as my love for the Lord grew like a wild fire, I literally began trusting Him in a very child-like manner.

At that point in my journey with God, I was unaware that he actually *wanted* me to become like a little child. It just happened. He washed over me like a spring rain, resurrecting a believing part of my soul that had hardened and died. And, *Oh – Did I believe and trust*! Oh – Do I ever still!

I will say of the Lord, "He is my refuge and my fortress, my God, in whom I trust."

Psalm 91: 2

Only in very recent years, did I discover C.S. Lewis' *The Chronicles of Narnia*. The first book in the series is my favorite: *The Magician's Nephew*. Polly Plummer and Digory Kirke were the first 2 children to discover the heavenly land of Narnia. The other-worldly Aslan commissioned their first great adventure there, and when they ran out of food on this mission,

Digory suggested planting into the ground the last piece of toffee that came from Polly's pocket.

"Why shouldn't this turn into a toffee tree?" he asked.[3]

How amazingly wonderful! What faith and boldness! What imagination and creativity!

And the tree grew toffee the next morning.

Narnia: A land where anything is possible. A land where God's goodness and pleasure over us reign supreme. A land where child-like faith and innocence are valued over worldly success and power. A land that turns conventional wisdom on its head for the sake of beautiful foolishness!

…A land where a new adventure rises with every dawn. A land where God is a jealous roaring lion, fiercely protective of our hearts, but He is also a magnificent and majestic lion who calls us to Himself… with his invitation as softly flowing as his mane, as He lavishes his love on us and pursues our hearts.

It sounds like heaven on earth, and I am here to tell you, that is what it is. This is *exactly* the land that we live in when we abide in God. God is bringing His kingdom back, and it doesn't start when Jesus returns. It starts here and now. With you and with me. Come Lord Jesus!

Truly I tell you, unless you become like little children, you will never enter the kingdom of heaven.

Matthew 18: 3

I left college much like I was leaving the promised land. It had been my life's dream, up to that point, just to be there. And my time there had given me far more than even I could've expected: Not only friends, experiences, memories, and independence, but salvation as well. God supernaturally rescued me from my path of destruction and set me on a journey of healing, growth, love, mercy, blessing, and adventure.

Literally miracle after miracle He performed early in this journey. There is a saying I heard later in my Christian life, "If you need the Lord to provide or to answer, ask a new Christian to pray!"

My prayers were not only childlike – they were constant. I begged, and I pleaded! There was so much I needed to know, so much I needed – *period*. I talked to God about anything and everything. I asked for things earth-shattering, like comfort in pain, reprieve in tears, guidance in uncertainty, and His voice in the darkness. I requested small things too, personal to me, things I now call "pearls."

"Lord, show me a small fractal of your light and beauty today, I long to see your glory and splendor... something wrapped in an invisible satin bow, a gift just for me, that only my heart would know is from You."

And God was only too happy to impress His newly adopted daughter with His strength and power, beauty and majesty, goodness and kindness. He delighted over me, and I in Him. He gave me things like a hummingbird perched on a branch, a love ballad on the radio (that is *really* God singing right over my soul), or finding something I had lost (which happens quite frequently – both the losing and the finding. Insert smiley face emoticon.)

I can honestly say, not so much has changed from that perspective. If anything, I have only *grown* in love and dependence, in faith and expectation. But there is something fantastic and magical about experiencing it all for the first time, just like the first time Lucy opened the wardrobe door to Narnia.

...Truly I tell you, if you have faith as small as a mustard seed, you can say to this mountain, "Move from here to there," and it will move. Nothing will be impossible for you.

Matthew 17:20

A year after I committed my life to Christ, my college graduation was approaching. I had applied to five graduate schools for Speech and Language Pathology. I had, by late April, received four rejection letters. In early May, the fifth letter arrived. It was far too thin, far too small. But sometime before the day I that pulled the letter from the mailbox, in my heart, I was already beginning to suspect this vocational tract was not God's choice for my life.

And far from being disappointed upon reading the fifth and final rejection, I was ready. Almost excited. Expectant, at least.

I sat down and prayed, "God, I think I have already figured out that this is not what you want me to do with my life. Though it doesn't make sense on paper that I wouldn't get in (my raging pride and narcissism), it makes perfect sense that you are just trying to guide me to whatever it is that you *do* want me to do. Oh, and by the way Lord, what would that be?"

And God's response to my question made no earthly sense whatsoever to me at that time, but I very clearly felt the Lord telling me to be (wait for it) – a church secretary. Almost as if he was saying, "How else are you going to meet Christian people when you move to a new city?"

I grew up in Tennessee, moved to North Carolina for high school, and my parents moved to Alabama when I was a freshman in college. Birmingham was the city to which I was going "home" in less than a month, without a single graduate school prospect on the horizon. Additionally, I did not know a single soul there besides the members of my family.

Very shortly after my prayer time with God about the immediate future of my life, I had phone conversations with both my mom and my cousin, Susan. Both live in Birmingham. With much passion and excitement, I explained to them both, at separate times, "what I wanted to be when I grew up:" a secretary. You can imagine they were a little surprised at the complete change of course in my career path.

(Now hear me say, being an administrative assistant in an office is an incredibly noble profession – these men and women are the face and flavor of the whole show. The first impression! But here I was, with four years and many dollars spent in paid tuition on a certain trajectory – graduate school – seemingly down the drain.)

So I told my mom and Susan, both of whom I knew would listen open-mindedly in faith and surrender. Both women were extremely supportive, loving and kind. And they held from me what I am sure was going on in their heads: shock and confusion. They silenced any doubts they may have had about my intellect *or my sanity*, and they veiled any desires they had to laugh out loud. Instead, they both agreed to pray.

I had asked that they pray with me that God would reveal clearly *the* church where I was to become a secretary. They must have actually prayed that I would clearly hear what the Lord wanted for my vocational future, sensing surely that I must have misunderstood His voice. But not a week later, I got a call from Susan, as I was packing to come home. She told me that the secretary for her church's counseling center had just resigned, and the director was looking for a replacement. [4]

Call to me, and I will answer you and tell you great and unsearchable things you do not know.

Jeremiah 33: 3

I interviewed immediately after coming to Birmingham. Upon entering the office of the director, I was struck by the number of degrees on his wall. Masters, plural, and a doctorate or two. Multiple schools, multiple degrees. I was honored to be considered, but I was intimidated as well.

His calm and kind demeanor was almost unnerving, especially to someone who had known God for about half a second. And as if my interview had not been enough to undo me, fresh out of college, the director gave me a personality test after my interview: The Myers Briggs Type Indicator (MBTI), about which (by the way) he had written a doctoral dissertation.

He had his current secretary score the test immediately, and he informed me that I had failed. Not really. You can't fail a personality test, I guess. But needless to say, my personality was not suited to office work, detail management and number crunching. Nothing could be truer, I have since learned. (The MBTI is amazingly accurate.)

But... and this was the "but" on which all my hopes hinged... he would hire me as a fill-in for a week or two until he found his permanent replacement. He knew I was leaving, anyway, to backpack my way through Europe in about that amount of time; he agreed that I could work until I left for the trip, which had been given to me by my grandparents as a college graduation gift.

Good enough. I was thoroughly impressed with God and His voice, which had spoken to me loud and clear.

I prayed, "Thanks Lord! So I guess I better use this platform, use this blessing, use this answer to prayer, *pretty quickly* to find some Christian friends, so that I will have some waiting on me here when I return from Europe."

Turns out, my job was waiting on me too. The week before I left for Europe, Dr. Haygood called me back into his office and offered me the job permanently. My hard work and determination had made up for my God-given deficits. After all, I was a "feeler" not a "thinker." I was "judging" not "perceiving." And "intuitive" not "sensing."

The man who was a pastor, a professor, and also a gifted Licensed Professional Counselor, became a mentor, a friend and somewhat of a father-figure to me. I spent the next 2 years of my life in his company and under his tutelage.

How great is our God! How wonderful the journey with its twists and turns and all His blessings!

God used a job that was not at all suited for my personality type (administrative assistant)...

... to lead me to graduate school to be a counselor (a job perfectly suited to my personality type, but not aligned with my actual desires).

...to later lead me to jobs completely aligned with my spiritual gifting of evangelism and discipleship, *as well as* my passions *and* desires – missions, mercy ministries, *and writing.*

I ultimately felt destined for a life mingling my love of words with my love for God.

I began my vocational life (in college) thinking that I wanted to be a speech pathologist to work with the abnormalities of language and disordered speech in others. And I wound up desiring to be a vessel of speech and language, myself, for God. He was The Great Speech Pathologist in my life, not I in the lives of others. He took my fumbling, faltering lips and spoke in and through me. The irony has not been lost on me.

...Do not worry about what to say or how to say it. At that time you will be given what to say, for it will not be you speaking, but the Spirit of your Father speaking through you.

Matthew 10: 19b-20

I had a new name, and it had nothing to do with my education or vocation. It had nothing to do with my achievements or failures. No longer defined by my past, I had a new future. Because Jesus' tomb was empty on Easter, the whitewashed tomb of my soul was filled with new life in Jesus. Because his blood was poured out, my life has been filled up.

I have come that they may have and enjoy life, and have it in abundance – to the full, until it overflows.

John 10: 10b

Chapter 2 | She is My Sister: Angamita Susan

In 1994, around the time I was graduating high school and entering college, running *from* life, running from God, there was another young girl, on the other side of the planet, running for her life and from a vicious enemy.

Angamita Susan, Amanacholi by tribe, was born at home in a thatched hut, which was constructed of grass and poles, in the Amuru district of Gulu in Northern Uganda. Her hut was "deep in the village." American translation – in the bush (and in the middle of nowhere). She was born sometime around 1983, placing her at approximately age 11 in 1994. Even today, she does not know her exact age.

(She later told me she thought she was 27, by estimating her age based on several childhood peers, with whom she has recently reconnected. This age puts her having been born in 1985-1986, not in early 1980's, which shows the real void of information about her age, not to mention so many other things. Holes in her childhood, holes in her history.)

Though she was one of 4 children, 2 older brothers and 1 younger sister, she has no one left to ask questions of her age or her history, as everything and everyone from her former life was stolen from her in the blink of an eye. Her parents were taken from her, all of her siblings, and her childhood, which was over before it started. The little that she held dear and familiar, shattered in a moment.

Joseph Kony, warlord of the brutal LRA, stormed into the Kirandongo district of Gulu, Uganda, where Susan lived with her family. With a maniacal focus, aimed at ravaging the peaceful, largely agrarian tribes of people in Northern Uganda and beyond, Kony and his henchmen attacked, along with countless troops of child soldiers. These young boys are literally ripped out of their homes, ordered to join the LRA and kill on command, or else be killed themselves.

The horrors of the Lord's Resistance Army are brutally endless. Young boys captured and ordered to murder their parents immediately on site. If a boy chooses not to kill, he is shot in front of his brothers, all witnesses to Kony's unconscionable and swift assassinations.

The next in line is given the same command: Kill or be killed. Kony and his army steal young girls to use and abuse them, and they throw innocent young boys into the hellish nightmare of their twisted plots and schemes.

Susan's childhood memories are filled with unending awareness of such violence and fearing for her life. Her town was unstable, as was the pulse of her own family. Susan was very close with her "friendly" mother; her father was a local carpenter, but he was also an alcoholic and often absent. He did just enough work to allow the family to scrape by. She remembers her parents fighting one time when he was "in love" with another woman.

Susan told me, "He spent all of his money on beer and women."

Susan has memories of this family tension against the backdrop of Kony's inhumane tortures: land mines, slaughtering by force, bodies dismembered and faces cut at the ear and mouth. She recounts how Kony would kill people, cook them in pots, and serve them to their own family and neighbors to eat. If you did not eat, you were killed.[1]

By the middle of the first decade in the 20th century, the world seemed to wake up to a trend in Uganda – children who walked miles in the afternoon to the nearest city or populated area in search of heightened protection from the LRA at night. Western news venues reported widespread accounts of these "Night Commuters" in every media outlet.

Who knows where, how, and when this visible population of children began to form? Susan had never heard of the term coined to describe this generation of children, but it is certain that Susan's family was no exception when it came to seeking refuge in the dark of the night.[2] Her family would leave their hut each night around 6 p.m. to sleep on the ground in the bush in an effort to save the children from being stolen, to prevent their lives from being taken, even from death by fire, as Kony was known to trap people in their huts and then light the hut on fire.

What kind of childhood must Susan have had? It seems she did not have one at all—it was stolen from her like the night came and stole her safety, shattering any residual hopes of protection and refuge.

Unless you have experienced night without any electricity, and often without moonlight, it is hard to describe the nights in rural Uganda. On my trips there, I might describe them as serene, peaceful, quiet, still – in comparison to the "noise" in America. However, for Susan, they were anything but. The sun went down and the night brought the beginning of living nightmares. Night was not just scary, as it is for some children. It was horrifying. Not just imaginary monsters lurking, but real and vivid ones.

My daughter recently told me at bedtime, "Mommy, I am scared."
I was immersed in Susan's story when this conversation began, and my initial response was visceral flinching, my own fear fighting back. But I came out of the computer world in my head for a moment and asked Hannah Whit why she was scared.

She replied, "I am nervous about auditioning for a play if I join the theater club."

Her fears cut me to the core when I considered and contrasted the fears that Susan had experienced at the very same age.

Here is my sweet and sensitive girl, with her anxiety rearing its head again at night, but in the safety of a locked home, made of brick walls and protected by a security system! And within a country that has provided me the opportunity to buy and own a cell phone, not to mention the infrastructure of land-line telecommunications we have here, should I need to call for help. And in the end, someone will be on the receiving end of a 911 emergency request, should I need it, with law enforcement ready to respond and assist.

30

Susan was raised in a thatched-roof, one-room, open-door, mud hut. She might have had a neighbor or two hear a cry for help, had she given it, but what good would a few unarmed civilians do (without the assistance of police or military) against mobs of rebel soldiers.

Hannah Whit was concerned about an extra-curricular activity, not her life, nor mine. And she was not alone, even in those fears; I calmed and listened. Hugged and comforted. Susan – in the most literal sense possible had no one, in the blackest, darkest nights of her childhood.

I wait for the Lord, more than watchmen wait for the morning, more than watchmen wait for the morning.

Psalm 130: 6

How alone and afraid Susan must have been! How thoroughly and completely frightened! And then, after dark one night, in a blanket of pitch-black, months into one of Uganda's rainy seasons, one of Susan's worst nightmares became reality.

Bullets sprayed everywhere, bombs exploded, a mass chaos of people running for their lives, sprinting for escape. Many people were gunned-down during this time. Susan was with her whole family, all together, running and trying to escape the attack. In the mayhem, she was completely separated from her mother and sister.

Susan saw her father, Zachariah, murdered in front of her face. "He was shot dead immediately. He died on the spot."

But there was no time for this young girl to say goodbye. To stop and wonder why he never loved her mother, why he never loved her. Why he didn't provide for or protect them, and why he couldn't protect her now. She didn't stop for one second in her own narrow escape.

She made it out with her life, but not without a bullet in her own arm and shrapnel in her stomach and leg. She ran until she could run no longer. She was finally rescued and taken to a U.N. refugee camp for the "internally displaced" in Kiriandongo, a neighboring district between Gulu and Masindi. She was given medical treatment there also.

"It was a mzungu (white person) doctor who was treating me, and she loved me so much," Susan recounts as visible joy washes over this normally shy and quiet woman. She showed me her scars as she explained that even now, sometimes the bullet wound in her arm swells and causes pain since the bullet itself was never removed.

In all of the years since this horrific day, she has heard nothing of her kind mother or any of her siblings.

She did say that there was a fire one day at Family Spirit, the orphanage that she helps run. Of the few officials who came to investigate the cause of the fire, one was from her home district in Gulu of Amuru. This Masindi Policeman, Okidi, promised to go and ask if there was any clan member left. He said he would ask if any person had heard the story or whereabouts of her remaining family members, but she has never heard back from this man. Susan thinks he got transferred to another place, to another district for work.

She supposed her father's body was never rescued, never buried. She assumes he was "just left to rot."

"I do not think I will ever see any of my parents again, neither will I see the rest of my siblings. I thank God that he has shown me new people like you to be part of my family. I feel so happy when you call me sister."

Do not hide your face from me when I am in distress. Turn your ear to me; when I call, answer me quickly.

Psalm 102: 2

When I began writing Susan's story I was a bundle of emotions. Sometimes the pain of how I experienced her story, marinated in it, would not go away. Like an open and untreated wound, it would just ooze and fester. It consumed me at times.

Sometimes I was angry with God. I came to Him with a million questions and accusations. But He calmed and comforted my ranting and raving, as He always does.

His truth and love brought me out of my insanity-induced rages, not necessarily back to my senses (for He is incensed over the same things as I). Rather, He brought me back to Himself – He led me back to the rock that is higher than I (Ps. 61: 2). Back to trust, back to surrender, back to the realization that His plans are always better…

"No, His plans are *perfect*," I had to remind myself. I preached it to myself like the Psalmist in Psalm 42, even when the circumstances I sat in said otherwise.

More often, while writing Susan's story, I became entirely disconnected, apathetic toward writing and apathetic toward the God who called me to do it. It would get to be too much, the job became too daunting, and I too powerless to process it all in my heart, much less on paper.

I heard and sometimes blindly accepted many of the enemy's lies: It is too hard; I am nobody, certainly not a writer; It's not worth it; I don't have enough time; I don't have enough energy; I don't have what it takes. I would give up, and instead of facing my fears of failing, I would insulate myself by shutting down in apathy. If feeling becomes too difficult, then just don't feel at all.

Forget. Become numb. Run away. Procrastination, lack of follow through, ADHD – these are a few of my "favorite" things. (ADHD as I know it – "Attention, Disobedience, and Heart Disorder")

The writing of Susan's story was no different. In my longest season of running *from* God, running from writing, He began calling me back to Himself, "Yet this I hold against you: you have forsaken the love you had at first" (Rev. 2: 4). Forsaken my writing, forsaken my God, forsaken His calling during this season.

He whispered me home to His heart, again and again. He began showing me what my sin might cost. Forget my own satisfaction of completing a job, any job, for once in my life; forget the enjoyment of His glory expressed in and through me, of being used by the God of the Universe. ("Who is man that you are mindful of him?" Ps. 8: 3)

He kept bringing me back to the reality of the lives affected, Susan's life at the top of the list, as the mother to all these children. Susan who had, herself as a child, been orphaned, neglected, forgotten, cast aside, abused and abandoned. There was, there is, too much at stake.

He convicted me: "Come back close to my heart. I haven't gone anywhere. Allison, just turn around."

My friend, Beth Jones, reminded me, "God in his kindness leads us even to repentance." We cannot even turn back to Him on our own. I had looked down from the computer, looked away from God, but God in His kindness, in His patience and forbearance with me, put my face in His hands and lifted my gaze back to Himself. (Romans 2: 4)

He used Susan, herself, to assist.

Susan's emails always draw me in – not only into the desperate reality of her situation and the unjust disparity between our worlds and lives, but also they draw me back into the sisterhood we share and the love of God that covers and comforts us both. And as our relationship continued to deepen, the cords of feeling and fellowship twisting tighter between us, I saw further and further into her heart and life. Further and further into the heart of God.

Oh, the depth of the riches of the wisdom and knowledge of God! How unsearchable his judgments, and his paths beyond tracing out! "Who has known the mind of the Lord? Or who has been his counselor?"

Romans 11: 33-34

I was sitting in the drive-through line at Chick-Fil-A, one day, during the season I was struggling with writing Susan's story. I checked my email. When I saw a new email from Susan, I did what I do – I frantically fumbled with my phone. Finger flicking and jabbing, screen sliding and scrolling.

Because I know it is hard for her to find time to answer. I know the Internet service – ha, the electricity to start – is shoddy. I know she is hard-pressed to find a moment of time not nursing or cooking or parenting or teaching or disciplining one of her two boys, or one of the over 200 orphans that swarm and circle her at any given minute. I knew that I would hang on every word in her email.

I knew I would relish the communication from my faraway friend, and I began devouring another new email from Susan, hoping to complete it before I got my food and had to drive away. And as I read, I was broken again. Broken anew.

I was broken for the things and the ones that break the heart of God. Broken under the load Susan carries, but glad to lift even an ounce of the heavy, impossible burdens of my sweet Ugandan sister by simply crying with her on the other side of the world. My heart was broken. I lifted it, and I lifted her, up to the One whose body was broken too.

By the time I received my value meal, I was wiping tears from my face. I drove on to Costco, a few hundred yards from the fast food joint, but my heart was a few thousand miles away. It is hard to put food in your mouth when there is salt water coming from your eyes and snot running from your nose. Easy, on the other hand, to understand how tears can become one's food (Ps. 42: 3).

It was two in the afternoon, and I hadn't eaten since my early breakfast. My stomach was churning and turning, but I choked down just enough food to quiet the audible protests of my belly, even as I choked back the sobs. There I was, sitting alone in the parking lot, wondering: *Does Susan ever get to be alone? To do anything... alone?*

"Look at me," I thought. The luxury of a babysitter. The luxury of hot chicken, atop fresh vegetables, served on a salad for my drive-through convenience, ready five minutes after I ordered it. I didn't have to kill the chicken, tar or feather it. I didn't even have to cook it. I didn't throw my hands up to heaven and praise God for this prized rarity – MEAT TO EAT!! Meat is reserved at Family Spirit for only very special occasions like Christmastime.

I take for granted the over-abundance of healthy foods, the abundance of delicious and disgusting *junk* even. Anything available to me at any given time I want it. I have the means to purchase it, and I live in a country that readily offers it.

And as I lingered longer in the parking lot that day, crying tears alone in my car, I tried to eat a little more of the food that I purchased for myself. And I thought of "the bread of adversity" Susan had eaten her entire life. (Is. 30: 20)

Why Lord? Why was I sitting outside the emperor of the supersize stores worried about having to return a towel, while Susan sat with next to nothing worried about living long enough to see her boys grow up?

And why was I returning the towel in the first place? I had accidentally purchased two different sizes. I meant to buy two bath towels, but I discovered when I arrived home – only one was a bath towel. The other was a bath *sheet*. Turns out, we are supersizing towels, too, because a bath *sheet* is a bath towel of epic proportions.

And I had gotten *white* towels, of course. Unmovable in the parking lot, I was needing to go in and exchange my bath sheet for a normal-sized bath towel, and I began staring at the whiteness now. Something that white would last about half a second in Uganda's red clay, while I had gotten 13 years of mileage out of my last set of white guest towels.

I was spiraling. Down. Back to the heart of God. He was drawing me back in. Drawing me back home.

When I get honest, I admit I am a bundle of paradoxes. I believe and I doubt, I hope and get discouraged, I love and I hate, I feel bad about feeling good, I feel guilty about not feeling guilty. I am trusting and suspicious. I am honest and I still play games… To live by grace means to acknowledge my whole life story, the light side and the dark. In admitting my shadow side, I learn who I am and what God's grace means. As Thomas Merton put it, 'A saint is not someone who is good but who experiences the goodness of God.'

Ragamuffin Gospel, by Brennan Manning[3]

Susan escaped Kony's army with her life, but what of her heart? Her body was terribly injured – was her heart not handicapped beyond repair? Was her soul not completely carved out, hollow, and empty?

By this stage in her young life, Hannah Whit's days have been filled with love and care. She sees the doctor yearly for check-ups, and she gets medicines when she is sick. She finds relief from something as simple as a fever. Tylenol is not a luxury for us, nor is it for 90% of Americans – it's as commonly found in homes as peanut butter is.

Susan's life was devoid of all these things to begin with… before her life got unimaginably worse.

I was trying to imagine a little girl just slightly older than my Hannah Whit - alone. I was trying to imagine Susan, there, completely alone with no one in the world. She had nothing. And now she has no ONE. Not just unfavorable, depressing circumstances, but unthinkable violence. She lived a nightmare that would crush an adult, let alone a child. Where does a child put these events? How does she process them?

She has seen her father massacred in front of her; she has been separated from her mother and from her siblings, left to wonder about their fates for the rest of her days; and she has travelled countless miles, on foot, likely without shoes. And this is just the beginning of her troubles.

How could an 11 year old survive so much? And have more still to survive?

Even though I walk through the valley of the shadow of death, I fear no evil, for You are with me…

Psalm 23: 4a

When Susan came to live in the UN refugee camp, she received a blanket and a place to sleep in a tent. Others slept on the ground outside the tents. Members and overseers of the camp helped Susan make local contacts, where she could go and work small temporary jobs (as a preteen!!), but she never found a permanent place to settle. She stayed mostly at the camp for the first two years after she was driven from her home. Susan was a child, in a crowded sea of forsaken people, but very much alone. She received a daily ration of food from the camp, but went to a local well for water.

One day, at the well, she met a woman. "She appeared to be sad to me. I told her about myself, and she asked me if I could go and stay with her in her house. I accepted, and I went with her. To my surprise, the woman was a barmaid. She sold beer, and – I am sorry – she began selling me to men. She would make the men use me for sex and pay her money." Susan was around 13.

I swallow her shame, and it chokes me. My heart is undone that Susan felt the need to apologize to me. That she has convinced herself that any part of this could be *her* fault. That Satan ensnared her in slavery and enslaves her still in self-condemnation.

Lord, where were You at this well? To the Samaritan woman, You showed her Yourself and Your life and the water that wells up to eternal life. Why did You allow evil to consume an innocent life, the life of a helpless child? Had she not been through enough?

Questions. So many questions. I am filled with questions for God. Filled with sadness and doubt. Anger and confusion.

I rage in humanity, in my questions and in my limited knowledge. Too blind to see the bigger picture. Too personally involved to see *Your* involvement, Lord. Thinking, here and now, that I know best, when I didn't even know Susan, there and then.

But You did know her. You do know her. You loved her then, and You love her now, Your precious and beautiful daughter. She is a daughter of the King, an honored woman; You are enthralled with her beauty. (Ps. 45: 9-11)

You also raged at her accusers, on the cross. You claimed her there for Your very own. You bought her at a price – the price of Your life, which You freely laid down to rescue her. And You know the plans You have for her, to give her a hope and a future (Jer. 29: 11). You work all things together for good, Lord. (Rom. 8: 28)

What, then, shall we say in response to these things? If God is for us, who can be against us? He who did not spare his own Son, but gave him up for us all – how will he not also, along with him, graciously give us all things?

Romans 8: 31-32

I'm searching. Searching for pearls in the miry pit. And God's Word is full of jewels. Full of life.   And it does not return void.
Again and again, I'm preaching the Truth to myself, because the reality of the world and the promises of God's Truth sometimes seem so far apart. I don't cling to the Word, I don't preach it to myself, and I don't write it

because I am being trite in the face of impossible suffering. I don't say it to offer hope to Susan, or to the reader, but mostly to offer hope to myself. I do it to feed myself the cure when the enemy has poisoned and infected me with his lies and his destruction, in my life and so much more in Susan's.

I'm holding on to Jesus, because He's all I have in the storm. And I trust Him to calm the waves, to work the miracle. I'm offering my doubts a dose of faith from the pharmacy of God's Word. I say it to myself over and over and louder and louder not in spite of the fact that I cannot actually see it, but exactly because of the fact that I cannot see it. So in my blindness, the Master can lead me with His Voice. So I can hear Him, though I cannot touch Him.

Why, Lord, do you stand far off? Why do you hide yourself in times of trouble?
Psalm 10: 1

And I figure, if the psalmists have asked the question, if the prophets and the great heroes of the faith have asked the question "Why?!?!" then I can ask it too. Even Jesus, on the cross, in cataclysmic suffering and separation from God asked, "Why?"

"My God, My God, why hast Thou forsaken me?" (Matthew 27:46)

So, I give my questions to God.

I have real doubts, real problems with my faith, but I have a God who is more real to me than the pain I see around me.

I don't trust because it is easy; I trust because the power to do so comes from The Power Source. I don't believe, in the face of such suffering, because I have lost my mind; I believe because God has formed my mind in His perfect image. And though my brain is incredibly crafted and unbelievably complex, I also see its limitations: *I do not possess the mind of God.*

40

Yet, I believe, because my mind is being renewed and transformed by the Spirit of God. I believe in the very real presence of Evil, but also in the conquering and consuming power of The Victor.

Psalm 10 continues:

In his arrogance the wicked man hunts down the weak,
who are caught in the schemes he devises.
He boasts about the cravings of his heart;
He blesses the greedy and reviles the Lord.
In his pride the wicked man does not seek Him;
In all his thoughts there is no room for God.
His ways are always prosperous; your laws are rejected by him;
he sneers at all his enemies.
He says to himself, "Nothing will ever shake me."
He swears, "No one will ever do me harm."
His mouth is full of lies and threats;
Trouble and evil are under his tongue.
He lies in wait near the villages; from ambush he murders the innocent.
His eyes watch in secret for his victims; like a lion in cover he lies in wait.
He lies in wait to catch the helpless;
he catches the helpless and drags them off in his net.
His victims are crushed, they collapse; they fall under his strength.
He says to himself, "God will never notice; he covers his face and never sees."

"Arise, Lord! Lift up your hand, O God!
Do not forget the helpless.
Why does the wicked man revile God?
Why does he say to himself, "He won't call me to account?"
But you, God, see the trouble of the afflicted;
You consider their grief and take it in hand.
The victims commit themselves to you;
You are the helper of the fatherless.
Break the arm of the wicked man;

Call the evildoer to account
for his wickedness that would not otherwise be found out."

The Lord is King for ever and ever; the nations will perish from His land.
You, Lord, hear the desire of the afflicted;
You encourage them, and listen to their cry,
defending the fatherless and the oppressed,
so that mere earthly mortals will never again strike in terror.

If I did not know better, I would think a modern day Ugandan Christian wrote Psalm 10 about Joseph Kony and the LRA. About local villages. About the "Night Commuters." About sex trafficking. But Evil is an age-old story, as pervasive in the past as in the present. The thief has come to steal, and kill and destroy, but God has come that we might have life, and have it to the full. (John 10: 10)

The promise of God is this: Love Wins.

I can offer promises, *His Promises*, not only to the pain in the world, but to things in Uganda, specifically, that rip my heart in two. I can accept that there are things I won't understand, precisely and exactly because of the very observable, very rational, very scientific, very biological fact – *I am not Divine.*

And I hope in God in the face of incredible pain, not as a consolation prize, but because I truly *prize* God – and because he first prized me.

Whom have I in heaven but you? And earth has nothing I desire besides you.
My flesh and my heart may fail, but God is the strength of my heart and my
portion forever.

Psalm 73: 26-27

After 6 months captivity with the barmaid, a "very old" neighbor woman (who was 40 or 50) rescued Susan. She discovered that Susan was being held as a sex slave, a child being brutally used, being led to believe it was a legitimate exchange for a place to live. Susan was led to believe it was a job she had chosen, and not evil chosen for her by a violent and twisted enemy.

This neighbor had herself been displaced, but she had found a way to earn a living. She freed Susan and brought her into her own home to guide, protect and care for her. The woman's name was *Angel*ina. I gasped; I came up for air when Susan told me her name. God rescued Susan, I am convinced – He sent a living angel to do it.
"Angelina was the next door neighbor to the barmaid. She had several times found me in tears, then began to ask me why I always appeared that way."

Angelina brought her to the Catholic Church she attended, and introduced Susan to her priest, Father Magezi. He paid for her tuition, so she could go to school, but he died in 2001. Susan was in Senior 2, at that time, and she had two years left until her high school education was complete.

Angelina then petitioned on her behalf again. She took Susan to the head teacher of the school and told her about Susan's life. The headmistress agreed to let Susan complete her studies free of charge.

The angel of the Lord encamps around those who fear him, and he delivers them.
Psalm 34: 7

Susan was a good student. Her interest was nursing. But after Senior School, which she attended for free, Angelina did not have the money to personally pay for Susan to continue studies elsewhere. She lived with the Angelina for about 4 years, until she was around 18.

Susan had begun praying for her future, and one day there was a woman from the Catholic Church who told her about the Philly Lutaaya Initiative; Philly Bongole Lutaaya is considered an AIDS hero and champion in Uganda. Susan went before this organization, which had been given grants to support orphans, as well as youth and children suffering from HIV. One of their proffers was education.

At this time, Susan did not yet know she was HIV positive, but the Philly Lutaaya Initiative informed Susan that they could help her. And they did. They brought her to Family Spirit, which was still in its conception. Susan would help on the property, and in exchange, the Initiative paid for her to continue her education – but in a school that taught and trained nursery teachers, not nurses, for this would equip her to teach at Family Spirit.

Shortly after her support began, children began arriving at the initial property held by Family Spirit. Susan discovered many of them herself. This was about 2002, and Susan was going on 19. She cooked for them and washed clothes. Susan told me, "I could do a lot of work there as the eldest child."

After about one year, the number of the children had increased to around 30. There was no money for food or school for the children. Susan recalls,

> Sometimes, there was just one meal a day, or just water that day. Isaac would go and beg for food in the community. Sometimes a passerby would donate food, even at 11:00 at night. When we would get food late like that, we would wake all the children up who immediately cried from hunger and confusion, to feed them the food that had just come in.

They would take anything that came in, whenever it came in. "Water with coffee and without sugar. Some days just a bowl of porridge."

Susan said they were never picky, always grateful "so long as we have put something in the stomach."

Susan's days got longer and harder. She would leave for her college classes in early childhood education around 2 p.m. after cooking and washing, and come back at 6 p.m. to pick up where she had left off with her work. It took her nine months to complete her education in 2003. In 2004, Family Spirit started the nursery school. Older and younger children alike, they all sat in the one "nursery" class together because Susan was the only teacher and *hers* was the only class.

The next year, when there became a need for the children to graduate to the next class level, Susan moved up with them. So in 2005, Susan began attending school again, a Primary Teachers College, to continue to keep her teaching credentials current with the children who continued to progress in grade level. A volunteer then came in to take over the nursery class position that Susan had left vacant.

Her new college was farther away, requiring that she stayed there overnight Monday to Friday, coming home only on the weekends. During this time, she became very sick and was losing weight without explanation. The horrible and deadly disease, which she had likely contracted in 1997 from the men who used her, had finally ravaged her insides and became evident outwardly. When she was starting to get show visible signs of illness, all of the students at school began avoiding her. She told me, "I was isolated and disliked."

Her condition worsened, and in June of 2006, she was admitted into Masindi Main Hospital for over 2 months. It was here that Susan was diagnosed with HIV. During this time, she was so depressed that she wanted to end her life.

The hospital referred her to TASO (The Aids Support Organization of Uganda), and Susan said she finally came "back to her senses" when she began her treatment and counseling there. The doctors, nurses and counselors of TASO gave her many examples of people "living positively" with HIV, a common slogan of encouragement in Uganda. (She and Isaac both continue their treatment there to this day.)

When she began receiving the free ARV (antiretroviral) medicines and consistent care, her condition improved. She felt well enough to return to school. Susan worried about how she would fare on her finals, having missed so many classes, but she said she passed her exams because "God helped her and guided her."

She completed the 2-year course in Primary Education late in 2006. Family Spirit grew again, adding another grade level.

Have mercy on me, Lord, for I am faint; heal me, Lord, for my bones are in agony.

Psalm 6: 2

Susan's story is just one of the countless tales of heartache, of people whose families were torn apart, and whose lives were senselessly shattered. How many others have questions about their age? Questions about their homes and families? Friends and relatives? How many have questions about their childhoods, piecing together horrific and traumatic memories? How many question God's plans for their lives, if there are any plans at all, or if there is even a God? How many like Susan, wonder if God really loves them?

Susan's Ugandan name, "Angamita" means "Nobody loves me," or, "Who loves me?" Surely only a parent in a difficult and dark place would name their firstborn girl in such a manner. Another "Why?" Another question that may never have an answer. But to the question, "Who loves me?" Susan is finding answers every day.

I will plant her for myself in the land; I will show my love to the one I called 'Not my loved one.' I will say to those called, 'Not my people,' "You are my people," and they will say, "You are my God."

Hosea 2: 23

Susan's name reminds me of Naomi in the book of Ruth. "Don't call me Naomi," she told them, "Call me Mara, because the Lord has made my life very bitter" (Ruth 1: 20).

Naomi was a desperate woman on a journey to her homeland. Susan was a desperate girl exiled from her home. My prayer for her has been, like my prayers for myself, that we will find our way home daily, to the heart of God, who turns the bitter into sweet.

There are many missing pieces for Susan in her own life, so I certainly do not profess to present a thorough telling of her story here. On top of what she does not know, or possibly has blocked, there are gaps of information from our different native tongues, from our different cultures, from the physical distance between us... but there are heart ties between us as well, highways that bridge the gaps, that fill in some of the blanks and heal some of the pain – our sisterhood in Christ.

I hesitate to compare us at all, because I simply cannot imagine the heartbreak she has endured. I cannot imagine suffering through the living hell she has experienced, which is as much like the story of Job as anyone I have ever known. Our lives have been as different as the colors of our skin, her beautiful dark ebony to my weathered white, but our journeys home to the heart of Christ have a few similarities, even as they are being woven together now, and we share that foundation who is the Solid Rock of our faith.

We are both adopted by Abba and have the same heavenly Daddy, which makes us sisters, the two of us with each other, with Naomi and even with the Israelites journeying to the promised land. Our Savior lived and died, loved and sacrificed, and reigns supreme for us all.

Both the one who makes people holy and those who are made holy are of the same family. So Jesus is not ashamed to call them brothers and sisters.

Hebrews 2: 11

Naomi's chosen name, "Mara" or 'bitter,' harkens back also to the Israelites Exodus out of Egypt and the waters of "Marah." Another set of circumstances marked by appalling despair. Yet also, another story where God works good from evil. Sweet from bitter. [4]

After the miraculous parting of the waters... "Moses led Israel from the Red Sea and they went into the Desert of Shur" (Ex. 15: 22a)...

"My God, My God, why have you forsaken me?" (Matthew 27: 46) The Father led his Son to a place of desertion so that Susan and I would never be forsaken. Even in her impossible pain, He never left her side, and He has never left mine. "Never will I leave you; never will I forsake you" (Heb. 13: 5).

"For three days [Israel] travelled in the desert without finding water" (Ex. 15: 22b)...

For three days our Savior laid by the dark winter of death in the tomb before proclaiming victory and resurrection, before ushering in the new life of Spring. He died for me and for Susan to have a new life, and He died also for us to find new life in Him. "If anyone is in Christ, he is a new creation. The old has gone. The new is come" (2 Cor. 5: 17).

"When they came to Marah, they could not drink its water because it was bitter. (That is why the place is called Marah.) So the people grumbled against Moses, saying, 'What are we to drink?' (Ex. 15: 23-24)...

When He was about to be crucified, "There they offered Jesus wine to drink, mixed with gall" (Matthew 27: 34)... Bile! Bitter and severe, he tasted it for us, in the crucifixion, to spare our own lives. We gave him poisonous gall and bitter suffering, and He gave us honey in return. He promised Israel a land flowing with milk and honey, and He gave us His Son, His Word, "More precious than gold and sweeter than honey" (Ps. 19: 10).

"Then Moses cried out to the Lord, and the Lord showed him a piece of wood. He threw it into the water, and the water became sweet" (Exodus 15: 22-25).

God showed us, too, a piece of wood, formed in the shape of a cross, which turned our bitter into sweet.   For me and for Susan. For all who believe. For now and forevermore.

...But I trust in your unfailing love; my heart rejoices in your salvation. I will sing the Lord's praise, for he has been good to me.

Psalm 13: 5-6

Chapter 3 | He Lifted Us Up: A Marriage on The Brink

Circled in Love

I met Adam in the fall of 1998, the year before Family Spirit was conceived. I had returned from Europe in early August, returned to the job that was held for me, filled only until I stepped back into it. Since I was going to be staying awhile, I decided to make good on the idea that God was bringing me this job for friends and fellowship, among so many other things. I began attending a Bible study at Covenant Church in Birmingham, the church associated with Covenant Counseling and Education Center where I worked. And in November, I finally left the denomination of my upbringing and attended a church service at Covenant with a friend from my Bible study.

That providential Sunday morning, my friend scanned the pews and saw a familiar face from her recent college days at Samford University, which happens to sit across the street from Covenant Church. She spotted Adam Hodges. It turns out, God brought me not only church friends from my position as secretary; he brought me a husband. It turns out, I married *that* man sitting in *that* pew. It turns out, Adam proposed to me *in* that same pew about a year later, December 23, 1999.

We began our life together in May of 2000, the same year that God breathed life into Family Spirit, the same year that the first children came into their home care program.

I had engraved "Eph. 3: 20-21" on Adam's wedding band, but I kept it secret until our wedding day. Man and wife, we left the church together, and I discovered he had engraved the same verse on my band:

Now to him who is able to do immeasurably more than all we can ask or imagine, according to his power that is at work within us, to him be the glory in

the church and in Christ Jesus, throughout all generations, forever and ever!
Amen.

Ephesians 3: 20-21

I had no idea this verse, and the passage before it, would come to shape my entire life, my worldview of God and His love. But the wheels would fall off first.

Dr. Haygood, my boss and the director of the counseling center, was one of the pastors to marry Adam and I. He lovingly taunted me all through our engagement, "You know, when you get married, the wheels will fall off." I would go into to his office to deliver a message or ask about rescheduling an appointment, and he would remind me in his graceful southern drawl, "One day... one day... the wheels are gonna fall off."

Sure enough, we were a few days into the honeymoon when it happened. I always figured Dr. Haygood would be right. He held multiple degrees and all the right titles for advice giving. Pastor. Teacher. Counselor. Besides, he was right about everything it seemed to me. All of his counsel. All of his recommendations. Everything he preached from the pulpit. God used him mightily. In thousands of lives, and in my life as well.

I figured he was right, also, because Adam and I had baggage that equated to our coming into the marriage with shoddy tires and no spare, as it were. But I also figured it would take some monumentally cataclysmic event occurring between us or around us to bring out the worst in each of us. Never did I suspect we would start losing wheels in the tropical paradise of the Cayman Islands, days into our marriage.

Apparently, it took only our developmental wounds and the depth of our own sin to force the wheels off very quickly.

Adam brought his laptop on our nuptial vacation, for the purpose of showing me his "honeymoon spreadsheet." You can imagine how that went over with his new bride. Every step, every decision, every turn we made was gauged by Adam's fine-tuned financial map. And he kept checking it… and checking it… and checking it.

Dinner? No we couldn't eat that night because we had exceeded our budget for the day. Outing tomorrow? You guessed it. Not in the budget. I finally broke, and I told him what he could do with his spreadsheet and his computer.

In fairness, I may be exaggerating slightly (but *only* slightly) about the starting point of our marital distress. It amazes me, though, how Adam's spreadsheet was such a good analogy for our first years of marriage, *with no wheels*. He had delineated everything in his mind for how our lives together should go – finances, schedules, and work.

And I had a different "spreadsheet" in the forefront of my own mind. Was he measuring up to my expectations of time spent together, romance, or priorities? We had two different maps, to two different destinations, and no vehicle to get us to either.

Each of us failed to measure up on the other's checklist. It caused heartache at first, then desperation. Eventually it almost completely unraveled our cord of three strands, had it not been for God in the middle holding us together. Our house became charged with anger, resentment, pain and brokenness.

Though one may be overpowered, two can defend themselves. A cord of three strands is not quickly broken.

Ecclesiastes 4: 12

In hatred and in ugly sin, Adam and I had thrown "divorce" at each other a handful of times in those early years. About 3 years into our marriage, I gave up. I gave up on our marriage. I gave up on Adam. And I gave up on happiness.

I even gave up on divorce. I surrendered that threat where it belonged – at the foot of the Cross. Christ died for my own plans to abandon Adam and also for the abandonment I felt *because* of Adam. He suffered for my malicious hatred of Adam and for my desire to jump ship like Jonah. I had given up on everything, *but I did not give up on God.*

And God ran after me, in my impulse to run away. By His wounds, I would be healed. I had made a commitment to God that I would not dishonor. I put a stake in the ground. In fact, the stake had already been erected for me in the Cross of Christ.

I went to the Lord and said, in effect, "Jesus, I have made the decision that I will not seek a divorce. The thought of doing so is forever cast from my heart. I cannot *stand* the man who lives under this roof with me, but I made a vow to him in Your presence, and in Your name, I intend to honor it.

"I am filled with doubt that Adam will ever change, that our marriage will ever change. I am fully convinced that our lives will be forevermore parallel, or will completely diverge. But Lord, I am staying with him, because you are staying with me. And in the meantime, and *by the way…* CHANGE ME!

"I am still here, and I am still open to Your hand working on my heart. Do not give up on me, even as I am effectively giving up on my marriage, because I am NOT giving up on You. Though I am tied to this man, as flesh has become flesh, I am tied also to You Lord, in a bond stronger than earthly marriage. For I am married to YOU eternally… and YOU Lord, You love me, *perfectly.*"

These words I uttered deadly seriously, in complete and utter pain and hopelessness.

Jesus brought to death the ideas we held about marriage in our hearts. In place of these, He raised his own love, power and sacrifice. He stepped into the middle of our living hell, and He rescued us both.

Surely he took up our pain and bore our suffering, yet we considered him punished by God, stricken by him, and afflicted. But he was pierced for our transgressions, he was crushed for our iniquities; the punishment that brought us peace was on him, and by his wounds we are healed. We all, like sheep, have gone astray, each of us has turned to our own way; but the Lord has laid on him the iniquity of us all.

Isaiah 53: 4-6

It took another few years, but things miraculously began to change. Adam was behaving differently, and I hoped I was behaving differently too. I doubted, at first, what I was seeing. But changes started sticking. The difference became the norm. There was never a fixed turning point, but slowly during my pregnancy with our second child (our first son), and the season before and after, our marriage made an unmistakable shift.

I wondered if it was the years of counseling. We started in pre-marital counseling, and we never "graduated." We never got "fixed," so I guess that is why we never got out. We are still – *happily* – in counseling today.

I wondered if it was the mentoring relationship Adam had gotten into with a man about 20 years his senior. I wondered if it was the discipleship group Adam had been involved in, Christian Leadership Concepts[1] – walking through a couple of years of close and deep fellowship with men his same age. I wondered if it was my final surrender, waving the white flag to God in defeat and desperation. I wondered, even, if it was our Austin – Adam having his first son.

But I think I knew deeply, too, that God used all of it, *and* none of it. It was the sheer grace of God lighting on our relationship, freeing us from the strangle hold of sin, lifting our burdens, healing our hearts. None of it would have been possible apart from His power and love, which he freely poured out for us and on us.

When God called me to Himself at 20, he saved me from myself. From the dead end path I was pursuing frantically. He saved me eternally, securing my destiny with Him forever.

And when I was about 29, he saved my marriage. Mysteriously, but very decisively. He saved Adam and me from destroying each other and destroying our family.

God's voice whispered goodness and love to my *own* heart, deep in its secret recesses, for at least the 9 years I had known Him. *Then*, I witnessed an impossible miracle relationally, between *two* hearts, and the Lord's whispers turned to shouts and sent me to my knees in praise and thanksgiving.

How could it be? To put such power in my marriage as to raise us from death! Why did He care so much?

I wasn't hurting for material provision, I was longing for supernatural provision. I hadn't been physically ill, just desperately heartsick. I had other wonderful family relationships and beautiful children, but the one to whom I had been joined in flesh had become my enemy. Yet, God did not part those he had joined. He did not leave us or forsake us.

He actually had given us that which we never conceived we would *actually need*, when we engraved it on our wedding bands: "more than we could ever ask for or imagine." And this first miracle was only the beginning of that promise being fulfilled.

I will repay you for the years the locusts have eaten...
Joel 2: 25a

Road to Africa

In 2003, I was rejoicing over the birth of our daughter, but simultaneously was at about the worst place in our marriage.

Hannah Whit was born prematurely, weighing in under six pounds. I never imagined I could love such a tiny person so immensely (all 95 ounces of her), and yet, feel so abandoned by the person who brought her into the world with me.

No longer was I alone in the world to care for myself. I was alone to care for myself *and* a totally dependent other. Alone in the middle of the night, alone during the days, often alone on the weekends.   Alone to figure out how to feed, bathe, and soothe a baby, when I couldn't even soothe myself. My tears and my own pain drained me emotionally, and now I was drained physically as well. I was in the depth of my circumstantial depression in our marriage. The darkness had not yet seen the light.

But in the darkest hour of our marriage, he began to reveal a darker place still: a brokenness far beyond what I could imagine. A pain that, by far and away, overshadowed my present reality and my small existence. One Sunday, our pastor briefly mentioned AIDS orphans in Ethiopia as I held newborn Hannah Whit in my arms.

Can you imagine the stark contrast? Here is this perfect and lovely, beautiful and healthy five-pound blessing, wrapped safe and warm in loving arms and clean, pink blankets. Adored by parents and grandparents and 5 great-grandparents: she was the first child for us, the first grandchild to all of our parents, and the first great-grandchild to 4 of the 5 great-grandparents. Who could possibly be more loved or more spoiled?
And on the other side of the world, so many lives filled with unimaginable pain, loss, grief, abandonment, disease, suffering, filth, and desperate, dire need.

I couldn't possibly love any more, this one whom God had placed close to my heart, tight in my arms... but what about the ones so far away, longing for arms to hold them closely? Born without parents, whose mothers had often been finished off by the toil of labor, having given in to the disease they also carried. Many of these orphans were given only one thing, left with only one thing in the world: the HIV they contracted at birth.

My heart, though broken in the confines of my personal hell, shattered under the weight of such tremendous suffering.

Very truly I tell you, unless a kernel of wheat falls to the ground and dies, it remains only a single seed. But if it dies, it produces many seeds.

John 12: 24

God planted the first of many seeds, but they were covered with several more years of earth and soil, and pain and darkness. He was still bridging my newfound faith and fledgling love for Him with my new marriage and fledgling love for Adam, over the highways of amazing transformation and sanctification. God grew both my love for Him and my commitment to Adam.

He grew my faith, increased my trust and belief, my ability to surrender and to see truly, that, "With God all things are possible" (Matthew 19:26). I began to see how life was a living parable for His grace and mercy, His reckless pursuit and mysterious ways, His unbelievable miracles and incredible gifts. But even as He began healing my broken heart in my marriage, He was shattering it anew in different and deeper ways.

When Adam and I saw the light again around the time Austin was born in 2006, the seedling that God had been watering deep in my heart pressed upward on the soil and outward into reality. With our marriage rescued from the depths (or at least aboard a lifeboat), God had my full attention. What started as a whisper of suffering, in a church announcement in 2003, became murmuring all around me by 2007. I couldn't have escaped what God was putting in front of me around every turn, not that I was trying to.

God brought Africa across my path and into my view more and more: I had friends who served in an orphanage in South Africa for 2 years.[2] I read book after book about orphans, and their pain and suffering, which shredded and tilled the soil in my heart (*There is No Me Without You*[3], *The Lost Daughters of China*[4], *Lost Boy No More*[5], *28 Stories of AIDS in Africa*[6]). And I was inexplicably drawn to these books, the more and more I read.

During the same period of time, books about *"Crazy Love"*[7] and *"Radical"*[8] living in Christ, books about the *"Generous Justice"*[9] of God and *"The Hole in our Gospel"*[10] convicted me of my part to play. Even *American Idol Gives Back*,[11] of all things, God used to break my heart for the things that broke His heart.

I sat in front of the images flying across the TV wailing and saying, "No, Lord, no. This cannot be possible," and, "I can't be witness to the problem and not be a part of the solution."

In the spring of 2008, my mom and I were consumed with the passion of one 13 year-old girl, Ellie Ambrose. We sent out letters and raised a few thousand dollars for her ministry, "Ellie's Run" which fed, clothed and schooled children in the slums of Kibera, Kenya.[12]

It forced us to reassess our small business, and we decided to stop retailing stationary and gifts for fun, and start selling t-shirts for the Kingdom. Instead of reinventing the wheel, we designed and manufactured a t-shirt that we could use at any function, in any place, *at any time* to raise money for any charity we desired. The first shipment of shirts didn't come for three years, but the seed had been planted and the work was set in motion.[13]

And later in 2008, Adam and I, along with Anne and Nate Morrow, friends from our church, hosted a small get-together for another young girl, 19, named Katie Davis[14]. She is another Christian soldier, who was living radically and crazy-loving on the other side of the world. For a couple of years, we sponsored children and promoted her ministry to our friends, and by the time Liam was born in 2009, I had begun praying not, "How Lord?" Not, "What's next?" But, "When, Lord? When am I going?"

When will I wrap my own arms around these precious ones? When will I put faces in my hands and babies on my lap? When would I get to put Band-Aids on flesh wounds and pour my whole being into heart wounds? I wanted the Lord to turn my sending and my giving into going.

My heart was 6 years in the process of being completely broken for a place I had never been, and I wanted to GO.

He will stand and shepherd his flock in the strength of the Lord, in the majesty of the name of the Lord his God. And they will live securely, for then his greatness will reach to the ends of the earth.

Micah 5: 4

That same fall that Liam was born, 2009, I embarked on a 3-year bible study by Randy Pope, "Journey,"[15] with 8 other women. One of these 8 women was Anne Morrow. In our initial weeks together, Anne asked us for specific prayers regarding Africa as well. She told us, "The Lord just keeps saying 'Africa,' and I don't know what that means."

We prayed all year for the Lord's clarity and for her discernment. By the same time the following fall, she was on her way to Africa, accompanying church friends of ours (Drew and Tara Maddux) who went to adopt their 2 little boys in Jinja, Uganda.

Anne had prayed, "What does this mean, Lord? Africa?" And found herself on a plane to Uganda. In my own brokenness for the continent, I knew *exactly* what it meant for me from the very beginning – *I wanted to go.*

So in the 2nd fall of our Journey group, 2010, I committed to God to pray for a year (a challenge of "The Radical Experiment"[16]), and I trusted that He would show me within that year: Where I was going and how I was going to get there. (I even begged him to show me if it was not Africa, but some other continent, some other country where I was to journey. I waited with open hands.)

This waiting was to be both the end of one longing and the beginning of another. My prayers began to show me another bridge, and another highway, between one season of my walk with the Lord and the next. Though I had many times surrendered my pain over Africa and my desire to go, I was now drawing a line in the sand. I officially and methodically left it all in the hands of the Lord, in the fall of 2010, not long before Anne spent her first of many days in Africa.

As I left my plans and desires with the Lord that fall, I couldn't miss the mighty hand of God in the Morrow's hearts and lives. He was bringing Anne and Nate to the realization that adoption was to be a part of their family's story. In March of 2011, they met newborn Alinda Rose for the first time over Skype.

All of their questioning, all of their longing, all of their praying, all of their doubting was met by God with certain answers and precious blessing. Heartache and heaviness on both sides of the world united in hope and completion in two countries and in two families by the powerful highway of God's love and intervention. This is just a part of the very horrible, very dark, but very real crisis in Africa: extreme poverty that chokes even the most basic of needs, many joyful beginnings juxtaposed with painful endings.

But our God gives us "the oil of joy, instead of mourning, and a garment of praise instead of a spirit of despair" (Isaiah 61: 3). In our darkest hours he says to us, "I am not through with you yet... I have only just begun."

And there in that moment he provides for us a highway of hope. A highway from an orphaned baby to a family with open arms. A highway from a small hospital, in a small city, in a small country on the other side of the world, direct to Nashville, Tennessee.

I will not leave you as orphans. I will come to you.

John 14: 18

In the fall of 2009, when I began Bible study with Anne, she had been praying for the first time, "Africa? What does that mean?" In the fall of 2010, the second year of our Bible study, she *went* for the first time. And in the fall of 2011, the third and final year of our Bible study, she returned and met her daughter for the first time.

The Morrow's unfolding story had an unmistakable pull on my attention. And I am sure that I wasn't alone. Everyone in our Bible study was amazed, watching and waiting as God performed miracle after miracle in the Morrow's journey of trust and faith, in their desires to add a fourth child to their family.

To be honest, I was totally enraptured in their developing drama. So much so, that there were months where I completely forgot about my own longing to go. Plus, I *truly* had left my own questions in God's hands in total surrender... I knew He would show me His timing and His plans. I knew He would have some answer to my desires for the foreign mission field. When I asked Him to reveal His plans to me in the fall of 2010, I truly believed He would.

And so, somewhere in the spring of 2011, I had completely lost myself in the Morrow's story. Lost in wonder, awe, holy disbelief and life-altering excitement over these precious friends serving a mighty God and running with arms wide open to adopt their precious daughter. My desires, fully surrendered, had been almost fully forgotten. *Almost.*

Isn't this when God usually knocks us off our feet? Showering His blessing and showing His way, when we have completely abandoned our desires and "our ways" at the foot of His throne. It certainly had seemed that way in *our* marriage, anyway... God bursting forth the floodgates of heaven in when I had completely given everything over to Him. Why should it be any different with Africa?

After all, it is not until our hands are emptied that there is room to receive the surplus that God longs to pour in. We must first lower our hands, letting the tiny water droplets we cling to slowly roll off our palms. Then God, in His perfectly abundant nature, un-dams the waterfall to let rushing cascades spill forth, not just into our hands, but into our wide-open arms, into our expectant hearts and surrendered lives... even, and especially, through us into the lives of others. *Overflowing.*

So you can imagine my surprise when Adam asked me one evening in May of 2011, "Do you think I should call Nate and offer to go with them? You know, to go get Ali Rose?" (Yes! *I knew*!)

Adam and I were sitting in a Chinese restaurant celebrating his birthday when he asked me this. It was only a month after the Morrows "met" Ali Rose via Skype, only two months after she was born into the world. You can imagine my surprise when Adam said, "I am just going to call Delta and see how much a trip like this would cost!"

I was giving him any encouragement he may have needed in my facial expressions. (I really like to think I am a better encourager to him than God's Holy Spirit.) Then Adam joked, as an afterthought, "If I can get an *actual* agent on the line in less than 5 minutes, then it's a sign."

You can imagine my total surprise when an agent answered Adam's call within 5 seconds.

You can imagine my surprise when my fortune cookie said, "Sometimes the best action is just to take the first step." Now, I do NOT believe in fortune cookies or fortune-tellers or "fortunes," for that matter. But I do believe God has a sense of humor! And I wasn't just laughing, I was bubbling over with joy.

And honestly, I *still* didn't think of my own desires to "go." This was nothing shy of a miracle in and of itself. (*Not* thinking of myself!?) Not at any point did I try to put myself into Adam's story (or in God's story for

62

Adam). If Adam was going, then AMEN! After all, his trip had nothing to do with the prayers I had prayed for my own trip, right?

A couple of weeks later, I got a call from Anne one afternoon. She was almost hyperventilating, "What in the world?! Nate just told me that Adam called and offered to come with us to Africa. And I asked Nate, 'How in the world have I not first heard this from Allison?' It's either because she has had a coronary from excitement or because she doesn't know!!"

To say Anne was surprised would be an understatement – but can you imagine *my* surprise?

I didn't know Adam had called Nate! I didn't know that he had stepped beyond the radical idea in his head – *into action*. (I knew that Adam had talked about going two weeks prior, but he had said nothing to me since. I had no idea he had actually called Nate.)

So, I was able to tell Anne that both of her statements were somewhat true – both the "not knowing," *and* the coronary. I had come near heart failure when Adam had first brought it up, and I was certainly approaching coronary arrest with this news.

At the moment she called, I was still sulking in my disappointment that two weeks had gone by, and not a word from Adam. Calling Nate before getting a "second opinion" from me? What a bold and daring (and unusually out of character) move by my husband! I guess he knew, anyway, that his "holy spirit" (little "h," little "s") would have advised onward with both thumbs pointing up.

Our highway to Africa began early in our marriage, with God tugging at my heart, but through the Morrows – *and through my husband* – God would pave the highway there.

My ears had heard of you, but now my eyes have seen you.

Job 42: 5

Chapter 4 | The Story in My Heart : The Morrow Crew

I can't actually remember the first time I met Anne Morrow, and that's probably because, by now, it feels like I've known her forever. Anne's story is somewhat similar to mine – she was raised in a church-going home, but she didn't become a Christian until high school. Both of us came to Christ later in life, but Anne's story has the added element of romance. Her husband, Nathaniel, led her to Christ when they were dating in high school... on the side of a county road, in the cab of his old pick-up truck. As they say in our Southern neck of the woods, these are the perfect makings of a country song!

Anne's love for her husband and unwavering admiration of his faith continued to inspire and encourage her. When we began our Bible study journey together, in September of 2009, she was eager to grow in her own relationship with Christ, still spurred on by Nathaniel's example. She desired to grow in her own relationship with the Lord, just as she had seen her husband thrive in his journey with Jesus.

All of the women in our new Bible study were in a similar stage of life – moms with young children. And all of us possessed a deep desire to walk closely with the Lord and with each other, growing in intimacy with God, while developing a rich community within our group. I was coming into a fellowship of equally minded friends, and Anne was no exception.

The beauty of God's Spirit in Anne's heart is unmistakable. She is thoughtful, terribly witty, and always authentic – Anne is the real deal, the genuine article. Throw Africa into the mix, and it is easy to see how I was quickly drawn to her.

In those early days, however, neither of us had any idea that our different paths would merge right onto the same highway...

Therefore, if you have any encouragement from being united with Christ, if any comfort from his love, if any common sharing in the Spirit, if any tenderness and compassion, then make my joy complete by being like-minded, having the same love, being one in spirit and of one mind.

Philippians 2: 1-2

This is beginning of Anne's part of the story.

"This is the story in my heart," she starts. "It is the story of how the Morrow Five became the Morrow Six. It's a story written by the Ultimate Storyteller, who knows the details, knows the twists and turns, knows the climax and the ever after. It's the story of my finally deciding that I wanted to live *that* story. *His* story. It's the story of saying, 'Yes.'.....

All my life, in subtle ways, I've sought to control my circumstances, to play it safe, to hold this world, and the things of it, very tightly. This is the story of learning that my heart was made for freedom, to let go and to open my hands. To see that what spills out is beautiful, because it is a product of what He has first poured in. It is really a much better story than any story I could have written for myself.

The Lord spoke to me in 2008. He whispered into my soul, "Africa." What I didn't know then, but I do know now, is that he was inviting me to participate in a larger story. When I first felt Him stir, He revealed only a call to obedience. "Trust me, for I know the plans...."

Following the Lord into His plans, and going against my own planning nature, I took baby steps, inching my way toward trust and obedience. Those baby steps grew into giant leaps and found me on a plane to Uganda in October of 2010.

Although I was going with two of our dear friends, Tara and Drew Maddux, who were adopting two little boys from Jinja, I felt certain that the trip was *not* about adoption for me. I went not as a result of any specific calling, but only because I was responding to the call, "Go."

It was the first time in my life that I knew God had spoken to me, and I was simply responding in faith. I didn't have all the answers (in fact, I didn't have any of them), and I was scared out of my mind. But it was time to *live life* instead of watching from the sidelines. I was learning to walk with God.

Africa changed me. No doubt about it. I now had names and faces and stories that personalized those statistics that I had been hearing about the orphan crisis around the world. My heart was opened to those hurting and in need – to orphans both near and far. Still, when I returned home from Uganda, I did not feel a specific call to adopt.

At this time, Nathaniel and I were both sure, however, that we desired to have a fourth child. We also both assumed it would be a biological child. Thanks again to my planning nature – I thought I had it all figured out as to when we might begin trying to grow our family.

Was I fickle when I intended to do this? Or do I make my plans in a worldly manner so that in the same breath I say both, 'Yes, yes,' and 'No, no'? But as surely as God is faithful, our message to you is not 'Yes' and 'No'… For no matter how many promises God has made, they are 'Yes' in Christ. And so through him, the 'Amen' is spoken by us to the glory of God.
                                                              2 Corinthians 1: 17-18, 20

In December, shortly after I returned from Uganda, my husband attended a four-day retreat in Colorado. Before Nathaniel left, I said to him, "Will you ask the Lord if we are supposed to have a fourth child? And will it be a biological child or are we maybe supposed to adopt?" So, it was interesting that the teachers at the retreat instructed Nathaniel and the other participants, from the time they arrived, on how to have a conversational relationship with God.

While in the Rocky Mountains, Nathaniel was in one particular prayer session when he asked the Lord about our family make-up, and at 7:35 p.m. MST on December 4th, the Lord spoke to Nathaniel. He wrote the following in his journal: "You are to adopt. There will be more Morrows."

Nathaniel, taken aback, started firing questions at the Lord, "Who? Where from? How many?"

The Lord responded, "The rest I am not ready to reveal."

When Nathaniel returned home, he did not tell me that God had told him that we were to adopt. What he *did* tell me was that God was leading us to pursue His will as a couple. Nathaniel expressed his desires that we would be obedient to whatever God was calling us to. And if God's call was adoption, so be it.

In my planning nature, I reverted right back to trying to "get it all figured out." About that time, we were hit by a perfect storm of distracting and unfavorable circumstances in our lives. Our world was shaken, and due to where God had us in that season, it was clear that this was no time to get pregnant. Frustration began to creep in as the months passed, but the hold didn't lift. I was ready, and yet the circumstances forced us to continue waiting.

As days and then weeks slipped away, the focus of our prayer became, "What does God want for our family?" And, "What does He have in store for us?" We continued to wait and to listen for the Lord.

Wait for the Lord; be strong and take heart and wait for the Lord.

Psalm 27: 14

In early March of 2011, I left Nashville for the weekend to visit a friend in Columbus, OH. She had just delivered her first baby. Nathaniel and I again committed to being in prayer – to seek unity spiritually, while we were apart physically. We really sought to hear what the Lord wanted for our family.

Although my visit was a wonderfully blessed time with my friend and her newborn, I also came away with the realization that I did not long for another biological baby. I remember that before I left Ohio on Sunday, March 6th, I was wrestling with the intellectual certainty that I wanted another child, juxtaposed against the "sense" that it was not to be from me.

That same Sunday, Nathaniel sat in the prayer room at our church, reading his Bible and journaling. His question: "Are we supposed to adopt? Lord, I need to know - yes or no? Are we supposed to adopt?"

The Lord replied, "I already told you. *I told you in December.* You ARE going to adopt."

Nathaniel later told me, about his time in the prayer room, that an intense peace came over him, which he had understood as being resolution from the Lord. However, when he and I first talked about all of this, on March 7th, we were not quite so bold about telling each other *specifically* what the Lord had revealed to us both. I think we both just said, "Let's keep praying."

Needless to say, something was born in both of our hearts that weekend.

If only there were someone to mediate between us, someone to bring us together…
Job 9: 33

The next two weeks were hard for me. I asked those close to me to pray on our behalf that we would hear God in this, but the day-to-day waiting seemed unbearable. I had been ready to grow our family since late fall of 2010, so each day that passed I grew more impatient – *and* more excited. I had a sense of urgency, and I just kept thinking about how much I wanted another little one… and I wanted *her* soon.

That's right. Somewhere deep inside I knew I wanted a girl, another beautiful daughter to cherish. A sister for Lily, Luke and Jack. It was hard for me to admit – at least out loud – that I wanted another girl. When you conceive a child, it's not like you get to pick! But as I spent more time before the Lord and became more honest with myself, I knew I wanted *her*—and when I would close my eyes really tight... I knew she was not from me. She had a tiny brown face, big brown eyes and tiny hands and feet.

A very specific desire was growing deep in my heart, but I had no clue how that desire would be met. Again, it felt too crazy to even speak aloud.

The week of our spring break, Nathaniel and I were continuing to pray and seek, but we were not hearing much in return. I noticed every pregnant woman around me, but I also noticed every child that was obviously adopted. I grew frustrated and discouraged, but I kept searching and surrendering.

I was tracking my period and ovulation (*still* planning, just in case), while at the same time, I was doing internet searches for adoption. Ultimately, I would surrender everything, as part of my story meant laying down *all* of *my* plans. My heart was definitely leaning towards adoption (when I was not being fearful about it).

By the end of the week of spring break I was really wondering, "What in the world?" I did not want to try and get pregnant, but I also did not feel peace about the traditional adoption process. I honestly wanted the Lord to lead us, but I wondered where it was all going... and when. I had come to the end of myself. Which was precisely the place I needed to be.

Take delight in the Lord, and he will give you the desires of your heart.
Psalm 37: 4

When I went to Africa with the Madduxes, I travelled with another mom from Nashville, Mandy Gallagher[1]. She is truly my sister in Christ, and during the trip, we were bonded for eternity. But the path Mandy and I shared together also crossed with two American nurses, Abigail and Leah, both serving one year with a medical initiative in Masindi, Uganda.

At the time that we met them, they were caring for 5-month-old twins who were newly orphaned. These babies were fighters – they were just beginning to turn a corner and thrive under the unconditional love and care from the nurses. As only the Lord could orchestrate, Mandy and her husband, Mike, would later adopt these twins.

She is now their forever mother, and they have a very full and beautiful family that we are privileged to know and love. After the trip, we saw the Gallaghers frequently, but I also continued to keep up with Abigail and Leah through their blogs and occasional emails.

On Monday, March 21st (not 6 months after my first visit to Uganda), my phone rang, but I missed the call. The caller ID showed that it was Abigail calling from Uganda. She left a very calm voicemail for me, saying that she had something for Nathaniel and I to pray about.

Abigail and Leah had been called in to check on a baby girl who was just two weeks old, born on Sunday, March the 6th - *the same day* Nathaniel and I knew we were being called to adopt. CONFIRMATION!

The baby had been left at Family Spirit Children's Centre, a place that was not well equipped to care for infants. I listened to the message and burst into tears. I was hysterical. I called Nathaniel, who picked up and immediately assumed something horrible had happened to me or to one of our children.

After I was able to sputter out the news, we were both just quiet for a minute. Nathaniel was literally speechless, and he said he would call me back soon. I frantically tried to call Abigail back, but the connection would not go through. I then tried to call another trusted friend, but wasn't able to get her on the phone either. I was shaking. I was crying. I couldn't sit still.

I went to the only thing left – my Bible, and I read about "perfect love that drives out fear." At this point the biggest barrier in my mind to adopting was fear of the unknown. Fear of what the future would look like. The Lord gave me the verse 1 John 4:18. I began to cling to this scripture, and He began write it on my heart.

There is no fear in love. But perfect love drives out fear, because fear has to do with punishment. The one who fears is not made perfect in love.

I John 4: 18

The rest of that Monday was a blur. We made contact with Abigail over email, and we set a Skype date for Wednesday of that week. Abigail also told us, as we shared our hearts with her over email, that she was praying about whether or not this little girl could or should be *her* daughter. Nevertheless, she felt as though the Lord was prompting her to reach out to us. We all committed to praying fervently about this baby girl.

Leah picked the baby up from the children's home, and Abigail, who had been in Kampala, started the long drive back to Masindi. She prayed all the way that God would show her immediately whether the baby was hers or ours. Upon arriving home, she walked down the dirt road to the hospital and met Leah along the way. As Leah handed her the baby girl, Abigail pulled the blanket away from her face. As soon as she did this, Abigail saw all of the faces of the other Morrow children flash before her eyes. In that moment, she knew that the baby's name would be Rose and that she would be a Morrow. CONFIRMATION.

After our long-distance conversation with Abigail, Nathaniel and I decided that we were going to keep it all close to the vest. Besides God, Abigail and Leah, we would not talk to anyone else about the circumstances or the prayers we were all praying. We have learned in the past that other voices

- even with the best of intentions- can get in the way of hearing the Lord.

Abigail and Leah had attached a picture of this baby girl to one of their first emails to us. When I looked at her picture, I felt as though I was falling in love. It was so strange and so beautiful at the same time. Then, on Wednesday of that same week, we saw her for the first time over Skype. I could hardly contain my joy! She was perfect. I couldn't stop thinking about her, nor could Nathaniel.

Shout for joy to God, all the earth! Sing the glory of his name; make his praise glorious.

Say to God, "How awesome are your deeds! So great is your power that your enemies cringe before you. All the earth bows down to you; they sing praise to you, they sing the praises of your name."

Come and see what God has done, his awesome deeds for mankind!

Psalm 66: 1-5

As the days passed we got more information from Abigail and Leah regarding her story. These journal entries were posted on their separate blogs:

From Leah:

> On Monday, Abigail got word of a two-week-old baby that had been assigned to Family Spirit. Her mother died from her C-section. Though Family Spirit is technically not registered as an orphanage, the social worker gave her to them for lack of another place to send her.
>
> Family Spirit called us because her umbilical cord had blood spurting out whenever she cried. Susan, the woman

who helps run Family Spirit, brought her to me to be checked. When she came in, looking exhausted from her duties as mom, school teacher, director, cleaner, etc., I knew the baby would be staying with us. And stay she has!

She was born on March 6th at Masindi Hospital. The story is vague and details are missing, but apparently her mom died from an infection ten days after her C-section. A.R. is now part of our family, and we can't imagine life without her. At two weeks, she is 6 pounds, 3 ounces, 21 inches, with a head full of hair.

She's healthy - her umbilicus is healing, and her oral thrush is almost gone. We are enjoying her baby noises and love carrying her in the Moby wrap. She's a pacifier girl through and through, and her color is officially purple.

From Abigail:

Our little Ugandan family has grown by two more tiny feet. That tiny sweetness, who is **ALINDA ANNA ROSE**, was born on **March 6, 2011.** She's just 2 weeks old.

When Leah and I first saw her, the word that immediately came to both of us was "grace," so we began calling her Baby Grace while we decided on a full name. Her mother's name was Rose, so we felt like we wanted to honor the woman who gave her life by letting her keep her mother's name. Grace Rose and Rose Grace didn't sound right to us…so we waited for the right name to show up.

For reasons I can't get into here… yet… the name Anne is very important to this baby. It was also my grandma's birthday yesterday, and her name is Anne. I looked up the definition also, and I found out that Anna means, you guessed it, "Grace." So, we're calling her Anna Rose.

Since she's so little, she's been coming with us to the clinic during the day. She gets passed around among the staff, and they love her! They gave her a Ugandan surname, Alinda (pronounced ah-LEEN-dah). The name means, "God cares" or "God protects." It comes from the verb "kulinda," which means, "to care for".

We love this verb because it was one of the first words we learned in Runyoro, the local tongue in Masindi. So many people have come up to us saying, "Webale kulinda abaana," that we finally had to ask someone what it meant. It means, "Thank you for caring for our children." Maybe carrying the name Alinda will remind sweet Anna Rose that God has cared for her since the day she was born and encourage her to one day care for other tiny orphans.

A good name is more desirable than great riches; to be esteemed is better than silver or gold.

Proverbs 21: 1

Ali Rose was born on March 6th, 2011, and I believe she was born in our hearts on that same day. Her mother passed away on March 16th, which happens to be my Dad's birthday. Her African name, "Alinda," we love, and it has Nathaniel's mom's name (Linda) in it. Within a day or two, I was calling her Ali Rose (not out loud, of course!). Again, I had this joy that I couldn't explain.

Nathaniel and I reached out with our news to a trusted friend, and she told me that it was almost like I was a pregnant new mom, gushing with the news. It was hard not to talk to *everyone* I came into contact with about it. We were in communication with Abigail and Leah on a daily basis. We asked God about starting the adoption process on our side of things, and we felt a resulting peace that we should go ahead and start the paperwork. Nathaniel and I were on our faces before the Lord, asking, "Is she our daughter?" Wanting the answer to be, "Yes," but only if it was His will. We began to get addicted to looking at her picture on the computer and reading the details of her daily life in Africa. I couldn't get enough. And I couldn't believe I was feeling this way!

Nathaniel and I exchanged some text messages in those first few days that I thought did a good job of saying what we were feeling in the moment. They went like this:

> N-   How are you feeling?

> A-   I can't stop thinking about her.

> N-   I know. Me too.

> A-   It's like I am falling in love with her from afar. How is that even possible?

> N-   Not sure.... God. We must wait on the Lord.

> A-   I know, but I don't think I am falling in love with her on my own accord...

> N-   I agree.

CONFIRMATION.

On Sunday, we went to church and I broke down (did the big ol' ugly cry) just thinking about Ali Rose and the fact that three weeks ago her Mom had given birth to her. Now here I was, on the other side of the world, my heart breaking to be her mother.

But Mary treasured up all these things and pondered them in her heart.
Luke 2: 19

Nathaniel seemed to be having an easier time that I did not talking to others about it. It was hard enough not discussing everything with friends, but I desperately wanted to talk to my Mom. I didn't necessarily want her opinion or her approval – I just wanted her to know about this huge thing in my life! I hadn't talked with my Mom at all about wanting a fourth child, so she had no idea that we had been praying for several months about growing our family.

Yet, on Monday the 28th, I was sitting in my minivan outside the parking lot of Wal-Mart. It was a week after we got the phone call from Uganda. My mom called me, and we talked for a little while. (I had kind of been avoiding calling my family, because it seemed too hard not to say anything). Somewhere mid-conversation my Mom said, "I just, by chance, was reading Abigail's, and then Leah's, blogs, and they have this new baby. I think she is supposed to be your daughter." CONFIRMATION (and BLESSING) from the Lord!

My mouth hit the floor! What?!?!? I mean, it was that crazy! I still didn't feel like it was "right" to be discussing it with Mom, although I did have such a joy just knowing that she had seen the baby and read a little about her story. I asked my Mom to pray for us, and I told her that I would fill her in just as soon as I could. Although, I didn't know exactly when that might be.

On Tuesday, the 29th of March, we got news that Ali Rose's HIV tests were negative. We had been praying for her health relentlessly. Nathaniel woke me up early that morning to tell me that her "rapid"[2] test was negative, and our eyes filled with tears. During this same time, we were under a lot of stress in a separate set of circumstances outside the adoption. So, when we got her results, it was shocking to realize how much more important her health was to us, than the other things which had once seemed so important. Priorities were being re-arranged in our hearts and our minds. CONFIRMATION.

We prayed consistently that God would draw our hearts to hers and begin to shape us into her mother and father. We also prayed that if it weren't

His will, He would turn us away. We asked for more confirmation and peace to know what His plan was for both Ali Rose and for our family. We prayed for Jack, Luke and Lily, that they would be transformed into big brothers and a big sister. We prayed for Abigail and Leah, and we praised God for the unbelievable gift they were giving us in caring for this child, who we desired to be our daughter.

But most of all we prayed for little Ali Rose, for her heart to know Christ. For her strength and wisdom and character. For her to know LOVE right from the beginning of her life.

It is right for me to feel this way about all of you, since I have you in my heart and, whether I am in chains or defending or confirming the gospel, all of you share in God's grace with me. God can testify how I long for all of you with the affection of Christ Jesus. And this is my prayer: that your love may abound more and more, in knowledge and depth of insight…

Philippians 2: 7-9

When I got a call from the lady at Catholic Charities with whom we would be working, I could only smile when she told me that her cell service was shaky as she was calling me from Pikeville, KY. I told her that I knew about Pikeville, and I felt an instant connection and happiness to be working with her. (My parents have spent the last 12 years in Pikeville.) When we had our first meeting with our social worker, it was amazing to sit on her couch and tell the story out loud (Nathaniel and I, together) for the first time.

I don't know the exact day that I knew, beyond a shadow of a doubt, that she was to be my daughter. I can't pinpoint the precise moment, but somewhere deep within me I began to have an overwhelming peace and joy. She was a gift from the Lord, and I would consider it a privilege to be her mother on this earth.

I think I might have felt God's peace over this a little bit sooner than Nathaniel. However, I never felt the urge to pressure him or figure out where he was in the process. I felt that if this was truly from the Lord (which I believed it to be), then He would bring Nathaniel and I into unity.

On the morning of April 8th, a CPA (Christ Presbyterian Academy) freshman greeted Nathaniel in the high school parking lot. She wanted to tell him about the strange dream she had the night before. In her true teenage way she said, "Just so you know Mr. Morrow, I had a dream that I went with you and your wife to pick up a baby girl from Africa."

Nathaniel, in his best principal tone (trying not to let his voice crack), "You better stop having crazy dreams!" CONFIRMATION.

Nathaniel also received a call from our pastor. Carter[3] had committed to praying for us, but it was never his style to give us advice one way or another. However, he told Nathaniel, outright, "As crazy as it sounds, I believe the answer is, 'YES, she is your daughter.'" CONFIRMATION.

God gave us both such unique and affirming confirmations at each step.

I have given them the glory that you gave me, that they may be one as we are one – I in them and you in me – so that they may be brought to complete unity. Then the world will know that you sent me and have loved them even as you have loved me.

John 17: 22-23

April 8th, 2011, was the 16-year anniversary of my first date with Nathaniel. We had, on that day, officially been together for half of our lives. Weeks earlier, I had booked a sitter so that we could spend the evening together on yet another special date. That morning, when I woke up, Nathaniel had sticky notes all over the house with little things that he remembered about that first date 16 years earlier. I smiled as I read and recalled each memory.

After dinner, we went to Centennial Park because it was a gorgeous evening. We sat on the steps of the Parthenon, and I read a note to Nathaniel describing my life since he had entered it. From falling in love with him while dissecting the fetal pig in Biology II class, to accepting Christ with him on the side of the road in his "Ole Blue" pick-up truck, to our wedding day, to finding our calling working with the inner city youth of Nashville, to the birth of Jack, to being stretched and called into the private school world of Christ Presbyterian Academy, to the news and birth of the twins, Luke and Lily. What an amazing adventure we had been on!

In my letter, I used the scripture Jeremiah 29:11-13, "'For I know the plans I have for you,' declares the Lord, 'plans to prosper and not to harm you. Plans to give you hope and a future. Then you will call upon me and come and pray to me, and I will listen to you. You will seek me and find me when you seek me with all your heart.'" I told Nathaniel how blessed I felt to get to spend this life with the love of my life and my best friend. I told him that I couldn't wait to see the rest of the amazing story God was writing with our lives.

Then Nathaniel gave me a card that he bought. I read the outside, but when I opened the card up, I found the last sticky note he wanted me to have. It said, "Alinda Rose will be our daughter. I am there!!!!! I love you!!!!"

We both cried. We prayed. We cried some more. And then… we went to Sweet CeCe's for frozen yogurt to celebrate!

Nathaniel and I shared more about what God had done in our hearts over the past 19 days. He had allowed us to fall in love with this little girl, and He had turned us into her parents. He had gotten us to a place where walking away from her would have been as impossible as walking away from one of our biological children. He gave us visions of her later in her life, of Nathaniel holding her beautiful face cupped in his hands on her wedding day.

The next day, Saturday, April 9th, we Skyped with Abigail and Leah, and we got to see her little face again.   She had grown so much in the first month of her life. We told them that our answer was, "Yes!!!"

Lord willing, we wanted her to be our daughter. On Monday the 11th, we shared the news with our children, and let me just say we could all learn something from children. Their willingness to love and accept without reservation was extremely powerful.

Every good and perfect gift is from above, coming down from the Father of heavenly lights, who does not change like shifting shadows. He chose to give us birth through the word of truth, that we might be a kind of firstfruits of all he created.

James 1: 17-18

In October of 2010, I traveled to Uganda in response to a call from God. In October of 2011, I returned to meet my daughter for the first time – it was literally almost a year to the day. I made a final trip with Nathaniel, in November of that same year.

Accompanied by the Doyles and the Hodges, we went to attend court and bring Ali Rose home in time for Thanksgiving. From start to finish, our journey was one not only of faith and obedience, but also of the remarkable plans and blessings God gives us when we surrender our lives to His provision.

Ali Rose's story was written into ours before the beginning of time. An amazing story, written by The Master Storyteller. God invited us to participate, and this time, I said, "Yes."

We are uncertain of the next step, but we are certain of God.

Oswald Chambers[4]

Chapter 5 | Three Growing Families : The First Trip

Until recently, I believed my road to Africa officially began at Adam's birthday dinner (2011), when he suggested going to Africa with the Morrows. However, during the writing of this book, I found out God had been working in my heart *much* longer than I remembered. I got a text from my mom. She sent it on Adam's birthday, of all days (2013), exactly two years after Adam's suggestion to go.

Mom: "Hey there. I found a really neat paper you wrote when you were 8. I'll save it for you. This is what it says (I'm using your third-grade spelling, etc.) –

> *If I had a dream it would be for all people in Ethiopia to it-*
> *least have one pair of clothes. Lots of food for one year. And*
> *to live until there old. It would be so nice. I feal sorry for*
> *them. I would hate to starve. Why do they have to starve?*
> *My family gave $50. I'd like to see all of them with smiles on*
> *their face. Last night I wished I could adopt one of them.*

"Hmmmm." Mom wrote, "Seems like this Africa thing has been going on for a while!"

My response: "No way. No memory of that!"

Mom: "Yep! January 16, 1985."

Me: "That is JUST crazy!!"

And, yes. It is crazy. Even crazier that Susan was born around 1985.

But the plans of the Lord stand firm forever, the purpose of His heart through all generations.

Psalm 33:11

Adam committed to go with the Morrows to Uganda in June of 2011, just a few weeks *after* his birthday, and we learned very soon that another Nashville couple was adopting as well (Ryan and Lindsey Doyle). Less than a month after Adam's decision to go, we sensed the Lord leading me to come along too, so we knew it was very likely that all six of us would be in Uganda together at the same time.

Adam had to surrender his very real fear that I could be physically harmed. After all, we were flying into Kony's homeland, a place familiar with terror and political instability. Idi Amin's brutal regime made Uganda notorious long before Joseph Kony. And though Uganda is now mostly peaceful, it is still a country bordered by other unstable countries, present or past, on almost every side (South Sudan, Congo, Rwanda, Kenya). We were flying to a continent so far away and so foreign that Adam had absolutely no idea what to expect, and all of his protective instincts were on high alert.

To make matters worse, he had to watch "Machine Gun Preacher" with Gerard Butler[1]. This movie was based on the real life story of a Christian whose newfound faith took him to Africa, protecting child soldiers in Southern Sudan from rebel military forces. While Adam was plotting and scheming defensive militaristic moves to shield me from harm, running and re-running tactical rescue plans in his mind, I was busy getting the things we might actually want or need: prescription anti-malarial pills, bags of candy and sheets of stickers for any kids we might meet there, and crisp, unmarked one hundred dollar bills with a date of 2006 or higher (for the highest exchange rate).

Adam packed rope and duct tape for purposes not yet determined. I collected sunscreen and bug spray. I got shots and immunizations, updated my passport, picked up odds and ends on every run from the house. In the days leading up to our departure, I crossed all my "t's" and dotted all my "i's."

In the challenge of the "Radical Experiment,"[2] I had asked God to send me within one year – I couldn't believe He had both answered my prayers *and* honored the timing. In addition, I couldn't believe I was getting two for the price of one – not only were Adam and I going together... but the Lord, in his perfect nature, had also actually purposed Adam to lead me there.

"But it's too wonderful!" like the *Jesus Storybook Bible* says, and continues, "Is anything too wonderful for God?"[3]

This journey trumped every adventure I had ever been on and surpassed every trip I had ever taken. Since the night we landed for the first time on the dark red Ugandan dirt, I have not stopped longing to return to the place that captured my heart. Subsequent trips have only tightened my heart's ties to the place and to the ones I have come to love so deeply.

The priest answered him, "Go in peace. Your journey has the Lord's approval."
Judges 18:6

We sat on pause from late summer until autumn, knowing that at any time, things could fall into place for the adoptions. At any time we might need to book our airline tickets on short notice and be ready to go within days. My parents were ready, as well, to jump in and take over with the kids. We had even lined up friends for all back-up childcare scenarios.

In October, we received word that the babies had court dates, and it was time to get going.

Eighteen hours of flying. Two significant layovers in between four airports. A day and a half of planes and who knows how many languages. I have been to Uganda three times now, and each time I have gone by a different way and a different airline. But that first trip, Adam and I flew to New York LaGuardia and then to London Heathrow on our way to the airport in Entebbe, Uganda. And it is a long, *long* trip. No matter how you slice it.

We landed for the last time – in Africa. I cannot say it to this day, without hearing it in the local tongue, "Ah-free-ka." We were finally there. You would have never known we had just travelled on an overnight flight from a major international airport by the way we deplaned.

We walked off the massive jet via a plane exit stairwell, down to the tarmac, just as if we had been flying an island hopper briefly from one small airport to another. We walked outdoors to the airport building, where we would walk inside and go through customs. We left Nashville when fall was arriving. We landed in Uganda on a sticky-hot night, and we had our bug spray on before we had our bags.

There we were, Adam and I together, on the other side of the world just before midnight. We knew the Doyles and Morrows were not far behind us on a different airline. We sat on our bags until their plane appeared. Then, I got my camera ready to begin chronicling this portion of their adoption journey through photos. I expected simply to snap pictures of their travel-weary faces, but we all had another surprise waiting.

The gals there to greet us, Abigail and Kara, had brought the babies. (Kara is another Nashville woman who has served in Uganda in many capacities, and for many years.) I ended up capturing images of the daddy's first meetings with their girls. It was not unlike a daddy meeting his baby for the first time in the delivery room. Not unlike, I suppose, our Heavenly "Abba" Daddy, who welcomes us into his arms and lifts us up high on wings like eagles.

The Spirit you received does not make you slaves, so that you live in fear again; rather, the Spirit you received brought about your adoption to sonship. And by Him, we cry, 'Abba, Father.'

Romans 8:15

If you had asked me where Uganda was located in Africa before we left for that first trip, I don't think I could have told you. Look for the biggest round body of water in the middle of East Africa, and you will find tiny Uganda sitting right on top. Uganda is called, "The Pearl of Africa," both because of its small size and because of its valuable crop resources. The soil there, thanks largely to Lake Victoria and to plentiful rain, provides several cash crops, coffee and sugar among them. The Kakira (the yellow package with the lion) and Kinyara facilities (miles and miles of beautiful plantations located within Masindi) are the largest among the sugar companies.

Uganda is slightly smaller than the size of Oregon in square mileage. However, there are approximately 37 million people in Uganda (compared with the substantially lower 4 million in Oregon), making it the 37th largest country in the world by population. Before we left, I wanted to know as much as I could about the country where we were going, located in the continent I so highly anticipated: the people and politics, crops and climate, languages and tribes, history and healthcare, wildlife, and even bugs. So, I read what I could, words on pages and words on the computer screen.

And when we left the airport, I kept my eyes wide open still, despite that fact that it was late and I was exhausted. I was ready to take it all in. That which was knowledge was becoming experience. No longer would I be reading in black and white... I would be experiencing, firsthand, with all my senses. Though the Lord had used His Spirit to till my heart, He was about to use His people and His creation to pull up fruit.

The information I had wasn't discarded, it was actualized, like the warm night wind wafting through the open van windows. "Wake up," it seemed to say as it whipped around. "You're here."

Emotionally, I was at the point of no return.

We drove from the city of Entebbe to Kampala, the capital city of Uganda, where we would spend our first few nights. Kampala is home to over 1.5 million, roughly 20% of the total population of Uganda, squeezed into about 73 square miles of land space. To grasp the relative size, consider that my hometown, Nashville, is about 500 square miles with approximately 650,000 people. A striking contrast. And far more so to be there, and to see what my eyes were seeing.

Nearing the city limits well past midnight, we tried to get our first glimpses of Uganda, but we caught more sounds and smells than sights. If you take a look at satellite photography of the world at night (a fascinating image easily found on the web), you will see very little light anywhere in Africa. Kampala has more bright spots than many places in Africa, but small fires surely make up the largest part of the nighttime illumination – there are roadside bonfires on the ground and makeshift grills set up in metal barrels, both of which lead the way into the city.

These fires, and the meals cooked over them, lent themselves to the smells we inhaled with the warm night air. There was certainly no lack of people buzzing around at this hour either – the voices of many foreign dialects swirled around our car, both from the many people who lived and walked alongside the roads and from their radios – some humming low, others blaring.

The guesthouse where we stayed on those first nights is mostly tucked away from traffic and noise. A good thing. We went to bed well near three in the morning according to the East African Time Zone. Who knows what time zone our bodies were in – we had traveled through eight within 24 hours. I fell asleep exhausted, but the next morning, I was expectant to see the many things I had missed in the dark of the night.

I awoke to noise. Humming, muted city sounds. People rustling in a kitchen. Foreign tongues. Foreign birds too, crowing, cawing and chirping. And light. There were no blackout curtains at Adonai Guesthouse, only screens on the windows... and the sounds passed through them as easily as the light. It was dawn in Uganda. It was our very first day in Kampala.

Before we could journey into the girls' small hometown, where the guardianship cases would be heard, the Doyles and Morrows had many initial details to attend to. The Embassy and a major medical center were on the top of their lists. They needed to get papers in order, and the girls needed complete physical examinations. This way, Ali Rose and Eden Hannah would be ready to leave the country, in the hopeful event that their cases were approved. So, they took the babies and climbed back into the van.

Our driver, Moses, would take them to all the places they would need to go, and he would help them with the details they must accomplish. Moses would be with us all week. In all that God was doing, in all He had already done... Can you fathom that God gave us a leader named Moses?

Zipporah gave birth to a son, and Moses named him Gershom, saying, "I have become a foreigner in a foreign land."

Exodus 2: 22

Adam and I could be of very little help with the "first things first," so we stayed back to assist Abigail on morning number one. Abigail was one of the two nurses who had fostered the baby girls. The other young woman, Leah, had already left Uganda to return home to America – she was engaged to be married. Both women had fulfilled their initial time commitments to their ministry organization - but Abigail was able to offer additional weeks and months of her life as a guardian to these two little ones. She sacrificed as long as it took to see these last two orphans home with their forever families.

Abigail, Adam and I would be left to our own devices in the guesthouse where we were staying. (It is much like an international youth hostel.) Abigail needed to get some baby items and first aid supplies at the supermarket nearby, "Nakumat." She invited us to go with her.

"How will we get there?" Adam asked, puzzled, as the transportation had left with the other families.

"By boda-boda," Abigail replied. These were the motorcycle taxis, the primary method of transportation, which weaved in and out of absolutely unbelievable, chaotic, and dangerous traffic. Most Ugandan cars have no seatbelts, so you can imagine how primitive (and dangerous) the lesser forms of transportation are still.

Adam quickly shot a look at us both and, *without pausing*, he said *in more words than one*, "No."

This was a suicide mission he would not accept. My brain was following his lead, but my heart dove into the arms of the God who had gotten us there in the first place.

"Can I go?" I asked permission from Adam (A.K.A. self-appointed commander of the imaginary international SEAL team).

Another leap of faith by my husband, letting me put myself in harm's way... letting me go out, in the first place, into a dangerous, unfamiliar and unknown world – *alone*. With only another woman at my side. "Yes, but...." he said.

"Yes, but..." he repeated, "be careful. " And it gets better, "Wear a helmet if the motorcycle driver has an extra one."

Ninety-nine percent of boda drivers (by visible statistics) do not wear motorcycle helmets themselves, much less do they carry around extras for the (sometimes 4) other passengers they cram onto the seat behind them. Besides, where would they even put "extra" helmets? Think about it.

But, "Yes..."

"Yes, honey. I will wear a helmet if he has an extra one."

He protected us on our entire journey and among all the nations through which we traveled.

Joshua 24: 17b

For most of my first trip by boda, my eyes were shut tight. It was horrifying. I will admit it. Heavy traffic, few regulations – *or regulators* – and roads riddled with bumps and potholes. Every pass by another boda, car, or bus, coming or going, was a new sweep with death.

I have since learned that boda accidents are one of the top causes of death in Uganda, behind AIDS and co-morbid diseases. And I have since witnessed firsthand a boda-on-car accident, as a bystander on a sidewalk. But I did not know the statistics then, nor had I had any personal experiences. I just kept my eyelids drawn during the close encounters. And I held on to Abigail as if my life depended on it, because – it did, in fact.

It was in this scenario that Abigail and I began to get to know one another, trading life stories. How we had come to know the Lord and, in particular, how we had come to Africa. There were many quiet lulls, as well as abrupt standstills in our conversation, depending on our speed and relative distance to other moving objects. But from the guesthouse to the market, and from the market back to the guesthouse, we began exchanging information about our journeys.

I started by telling her how God began to light a fire in my heart for Africa when Adam and I were first married, and how God had since been wooing me to care for His children there. I told her all of the ways God had thus far moved in my heart, from Carter's sermon early in our marriage, up through the more dramatic events of the past year. I ended by telling her what my recent summer had been like, preparing to depart for this very trip… waiting to leave…

I explained to Abigail how we had travelled from Nashville to Memphis that July to get a car for Adam. It was the best price Adam could find, and we were driving the three and a half hours to make the purchase. I had looked forward to that extended day trip, because I expected to be alone in my own car on the return leg. Alone to reflect on where God had us, from where he had brought us, and alone to pray for the days leading up to our departure for Africa.

As it had turned out, our childcare arrangements fell through for the older kids, and all my previous expectations for the trip vanished. I wouldn't have time to reflect and talk with Adam on the way to Memphis, nor would I have time alone to reflect and talk with God on the way home. We would be plus two.

After dropping off two-year-old Liam, the older kids watched a movie on the way to Memphis. I drove and Adam slept – this is not at all an uncommon set-up on our trips. Adam drives a lot with his job, so he rarely drives on family excursions.

Since Hannah Whit and Austin were plugged into the movie via headphones ("The Lion, The Witch and The Wardrobe"[4]), and Adam was sawing logs (It is unbelievable to me that he can sleep in the vertical upright position.), I did end up having some prayer time the first leg of that drive. I prayed about Africa; I prayed about God's will for our trip and beyond. However, my prayers ended about an hour later, when the kids began talking again in the back seat.

Abruptly, the headphones were off, and just as abruptly, so was my conversation with God. I eavesdropped instead. My first- and second-born were talking to each other:

Austin said, "We need another child in our family like the Pevensie's (in Narnia). They have four. We only have three, so we need another one."

"Yeah," Hannah Whit added, "We need a 'Lucy.'"

Based on the conversation that God and I had just been having, I wondered – in listening to the kids, was I still listening to God? I wondered if God Himself were trying to say something more to me *through* their conversation. After Hannah Whit was born, our next girl name was "Lucy." But I had given birth to two boys... an "Austin" and a "Liam." No little girls to name "Lucy."

With God driving my thoughts to Narnia, my mind drifted to Lucy Pevensie… her childlike love for Aslan and His rapture over her. During the year leading up to Africa, I had discovered *The Chronicles of Narnia*[5] series. Through these books, God was speaking very powerfully in my life – He was showing me the nature of His love for me. So, I started to wonder if my desires for God and for Africa were about to collide with His plans for our lives. Perhaps a Lucy was involved?

After I recounted this recent trip to Memphis to Abigail, I also started to tell her about the morning we left for Africa – my cousin Leslie had given birth to her baby girl. News was delivered to me when we were in the car on the way to the airport. Leslie named her little girl "Lucy."

And then, I would have told Abigail about our first commuter flight from Nashville to LaGuardia – how Adam and I sat in the very rear of the plane, right behind a family of four. There was a Mama and one little girl on the left side of the aisle; the grandmother and a slightly older girl were across the aisle, on the right side of the plane. The two women and the two sisters chatted the whole length of our flight, but it wasn't until we landed in New York that we heard one of the little girls say to her younger baby sister, "Look what I drew for you, Lucy!!"

However, I didn't even get a chance to tell Abigail the last two stories, at least not initially, because she stopped me cold after I told her about our Memphis car ride. She said, "You know there *is* a Lucy in this story, Allison."

I gasped, choking down sobs, as if God had stopped my narrative to tell me Himself.

I had been in Africa for less than 12 hours, and I had known Abigail for only half of that time. We were really still introducing ourselves to each other – and boom! There I was again, embraced by a personal, loving, amazing God.

What an immediate confirmation for our trip. As if I had even needed it. God had been holding us in the palm of his hand all along, and here I was, right off the bat, getting a loving squeeze.

Abigail told me how she had tried to name all of the girls "Lucy," first Ellie (one of the twins), then Ali Rose, then Eden Hannah. However, it had never seemed right to both her and Leah.   Their other names had fit them best for better reasons.

Abigail said she even tried to give the name "Lucy" to a dog they adopted for a while.

I didn't know what it all meant – *I still don't*, but I knew God was guiding. I knew this trip to Africa was not to be our last. I knew that this first trip was just the beginning of a long-term relationship… with a Lucy, or a special child… or lots of special children… on the other side of the world.

I led them with cords of human kindness, with ties of love. To them, I was like one who lifts a little child to the cheek, and I bent down to feed them.

Hosea 11: 4

After our second boda deposited us safely back at the guesthouse, we waited for the Morrows and the Doyles to return. There was still more in store for our first day, but we needed the van. We were going to an orphanage past the outskirts of Kampala, too far to pay additional fare for a boda. It would be my first chance to love and serve children! I was anxious to get there, but I was also *just anxious.* Period.

I told Anne, before we left for Africa, that I was worried about a potential, emotional freefall. You see – I am a crier. And that is putting it mildly. So many tears I have cried in America for these precious orphans, and for their stories of loss, abandonment and need! I was afraid that actually arriving at this first orphanage would be my complete undoing.

Anne comforted me with her words. "You never know… you just might surprise yourself. I found that by the time I actually got here, I was cried out and in 'task' mode. I was too focused on loving and helping, hugging and laughing to be worried about crying," said Anne, a fellow crier. "Good," I thought. "Maybe I will have a similar experience."

Not at all, I found out later, when we took the van to the orphanage. I started crying as I approached the concrete slab, which was used as a front stoop, and I didn't stop for hours. I cried on and off the whole time we were with the babies – and increasingly so later, when Abigail said we would be leaving soon. I finally had to put on my sunglasses *inside the building*, as I sat holding one of the infants. Eventually, I excused myself, just a little before Adam and Abigail followed.

I was a complete mess. I had, as predicted, come fully apart at the seams. Adam and Abigail were talking most of the trip home, but I was unable to join the conversation. I apologized for my state, but I was otherwise unable to speak on the hour-long return trip home.

I continued to hide behind my sunglasses and silently sob. So many emotions raged inside me, first of which was my desperation. Why on earth did we have to leave, when everything in me felt as heavy as lead to stay? For another hour. Another day. For forever.

I was embarrassed. For myself and for Abigail. I knew Abigail and I had forged a fast bond earlier that morning, and I thought my blubbering might threaten to compromise our new friendship. I had exposed myself – and the mess that existed inside me.

Had I embarrassed *her* at the orphanage? Were my tears *too stark a contrast* among the more calculated daily caregivers? They job was to comfort babies – the last thing they needed was a foreign-speaking adult to look after.

I was worried, also, that I was embarrassing Adam. "Isn't this just what he expected?" I thought. That I would be so predictable. So glaringly obvious.

He had taken a leap of faith, and instead of being quietly grateful for his leadership on this trip, here I was, quietly out-of-control.

I was sad, and I had sunk beyond reach. When my bleakest picture of Africa became reality, sadness turned to despair. It was as if I had secretly hoped that *it wouldn't be* as bad as I had imagined *it could be*, and then, it turned out to be worse.

It was as if I secretly wished that being there, to actually HELP – might make me feel... *helpful.* When in fact, I felt even more helpless.

"Well, Anne, I have not lost my ability to produce tears." I tried to cover my embarrassment with comedic understatement before dinner. And inside, the pieces continued to unravel.

As she stood behind him at His feet weeping, she began to wet His feet with her tears. Then, she wiped them with her hair, kissed them and poured perfume on them.

Luke 7:38

The pain of the hurting around us, and the otherworldly joy at God meeting us in it, was increasingly trumped each new day. Tears, fears and questioning pushed on one end of the extreme. However, each time God stretched us, he then met us at the other end of the faith spectrum.

Each passing day, the trials became seemingly more indomitable, but God became seemingly bigger and more powerful. God's miraculous presence became the norm. Surrender; Belief; Prayer; Praise. These things didn't seem to be options.

They were more like breathing – vitally necessary and almost involuntary. And I started to understand what daily life was really like for the early believers in the book of Acts...

They devoted themselves to the apostles' teaching and to fellowship, to the breaking of bread and to prayer. Everyone was filled with awe at the many wonders and signs performed by the apostles. All the believers were together and had everything in common.

Acts 2: 42-44

Our second day in Uganda brought another emotional trial for me, which I failed anew, in terms of composure.

The Morrows and Doyles would be in the van again on "official business," so we would again need an alternate method of transportation. But this time, we would employ an actual automobile taxi. Adam, Abigail and I headed deep into one of the worst slums of Kampala, looking for the doorway of a particular one-room dwelling.

There were no directions for navigating our way to her whereabouts, let alone street names or door numbers. There wasn't an actual door, in fact, just a door *opening* that we were trying to find. We zigzagged up and down, in and out, one path to the next. The byways we travelled were hardly fit for people to walk on, much less for a car to drive on.

Abigail was looking for a lady named Helen. This young woman, maybe 30, was giving her two young boys up for adoption. They were around 4 and 6. Helen had progressed from HIV to AIDS, and she worried she would soon leave her defenseless children alone in the world. She worried that they would watch her suffer and die, and be left then with no one. She didn't want her 6-year-old son to become father to her 4-year-old son, as is *so often* the case in Africa that it is hard to imagine – an entire generation of young children being raised by only-slightly-older children.

Abigail was not only taking the boys to a local clinic for some medical exams, tests and shots, but also she would talk to Helen on the drive. On behalf of the adoptive family, Abigail would investigate some of the unanswered questions about Helen's circumstances.

We found Helen's doorway among the hundreds of others that looked just like hers. It was bleak enough bumping up and down along the dusty, red roads – trails riddled with sometimes-impassable crevasses in the dirt, formed by seasonal rains, worn and weather-beaten. But to stop and actually look into a single room home, no bigger than my very small foyer… to find a woman named Helen and her 2 children waiting wide-eyed – this was another thing entirely.

This book is filled with words – words that tell just one beautiful part of God's larger, glorious story. But for a brief moment, these pages are aphonic…

I am not sure words can explain the complete and profound poverty. Nor can they explain the humble, neatly dressed, glowing woman who emerged. Her silhouette held a candle to the darkness. My mind drifted from the clefts in the road to the cracks in my breaking heart.

Adam and the driver sat in the front seat of a tiny car, while I sat in the back with Helen and Abigail. Each of them held one of the boys on their laps. I was sandwiched next to them, lost in tears and thoughts, drifting in the silence. It was like a knife in my heart that these two young sons were very near the same ages as my two sons were.

My God, what world are we living in where a mama feels her only option is giving up her flesh and blood, the boys she birthed and raised and cuddled and kissed? What world are we living in where these two boys could only stare silently, at a dark life ahead, without this beautiful woman they call Mama?

These boys had shared embraces with their mother; they had been tucked under her fragile wings; they had known the safety of her hand and the reassuring light of her smile, in a hard and ugly world.

And now, they were looking at a world without her.

What would their last day with her be like, assuming she was alive to hand them over to their adoptive family? What would it be like for all of them, knowing in that moment they would never again see one another? What would it be like if she didn't make it to their final court date, and instead they knelt at her bed side sobbing over her as she took her last breaths?

What was it like for these two precious boys right in that present moment, with their future looming and bearing down on them already? A future from which any mother or child, with a choice – *any choice* – would run fast and furious in the opposite direction? My God, my God…

We arrived at the clinic, and the boys received their shots. The older son tried to sit bravely, stoic. I had lost all courage, and I sat expressionless, as I thought about the bleak set of circumstances in process.

It wasn't the painful, passing shots that pierced me. It was the permanency with which this mother was slipping into the past of her children. It was a crushing present reality that they could not escape. There was nothing, it seemed, that any of them could do about it… just as there was nothing they could do about the disease that pursued Helen, unrelenting.

Abigail, however, offered hope to Helen about the boys' guardianship on the way home, "You do not have to do this!"

She relayed new information, "The adoptive family has offered to sponsor your children while you parent them. They do not have to leave you now; you do not have to give them up."

Abigail found out later that Helen had three other (older) children also – a fact which Helen was likely afraid to reveal at first, knowing that no one would want to split the children *or* take them all. Helen's survival instincts had taken over – those which directed her to look after her younger two, who could not look after themselves.

A loving mama was being forced to make unthinkable decisions – out of a host of subpar options.

Record my misery; list my tears on your scroll – are they not in your record?

Psalm 56: 8

The Morrows and Doyles were making slow progress on their visa checklists. They were ticking off the items under their control in Kampala, like the WHO (World Health Organization) and the Embassy. After months of journeying, the very last details were finally in play.

From the beginning, these two families never assumed they knew what their journeys would look like. They never assumed they knew best. They never assumed they could control or forecast the final outcomes. They prayed and surrendered.

Roadblocks and closed doors didn't crush them, because their eyes were on God, not the outcomes. Even blessings didn't capture their hearts with an unrelenting grip because they could see past the gift to the Giver. And until the end, they didn't assume they knew the will of God. Rather, they pursued the *heart* of God through both the triumphs and the trials.

But, they were approaching the final "trial" – where their cases would be heard in court. It would be safe to say, after many months of prayer and surrender, after many months of asking and waiting with open hands... the stakes were higher and higher. They had more money in and more time in than ever before. Most of all, their love had grown for the girls who would be their daughters.

Anne, Nate, Lindsey and Ryan were far from home, far from their 7 other children. They had spanned the globe, for what they hoped would be a final time (at least where the guardianship cases were concerned). Certainly, they didn't desire that the girls should ever leave their loving arms again. But even as they kept the babies close – they kept God closer. Their hands were always open to God's leading, His timing and His will, even as they simultaneously held the tiny hands and tiny hearts they so fully loved.

From start to finish, they never assumed it would be a cakewalk. It was a faith-walk. And they would need more faith than ever to walk the last mile.

Let us acknowledge the Lord; let us press on to acknowledge Him. As surely as the sun rises He will appear; He will come to us like the winter rains, like the spring rains that water the earth.

Hosea 6: 3

In just the space of a week, there were incredible highs and lows. But with every defeat, which would seem to point to the end, there was an impossible victory that followed. Every time we received bad news from one source or another, God provided hope from heaven: influential advocates and benevolent persons, in the right place at the right time.

The week we were in Africa, our emotions and expectations alike were on a roller coaster, from start to finish. Time and again, God provided light for the next step forward, just when all hope seemed to be lost. After a pattern of such highs and lows, laughter and tears, it was finally time to drive to Masindi – to let the story play out to the very end in the courtroom.

Our drive north was a case in point. We were not 30 minutes into our journey, when Abigail received crushing news regarding the cases. She got off the phone and announced the difficult information to everyone.

It was looking like an insurmountable obstacle. We exchanged looks of shock, speechless, like our words had been stolen from our mouths and our very breath stolen out of our lungs. Our hearts were dashed.

And yet, there we were, in the van on the way to Masindi. We were continually prompted forward *only* by God. He continued to lead the Morrows and Doyles ahead, beyond all human reasoning. We knew there was a purpose in our trip to Uganda, a purpose in our continuing to Masindi, and a purpose in following the girls' cases to the very end.

We did *not* know: Would their journeys end in adoption or were *all* of our journeys for some other purpose entirely? Or perhaps… both possibilities were in play.

Though we didn't know the outcomes, we held tight to our eternal, unchanging hope – The God of the universe who had brought us thus far. We also read familiar verses of peace and promise. Among them, Proverbs 21: 1 (NKJV). "The king's heart is in the hand of the Lord, like the rivers of water; He turns it wherever he wishes."

I cannot remember why, for the life of me, but in our stunned and saddened state, we began reading Noah's story in Genesis as we bumped along toward Masindi. Within a matter of minutes, we looked out our windows, and we saw the most utterly magnificent rainbow I had ever seen – unabridged in the clear blue sky.

The God of the Universe invented rainbows in His creative artistry. He used them as a sign of the promise he made to Noah. And there, in the middle of nowhere, as we read Noah's story – there was a sign of promise to us. That the impossible was possible.

Whenever the rainbow appears in the clouds, I will see it and remember the everlasting covenant between God and living creatures of every kind on the earth.
Genesis 9:16

The next day, I sat outside the courtroom with Adam and the Morrows, as the judge heard the Doyle's case. We waited on pins and needles, but we prayed the whole time. When the judge had given his ruling, Lindsey came out first, sobbing.

Within moments, we discovered, she cried tears of joy. Her tears washed over us as well. I collapsed in praise. We embraced one another in a warm group hug, but there was another hurdle yet to overcome. The Morrow's case was up next.

Our first concern and question was, "Would the case even be heard?" It was after 4:00 now, the time at which the court closes. The judge can stop his sessions even before the end of the workday, so we balked at the likelihood that he would hear another case. We also doubted that he would grant a second favorable ruling.

However, he did hear the case, and the outcome was identical. Not only so, but he also allowed the court reporter to stay past close. She could type up the necessary confirmative documents that very night.

There was nothing left to do but wait on these documents for the girls' dossiers, which would show the Embassy that the judge had ruled favorably – *twice*.

Sing to God, Sing in praise of his name, Extol him who rides on the clouds; rejoice before him – his name is the Lord. A Father to the fatherless, a defender of widows, is God in his holy dwelling. God sets the lonely in families…

Psalm 68: 4-6a

In disbelief of the events that day, we all headed to Murchison Falls National Reserve for a game drive. Only because everything had worked out (according to plan *and* according to schedule), were we able to spend the night at Paraa Safari Lodge. God had granted us another miracle. We had been at the mercy of so many others, any one of whom could have derailed the schedule by a day, a week, or more. But all of our plans were in God's hands, and He delivered to us: miracle after miracle. The Doyles had been given a miracle named Eden Hannah. The Morrows, a miracle named Ali Rose. The next miracle would have my name on it.

We headed to Murchison Falls, and this was another test of sorts. To get to the Nile, it was first necessary to trek through the jungle-like forests on the near side of the national reserve. We raced through because missing the Nile ferry meant missing the animals on the other side of the majestic river.

There were plenty of baboons to see on that initial leg of the adventure, but there were also tsetse flies. They flew fast and furious into any cracked window and stung quickly and not without pain. One might think you would just leave the windows up during the duration of the pest-affected area, but the oppressive heat won out every time.

Just when we would get up enough speed to potentially out-drive the moving flies, we would crack the windows ever so slightly in hopes of a small breeze to circulate inside the muggy van. The van was like the rest of the country, devoid of air conditioning, so we wanted moving air inside to prevent the feeling of suffocation.

Despite our best efforts, we had run-ins with the enemy flies. These flies carry African Sleeping Sickness in most parts of Uganda, but we had been told that the park flies were sprayed for disease. They would be harmless – other than the biting sting.

I think everyone walked away unscathed – *everyone but me*. I tried to completely cover myself with my gear and garments, but two flies stung me right through my clothing. In the end, however, the battle wound would be worth the cost in light of the miracle God had prepared in advance for me.

There was one thing I wanted to see on the savannahs of Africa, one present I hoped God would give during our time there – a lion. God had been awakening more of Himself, and more of me, through Narnia. I wanted to bury my head in Aslan's shining mane like Lucy, but I would settle for seeing him at a safe distance!

Beyond all odds, and overcoming all obstacles, our schedule had allowed for us to make the game drive, so I began to pray harder than ever that God would show me The Lion. All we had heard, more times than I wanted to hear, was that lion sightings were extremely, *extremely* rare.

When we made it into the park, I allowed my imagination to be completely given over to the God of Imagination. I could only wonder what it might be like to see the majestic creature in person, alive and real.

They will follow the Lord; He will roar like a lion. When he roars, His children will come trembling from the west.

Hosea 11: 10

Adam and I had been to Hawaii on a business trip earlier that same year. We sat at breakfast one morning in a restaurant that overlooks the Pacific Ocean. This part of Maui was positioned in an opportune place for whale viewing, and Humpbacks frequent the stretch of ocean near this restaurant in mating and migratory patterns.

There is even a huge bell at the restaurant which one can ring upon seeing a whale. I had never seen a whale, let alone any such wild animal in its natural environment, and I did what I do when I really want something – I prayed.

"Lord, pleeeeeeeease let us see a whale. I reeeeeally want to see a whale, Lord." I carried on like this out loud and in my head during the course of breakfast, but the meal came to an end. Finally, Adam said we *reeeeeeally* had to leave – it wasn't fair to make people wait in line for a table any longer. So, we walked away without having seen a whale.

Pray continually.

1 Thessalonians 5: 17

When checked into the lodge at Paraa, it wasn't long before we were back in the van to take on the savannah: an ancient front-wheel drive Toyota versus the land before time. No cage or roll bars did this vehicle possess – just a sliding door between us and many different types of animals. And sometimes not even a door – the men jimmy-rigged themselves with rope for a ride on the flat metal roof of the moving vehicle. Adam's packing list was finally making its debut.

Our guide jumped into our van with us. Hundreds of species of animals and birds live in the reserve, but I only wanted to see one – the king of the jungle. We kept talking about how the illusive lion is the hardest to find, the most unlikely to see, so I prayed again, just as I had done in Hawaii the spring before.

"Please," with a lot of "e's." And I upped the ante in a one-sided conversation with God…

> *Lord, when we were in Hawaii, I asked to see a humpback whale. It's OK, God. You said, 'No.'* (I like to tell God things He already knows.) *But NOW, Lord, I* really *mean it. This is far more important to me. You have shown me Yourself through Aslan in the pages of* Narnia. *Now would you* pleeeeease *do it again by showing me the real Aslan?*

We saw giraffes, the gentle giants. Graceful dancers, they run fast like a slow-motion sports replay. One curious calf, however, did not run away. He bashfully kept only his posterior in view, at first checking us out from the corner of his eye. This led to initiating a gradual game of peek-a-boo. His rear end never moved, but, like an acrobat, he stretched his neck slowly around until both his eyes and his tail were in perfect view. Hello, Baby!

We saw an elephant family marching through the plains: Daddy, Mama, baby, baby, all in a perfect row. We saw Ugandan kob (a type of antelope), African crested cranes, waterbucks, and hartebeests (another type of antelope), just to name a few. All indescribably incredible. But I wanted to see the Glorious Lion.

I questioned our guide, George, for the 75th time, about our odds of a lion sighting. George promised to ring him for me. He placed his cell phone on his ear in a mock call. "Oh Li-own," he said in a slow, thick African accent, "Dees ees George."

He pretended to go on in conversation for a minute, but then he lowered his phone to his chest and said to me, "I call him. He meet us soon." In honesty, I put some mystical hope in George's ability to "call forth" the lion. Please God, *pleeeeease*.

I spotted the first one – unbelieving. I jumped. I gasped. I screamed (*quietly*). Others confirmed. Miracle of all miracles. We were not only seeing a lion – but a mama and her two cubs playing in front of our van on the path ahead.

A miracle, but as far as I was concerned, also a problem. The daddy lion that lounged next to the vigilant mama was very young. He really looked no different than his betrothed. We had the extremely rare opportunity to see little cubs – *playing*!!

And sure, here was a grown lion too, and yes, a male. But he was no Aslan. He had no mane! He was just a young man. Where was the long golden hair glowing in the African sunlight?

I was certainly thrilled, but not quite satisfied, and definitely still longing. For Aslan.

George directed Moses to drive out to the riverbank for a while, and he promised me that we would return for another chance at The Lion before heading back to the lodge. We drove along the mighty Nile, and also right alongside an old, mammoth elephant, marching solo.

He ignored us, walking upward and onward. I guess he knew he could crush our car with the sheer weight that he carried, if only he wished it. He seemed completely unaffected by our presence. We were so close that we could see the folds and wrinkles in his aging skin, and the flies that buzzed about him. Massive ears waving back and forth, tail swatting, head nodding.

105

This was a special treat for Adam and I – we are Alabama football fans! But it was, alas, not the lion that meant far more to me because of what he represented spiritually.

Finally, we returned to the area where we had seen the family of lions. Mama was gone, probably out hunting, because it was dusk now. The sun had begun to set, lighting the plains like fire. We sat for a moment and waited.

We were about to give up, when against all odds, his face appeared out of the underbrush.

Aslan.

The moment was silent and serious, filled with awe and respect. It was completely different from the giddy excitement of the cub sighting. More than an exclamation point, it was an ellipsis – meaning "falling short" in Greek.

I was – *we all were* – short on words. I was quite literally out of breath, as if the air had been stolen from my lungs. I had inhaled in disbelief, but couldn't exhale for fear of disrupting the quiet reverence demanded. He knew he was in charge; we knew he was in charge. Everyone in the van was still and silent. I worshipped the Giver of good gifts, the giver of this Aslan, the One True Aslan Himself, and tears welled up in my eyes, stinging gratitude.

Adam took an unbelievable photo. I was too transfixed to move my gaze, much less the camera. Abigail took another. It is stretched on a 16 x 20 canvas. He is peering at us from behind the tall golden grasses of the savannah, standing in front of the dry thicket, which was his home. The light is perfect, and so is the subject. Even now, I can stare hard into his eyes and tears come quickly.

Printed on the bottom right corner are the C.S. Lewis' words, "Safe? 'Course he isn't safe. But he's good. He's the King, I tell you."[6]

His real name was Andrew, but one look at his beautiful mane, his mysterious and piercing stare, his solemn expression – I knew God had shown me Aslan. This blessing with my name on it: this land - a breathtaking panorama, and this powerful, glowing, regal creature. *This* was heaven coming down to earth. It made Narnia more real to me than ever before.

As Flannery O'Conner said, "I'm always irritated by people who imply that writing fiction is an escape from reality. It is a plunge into reality..."[7] In that moment, fiction became reality:

The eastern sky changed from white to pink, and from pink to gold. The Voice rose and rose, till all the air was shaking with it. And just as it swelled to the mightiest and most glorious sound it had yet produced, the sun arose. Digory had never seen such a sun... You could imagine that it laughed for joy as it came up... the Earth was of many colors; they were fresh, hot and vivid. They made you feel excited, until you saw the singer himself, and you forgot everything else. It was a Lion. Huge, shaggy, and bright, it stood facing the risen sun.[8]

The Magician's Nephew, C.S. Lewis

We spent the one night at Paraa, then we came back through Masindi the next day in hopes of obtaining the long-awaited documents before returning to Kampala. But we had one more mission in Masindi: stop and visit the orphanage where Ali Rose and Eden Hannah spent their first hours, before being moved into the foster care of Abigail and Leah.

Abigail told us the needs were great. She knew Susan and Isaac and many of the children, and we were excited to visit the facility and the kids. We expected to play for a while, and we would shower them with love and attention. We stopped at a roadside market to purchase bananas by the bunch before making our way to Family Spirit.

We handed out bananas and some of the protein bars we had brought for the trip. It looked at first like there would be some order to the process (lines formed and manners on display), but with over 200 kids and just 7 of us, chaos ultimately won the day. Beautiful chaos.

When the nutritional items were divvied up, we started all over again with the "sweeties," their term for candy – Dumdum suckers and Smarties rolls. An image I will never forget is 6'4" Nate Morrow with his hands up in the air, holding candy bags high, unable to move because of the swarm of children around him – the children's arms were in the air too, reaching for the rare candy treats.

Shortly after the candy bags were emptied in as fair and calm a manner possible, I noticed two little girls off to one corner of the dirt play yard. They were huddled close together. I figured they were probably trying to protect their candies from the masses, and I'm sure this is part of the reason they had withdrawn. But as I came in for a closer look, I realized they were swapping treats and taking turns.

One of the little girls took a lick of her sucker, then she held it forward for her friend to taste. The friend in turn, who had received Smarties instead of a sucker, popped a candy into her own mouth and then one into the mouth of her friend who held the sucker. They went on like this until the one sucker was licked clean down to the stick and the lone candy roll was nothing but an empty wrapper.

As had happened so many times on the trip before, I started crying. Each girl viewed a simple piece of candy as treasure to be joyfully contributed to another's happiness. Privy to the generous hearts of these little girls who had nothing, Halloween's recent passing flashed back before my eyes and hit me hard.   Free candy just for knocking on a door?

I remembered how, just days before, Hannah Whit and Austin had dumped their loot all over the floor in our house to compare and swap, an eye for an eye. But here were two little girls, who might not eat an entire bag of candy in the whole of their lives, sharing such a little bit so freely and giggling all the while.

As Jesus looked up, he saw the rich putting their gifts into the temple treasury. He also saw a poor widow put in two very small copper coins. "Truly I tell you," he said, "this poor widow has put in more than all the others. All these people gave their gifts out of their wealth; but she out of her poverty put in all she had to live on."

Luke 21: 1-4

Afterwards, the wrappers littered the dirt all around, and we made a quick attempt to clean up. We were then ushered to sit in plastic chairs, a place of honor, in order to watch many of the children sing songs and dance for us. I had no sooner taken my seat than I had one child on each arm, two behind me, one on my lap and another practically sitting on my feet.

A little girl to the right of me stroked my right arm, she slowed every now and again, but didn't stop the entire time of the performance – at least 20 minutes. The one to my left played with the rubber band and watch on my left arm, spinning it around and around, pushing the buttons, stretching the hair band. The two girls behind me played with my hair, patted my head or squeezed my neck – they also did not let up except for giggling every once in a while. And the one in my lap sat content the whole time, happy to let me embrace her whenever I could free my arms for a moment.

5 sets of arms, 10 hands touching, and another who seemed pleased just to sit at my feet. They were soaking it all in – drinking up as much as they could. When it was time for us to stand again, I cupped each little face, and I stared at their level into each set of brown eyes. "I love you, and God loves you even more." I told them all. "You are beautiful and special."

We sang one of our American worship songs for them, and we prayed for them before we had to leave. We left stunned at the conditions, hearts aching for having to leave them all behind. Ali Rose and Eden Hannah were on their way to a family in America, but what about the numbers upon numbers of others?

I thank my God every time I remember you. In all my prayers for all of you I always pray with joy because of your partnership in the gospel from the first day until now, being confident of this, that he who began a good work in you will carry it on to completion until the day of Christ Jesus.

Philippians 1: 4-6

Traffic turned our 3-hour return trip to Kampala into 8 or 9 hours. We were stuffed inside a muggy, slow moving van, without air conditioning in the heat of the day: 7 travel-weary adults and 2 restless babies. The end of our trip, however, proved to be perfect timing for vehicular entrapment: we laughed at the journey's funnier moments, and we celebrated God's amazing faithfulness. Through it all, our hearts returned to the kids at Family Spirit who were lingering, heavy in our souls.

Before Adam and I were delivered back to the airport, we had all decided that a lifelong relationship had just begun. We didn't yet have all the specifics, but plans took their infancy in that long van ride. There was a deep, profound understanding that this was *truly* only the beginning of something God had planned before the dawn of time.

Although it would be easy to think that our involvement in Uganda began with two adoptive families and two little girls, I am well aware that there is a larger story at play. The story was set in motion before *any of us* arrived on the scene.

It is certainly not because of this trip that there is now a group of people in Nashville advocating for an orphanage in Africa. It is not because of our original two home churches, Christ Presbyterian Church and West End Community Church in Nashville.

It is not because of two young nurses, Abigail and Leah, who fostered a handful of children in Uganda before our families ever arrived. Nor is it because of the medical organization with whom they worked. But all of

110

these things were stones laid on a trail, long before any of them came to be. Our story is the Lord's, from start to finish, from before our involvement, to whatever He has planned for the future. It is the story of how an incredible God, in His awesome power and His unsearchable mysteries, wove together the plans and hearts of the many players he called – and is still calling – into Masindi, Uganda. This is the story of His church, the body of Christ, which is not confined to a building and is not contained by a roof.

Dietrich Bonhoeffer wrote, "Where a people prays, there is a church, and where there is a church, there is never loneliness."[9] Our story is about a lot of people, from a lot of different places, who prayed a lot of prayers... all to partner with a couple in Uganda – to ease the loneliness, as well as the hunger and poverty, for one small group of children in Africa. It is also a story of how the Lord has used these sweet kids to change *us*.

I have always loved the limestone marker outside of the church in Nashville where my great-grandmother played the organ. It is the same church where my grandmother helped start the preschool program that all of my children attended. It is where my mom grew up and learned about Christ. The stone reads, "Westminster Presbyterian Church gathers here."[10]

Whoever fashioned that display had it right. The church is the body of Christ. It cannot be contained within walls, certainly not within Nashville or America. Our story is about a church body that gathers, from time to time, with members of the church body in Masindi.

For just as each of us has one body with many members, and these members do not all have the same function, so in Christ we, though many, form one body, and each member belongs to all the others.

Romans 12: 4-5

In my journal, shortly before we left for this first trip to Africa, I had written:

"Thinking of all the things we have all said thus far, and one stands out... 'God's got this.' Such a big thing is going on – way bigger than even the two adoptions." Nothing could have been more prophetic or true.

However, as it is written: "What no eye has seen, what no ear has heard, and what no human mind has conceived" – the things God has prepared for those who love him.

I Corinthians 2: 9

Chapter 6| I Will Fight for You : The Doyle Family

Though Anne and I have had more face time from attending the same church for many years, I actually met Lindsey a few years before I met Anne. When Adam and I first moved to Nashville in 2002, I almost immediately began attending a women's Bible study at Christ Presbyterian Church[1]. Adam and I didn't know where we would ultimately land with our church membership, but I was anxious to go ahead and get involved in fellowship with other women.

Lindsey led my second bible study group at CPC in the fall of 2003. The role she played in my life was crucial, because our first years in Nashville were also the early years of my Christian walk, the early years in our marriage, and my first years as a mom. Though I had not known Lindsey growing up, she is from my hometown of Knoxville. She attended high school with a few of the friends I knew from elementary and middle school. Her husband, Ryan, was a fraternity brother of Adam's at Samford University in Birmingham.

Adam and I fully settled in at West End Community Church in 2005, and we had all but lost touch with Lindsey and Ryan until the fall of 2011. All of our paths were about to cross again.

That was the fall we were heading to Africa with the Morrows. We soon found out, the Doyles were coming as well. They were adopting another little girl, Eden Hannah, who had been fostered by the same two young women that fostered Ali Rose. Both baby girls were living with Abigail and Leah in Uganda, awaiting their forever families.

This is the beginning of Lindsey's part of the story.

On October 6, 2011, Lindsey began recording the Doyle's story, "Here I am in the London airport writing this first blog post. Exactly two years ago I was here in this same airport...my heart in the same place....yearning with anticipation to hold my child. Two years ago, in 2009, I was headed to Uganda with Ryan to meet our precious son, Judah. Now I am about to cross into the 'promised land' again and hold that baby girl of ours, Eden Hannah Doyle.

"His path is not mine, and that is where I pray my faith will remain. Two years ago I yearned for our boy, our fourth child. Tomorrow the yearning will be over for our baby girl – the fifth Doyle. This is Lord's story of our journey to Eden, how He led us to her when we did not even realize we were searching...

"So here I am sitting in the London airport next to Anne, now my dear friend. Anne and Nate are adopting Ali Rose; Ali Rose and Eden Hannah will be forever friends. Theirs is a story of redemption and rescue, as is mine. The Lord picked Eden up, and He gave her to two that would wrap their arms around her and let her feel His love in a tangible way.

Tomorrow morning, sweet one, Mommy will be wrapping her arms around you in thanksgiving and love. Eden Hannah, it is time...

He is the one you praise; he is your God, who performed for you those great and awesome wonders you saw with your own eyes.

Deuteronomy 10: 21

Sometime in January of 2010, Bella, our second child who is sensitive and compassionate, "beautiful one," began to ask Ryan and me if we would adopt a baby girl. My response quickly and flippantly, without any regard to prayer, was always, "Sorry, Bella... I think Mommy is done for now. Maybe God is going to call you to adopt one day."

Bella kept on asking, and I kept on answering her in the same way. Not that Ryan and I did not want to adopt again, but we had just decided, "Not now. Not soon." Apparently, we thought that our plan was far better than the

One who was making the plans. "Our Plan" was to have our kindergartner, first grader, second grader, and third grader all grown, or at least driving, and then we would adopt a sibling group or maybe even twins. I so often think my plans are settled – how futile it is to make them on my own!

Bella kept on praying. In fact, she asked her entire class to pray that Mommy and Daddy's hearts would be changed to adopt a baby girl. Emma Lynn, our third child, bright and obedient, my snuggly one, decided she too was going to ask her class to pray that our hearts would be changed. Weeks began to pass, and people began to come up and ask us, "Are you adopting a baby girl? My child is praying that you are." Oh, to have faith like a child! No, we were not adopting, and I wasn't even praying about adoption.

But, as the Lord does in His mysterious ways, He was working in my heart all the while. My two little girls were praying and being faithful to ask God for a baby sister, and God was addressing their prayers – by addressing me. There existed areas in my heart that I had not fully released or surrendered, fears that were hidden deeper than I had known. God was saying, "I want those, even those. They are not yours to carry."

And the splendor is, that as I relinquished those old fears, new freedom came more and more. And as freedom came, my heart began to be open. I was open to whatever He had, even adopting a baby girl.

At that time Jesus said, "I praise you, Father, Lord of heaven and earth, because you have hidden these things from the wise and learned, and revealed them to the little children. Yes, Father, for this is what you were pleased to do."
Matthew 11: 25-26

Two years prior to meeting Eden Hannah, Ryan and I were in Uganda adopting Judah, experiencing for the first time the smells, the red dirt roads, and the people we have grown to love there. At that point, the Holy Spirit put it upon on my heart to be praying for a set of twins. I had no idea who these twins were, only that they were probably in Uganda and that they needed prayer.

It was the kind of prayer that doesn't stop after a few minutes. It was instead the kind of prayer that you soak in for a while – for days or for months, even for a year. Ryan and I prayed for the "set of twins" that God continually placed on my heart.

A year after Judah came home, I was still praying for these twins in 2010. I was in the carpool line at school, when a friend of mine, Mandy Gallagher, shared with me that she and her husband were being led to adopt. She was adopting a set of twins who had been extremely sick. Their mother had just died, and they were in Masindi, Uganda.

Tears streamed down my face and peace like a river washed over me. "Your twins –"I told her, "I have been praying for them. Even while they were in their mother's womb."

Before I formed you in the womb I knew you, before you were born I set you apart...

Jeremiah 1: 5a

Once I had relinquished my old fears, and allowed Him to turn those fears into thanksgiving, the desire to adopt a baby girl engulfed me. The Lord had my heart ready, for it was time.

In May of 2011, Ryan and I attended our girls' piano recital. Mandy, the wife of the couple adopting the twins, sat three rows in front of us. She looked up at me and simply asked, "How are you doing?"

I looked at her, and I didn't hesitate to be real by answering, "I am feeling the tug."

"The tug?" she asked.

"I know we are being called to adopt again, but I don't know what to do with it."

"Do you feel you are being called to adopt a specific child?"

My response…"A baby girl."

As soon as I said the words "baby girl," Mandy got tears in her eyes, and the recital began. As the music filled the room, Mandy texted me a picture. A picture of this tiny little angel…all wrapped up and swaddled…Eden Hannah Doyle.

Praise the Lord with the harp; make music to him on the ten-stringed lyre. Sing to him a new song; play skillfully, and shout for joy. For the word of the Lord is right and true; he is faithful in all he does. The Lord loves righteousness and justice; the earth is full of his unfailing love.

Psalm 33: 2-5

Even as the Lord intertwined our story with Mandy and Mike Gallagher's, He began to weave it also into the stories of four others…Leah and Abigail, and Anne and Nate Morrow. Our little peanut, along with the Morrow's daughter, was being cared for by two of the most inspiring and faithful servants I have ever known.

Leah and Abigail moved to Masindi, Uganda to work as nurses at a clinic. During their time in Uganda, they became foster moms to Eli and Ellie (the twins), followed by two other girls, then Ali Rose and baby Eden. Not only did they work at the clinic, but also they took on the full responsibility for these little ones. Their term at the clinic ended in May of 2011, yet they continued to care for these children until the last one was adopted.

They remained faithful in the newest portion of God's call on their lives – fostering these girls. They were steadfast during endless nights with crying babies, and they persevered through long days of chasing, cleaning, and caring. And they knew what was being asked of them. They had to have an open hand, for God had only called these babies into their arms for a season, to love them and then to surrender.

Eden Hannah will never know what it is like *not* to have arms around her. She won't know what it is like not to have a bottle or to have soothing words softly spoken in her ear, or kisses planted all over her face. She will never know the absence of these daily routines, these daily acts of unconditional love that most orphans never experience.

These two servants felt it on their hearts to have Mandy, the twins' mom, pray with them for the ordained forever-family for Eden Hannah. Mandy chose us. Leah and Abigail chose us. God chose us.

He has saved us and called us to a holy life — not because of anything we have done but because of his own purpose and grace. This grace was given us in Christ Jesus before the beginning of time…

2 Timothy 1: 9

In October of 2011, my first week in Uganda with Eden Hannah was such a busy, bittersweet, and blessed week. In the midst of trying to gather information regarding the adoption, I was able to catch a glimpse of Eden Hannah's life in Uganda.

Anne and I stayed the first few days in Leah and Abigail's home. It was a sweet time getting to know those who gave so much… getting to know, specifically, "her Leah." Our initial days there were full of "firsts"…her first bath, her first falling asleep in my arms, and her first time to roll over! Yes, I got to witness it. But in with the sweet was the bitter, too.

Baby William was just a month old and being nursed back to health by precious Kara, another Nashville gal serving God in Africa. Late one evening, William's I.V. would not flush, so Abigail had to transport him to the hospital in Jinja, Uganda. (This is where the girls were living at the time). She asked if I wanted to go with her to the hospital – it was the same hospital where Eden Hannah had been taken weeks before. Eden had been so sick that we didn't know if she would live.

So as I held tiny Willliam on the boda late that night, I imagined Abigail holding Eden on a boda late in the night, carrying Eden's own I.V. over her head, just the way we carried William's over his head. I imagined Abigail walking into the same hospital. And in witnessing that for the first time with William, I was overcome. It would be an understatement to say that our hospitals are much different than those in Uganda and that we are so very blessed.

In addition to the hospital trip that week, we visited the clinic in Masindi where Abigail and Leah served so faithfully. Just the sight of the patients' conditions was enough to shake me to my core. The first child we encountered had a cavity that had abscessed. A hole the size of a dime had formed in the skin of her cheek where the cavity was eating through, and her jaw was stiff and locked shut from bacterial infection. Yet, she gazed at us shyly and joyfully with a one-sided smile.

In America, a cavity is an easy fix. Dental care is something that so many of us take for granted, like Band-Aids and Neosporin. Why had something as simple as a cavity disfigured a young girl's face and threatened her life? Why was I born in a place where excellent medical care is so accessible? Why her? Why me? These weren't the last of my questions.

On our last healthcare facility visit, during those first days with Eden Hannah, Abigail and Leah took us to the hospital in Masindi. This hospital made the clinic in the village and the hospital in Jinja look markedly ahead of the times. It did not even have running water. No running water! I was hard-pressed to imagine care, much less surgery, without the aid of clean, fresh water.

The maternity ward at the Masindi Hospital hit my heart the hardest. Bare floors and walls, just bed after bed of women - no monitors, no medicines, not even a nurse except upon the very moment of delivery. And five hours after delivery, the woman is sent home – on a boda (motorcycle). When I delivered my babies, I had a whole birthing room to myself, a team of nurses and medicines at my request, and soft, gentle, encouraging words from family and professionals. These new moms were utterly alone, and in desperate poverty. Again came my question, "Why me?"

Beyond the birthing ward, others lay in the isolation ward, the children's ward, the surgery ward... So many questions for my heart to ponder, so much pain and suffering, so many lives lost, even on the day of our visit. Yet, there in the middle of it all, the Lord was fighting. Fighting for his children. Fighting for our baby girl. Though my questions still haunt me, so does my gratitude. I was, and still am, humbled and thankful.

Seeing the reality of rural healthcare in Uganda, I knew that Eden Hannah was a fighter too – tears filled my eyes for her in those places, just as they did for the others in such dire need of medical attention. For the conditions in the hospitals and the clinic. For Eden's survival against the odds. For God's hand on her life.

The Lord your God who is going before you, will fight for you, as he did for you in Egypt, before your very eyes, and in the wilderness. There you saw how the Lord your God carried you, as a father carries his son, all the way you went until you reached this place.

Deuteronomy 1: 30-31

Later that first week, Anne, Leah, Abigail, and I began to tackle logistics for legal guardianship. We traveled several hours to meet our lawyer. It was a comfort to greet the person who was advocating for their lives. Our lawyer helped us to make important decisions regarding the cases, but ultimately we left it up to the Lord to show us the way.

We encountered the closing of one door after another in Kampala, so we asked God for direction, to make His ways known, right or left. He made it clear that we should file our papers with the court in the girls' hometown of Masindi, but only a handful of guardianship cases had ever occurred there. We began asking for a miracle, for Him to move mountains.

Abigail then sought a moment with the judge, to respectfully ask if we should file in his village. She was not able to speak with him directly, but conversed with someone under him. This person directed without hesitation, "Of course you should file here." It was affirmation for us to begin the journey of pursuing our cases in Masindi.

Whether you turn to the right or to the left, your ears will hear a voice behind you, saying, "This is the way; walk in it."

Isaiah 30: 21

Though we naturally wanted to complete all the details for the legal guardianship cases in that one visit, our husbands joining us at the very end, it did not happen. Our paperwork in Kampala was completed in a timely manner, and our files were ready, but the court date assigned would require an additional trip. It was not far off, but we needed time to go home and be with our other children before we would return with our husbands (and the Hodges) for court. We would all spend the entire time between trips praying for the judge's heart to be softened and for him to give a favorable ruling.

As October passed in Uganda, I got to hold my baby girl every second of the day. Giving her bottles, taking her on walks, going swimming with her, playing noses, sleeping with her, and hugging her close to me. That is what my first days with Eden Hannah looked like, blessed by her every move.

But I also mourned the missing of October with my other four. I missed field trips, scarecrow days, football games, and just precious moments with them during this fall season. The end of our first trip in Uganda found me wishing for one second I could just wrap my arms around all five of my children and my incredible husband all at the same time. Then I visited the slums of Kampala... and met Helen.

She led us down the dirt path to her home. Her home was the size of my guest bathroom except without electricity, without running water. There was a mattress on the floor and a picture of her late husband centered on the wall above. I have never seen a home so sparse but so filled with love. The woman we met with was dying.

Her belly protruded and you could see in her eyes that she was not feeling well. She had gone to her pastor in hopes that her precious two boys, one of whom was extremely sick, could be brought to an orphanage – but the orphanage was full. An American family offered to sponsor the boys in school and help this mother with expenses or pursue guardianship of the two boys, whichever the mother chose. Whichever would give her peace, providing in the manner she desired.

Because she believed was close to dying, she looked at us again with tears, "I want them to have a family." Her love for her boys meant everything to her. She would make any sacrifice for them.

Next to the mattress on the floor was one tiny side table, and the only thing upon the table was her Bible, worn out, tattered, open to the Psalms. I thought of the sacrifice she was willing to make; I thought too of the ultimate sacrifice that our Heavenly Father made so that I could have life. Abiding with that woman put things into perspective in my heart, having been away from my family for so long.

After walking with her, I got back into the car and felt nauseated. I was sick with myself, sick with how lightly I take the sacrifice that my Maker made. Jesus died for me, pure and simple. And His Father gave His one and only son for me and for you.

This is how we know what love is: Jesus Christ laid down his life for us. And we ought to lay down our lives for our brothers and sisters. If anyone has material possessions and sees a brother or sister in need but has no pity on them, how can the love of God be in that person? Dear children, let us not love with words or speech but with actions and in truth.

1 John 3: 16-18

We first arrived in Uganda on October 7th, and we left Tuesday, October 25, 2011. We were in Uganda about two and half weeks, home about two and a half weeks, and then back to Uganda for a second time, arriving November 2nd with the Morrows and the Hodges.

The judge in the girls' village had asked to hear no more legal guardianship cases, but his staff continued to encourage us to go ahead and file there. He had approved only several cases in the past, so we trusted that God would move in his heart again for our cases. And we prayed (and prayed) to that end as well.

On November 9th, against many odds, the judge awarded us legal guardianship of Eden Hannah right before he awarded the Morrows guardianship of Ali Rose. This was a euphoric and impossible victory for us all. After overcoming seemingly insurmountable hurdles again and again, Eden Hannah was ours - forever! At this point, we thought there were just a few minor formalities left to check off.

The Hodges returned on November 12; Anne and Ryan returned a couple of days later. Nate and I stayed with Abigail to complete the final steps in securing visas for the girls' passports. We would need the passports *and* visas to leave the country – we obtained the passports Nov. 19th, but only the Morrows obtained the necessary visa.

So on November 25th, 2011, Abigail left the country with Nate and Ali Rose. I left with them, but very much alone: no visa. No Eden Hannah. On Thanksgiving Day.

So I say, "My splendor is gone and all that I had hoped from the Lord." I remember my affliction and my wandering, the bitterness and the gall. I well remember them, and my soul is downcast within me. Yet this I call to mind and therefore I have hope:

Because of the Lord's great love we are not consumed, for his compassions never fail. They are new every morning; great is your faithfulness. I say to myself, "The Lord is my portion; therefore I will wait for him."

Lamentations 3: 18-24

In total shock, after an unexpected turn of events with the American embassy, I had to leave Eden Hannah behind. After securing Eden's foster care with my friend Gracie in Jinja, I boarded our flight with sobs bearing down on my chest. I left without Eden in my arms.

"Thy will be done." Four words that I have prayed for years. Four words that are easy to pray – until they aren't.

During our whole adoption process, I prayed to have open hands – open hands for His timing to meet her, open hands for the court date and location, open hands for the ruling…. open hands to wherever He might lead. But when I returned to Nashville without Eden Hannah, I confess that I felt like a two year old throwing a tantrum, eyes shut, stomping around, hands tightly clenched – *not* opened. This is *not* how I thought it would turn out…. "Thy will be done."

My heart hurt beyond belief and my mind was fuzzy. It was a hurt that is even hard to describe, an emptiness that was so deep it made functioning virtually impossible. If I hadn't experienced her for six weeks, things *might* have been easier and the cries from deep within me *might* not have been so loud.

But, I had held her for days and nights that turned into weeks. She had become such a part of me that fall. Her tiny little cry became routine. I had learned when she needed a bottle or when she just needed to be held. I admit that I probably held her too much while I was with her in Uganda, if that's even possible. I never let her cry to fall asleep. Instead, I had walked her, whispered to her, prayed over her.

For six weeks, I had experienced her so thoroughly that I knew even her smells. Her smell after she had a bottle or her smell after a bath. I already knew her tiny touches – the way she would touch my face, lightly brushing it when her little eyes were looking into mine as I held her close. I knew the way she felt, her warmth from snuggling her close for most of the day, as she slept wrapped up around my body.

And then I had to leave her behind.

My entire being ached with her absence. I missed her, plain and simple. A part of me was missing, and every fiber in my being wanted to do something about it. But there was *NOTHING* I could do, except pray and trust, and try not to lose hope. "Be still my soul... Thy will be done."

I came home to an empty nursery. I would walk in and just glide on her rocking chair. Maybe that was a cruel thing to do to myself, but somehow it helped me feel closer to her. In her room, full of pink and white stripes, there were diapers and tiny clothes. There were brown baby dolls just waiting to be held by Eden's little arms. In the privacy and quiet of her room, there, I could be real with myself. I was *not* doing okay. It was beyond excruciating, but I was trying to remember at the same time, "He has me."

I knew and believed, as I always did before and as I always have since, that I serve a *good* God – a God who has my very best, and Eden Hannah's very best, in His heart and in His plans. I took great comfort in knowing that the arms I left her in, in Uganda, were arms that He had chosen before the foundation of the earth.

He knew Gracie would be rocking her, feeding her, loving her "for such a time as this."[2] He knew Eden would be in a home that exuded His Presence. When you walk in the front door of Gracie's house, you are engulfed and overwhelmed by the Holy Spirit. Her house is full of pure and raw joy –

just like her life. That was the home where I left Eden.

I was so grateful for that home and for Gracie. I was deeply thankful, but I missed my baby. And I was trying to hold on to the truth that He loved Eden Hannah so much that He chose his extraordinary servant, Gracie, to step up in my absence. I must confess there were days, though, that I did not feel the pure and raw joy myself. Days I just felt raw.

During the days between Thanksgiving and Christmas, the first days without Eden Hannah, Ryan and I began asking for prayers. We began asking for a miracle. We picked out Exodus 14:14 to be her life verse.

God had been fighting for Eden Hannah all of her little life up to that point, and He would continue to fight for her. The fact that she was still alive was evidence of The Lord fighting for her – I left her smiling and sitting up. At eight months, when she remained in Uganda with Gracie, she shouldn't have been alive. But our Savior had been fighting for her, and I believed he was fighting for her still – I just needed to *be still.*

Being still was not, and is not, something that comes naturally to me. But in my surrender, there was freedom. And in my freedom, there was peace. Jesus would continue fighting for Eden Hannah. He would continue fighting for me. I needed only to be still.

One quiet morning, soon after I left Eden in Uganda, Judah came downstairs to me - Lightning McQueen pajamas, morning breath, staggering still from sleep. He sat down beside me and told me he had had a bad dream about a storm in Africa. Before I could ask him what happened in the dream, he asked me, "What if you never adopted me? What if the judge had said, 'No,' and I wasn't in our family?"

Wow. He had never asked me those tough questions before.

I simply explained to him that Jesus had laid it on Mommy and Daddy's heart to adopt, because the Lord knew that Judah needed a family. I told Judah that the Lord knew it was *our* family, because he is *our* son. Then I assured him that, even if the judge had said "No," we would have continued to fight for him.

We would have continued to pray that the Lord work out a way for him to be in our family. I wasn't going to describe the appeals process to a six year old, but I relieved his doubts: even if we hadn't gotten the news we had wanted, we would have never stopped fighting for him to be with us. We never stopped fighting for Eden Hannah either. Nor did God.

The Lord your God will fight for you; you need only to be still.
Exodus 14: 14

At Christmas time, we were still without our fifth child. There was an ornament hanging on our tree with one word, "HOPE."

"**Hope** – a desire accompanied by expectation of or belief in fulfillment."[3]

I never really understood the word "hope" until 2002. Even today, when I see or hear this word, I am immediately transported to the year that my father, Lynn, was diagnosed with a brain tumor. I remember where I was standing, what I was doing, and the nauseous feeling I had when I heard the words.

His tumor was termed a butterfly tumor. Which is ironic, because if there is one symbol significant to me, other than the cross, it is the butterfly – representing new life. But a butterfly tumor does not represent life. It is a cancer that spreads to both sides of the brain, and in most cases, it means death, because most butterfly tumors are inoperable.

In Daddy's case, his tumor was inoperable. He was given six weeks to live. Those were the most hopeful six weeks of my entire life. Noah was three months old, and after much prayer, Ryan and I decided that I should move from Nashville to Knoxville to live with my daddy during his last few weeks. With each new doctor's appointment, with each new drug, and with each new study, we were hopeful. I kept begging the Lord for a miracle. Yet, in my heart of hearts, deep down, the Lord allowed me to know that Daddy was not going to live. I knew I needed to make every day, hour, minute, and second count...

Years before Daddy got sick (I remember it like it was yesterday), we were eating Chinese food at one of his favorite restaurants. It was just the two of us having dinner. I was in college and so hopeful about our conversation. I had tried to muster up enough courage to talk to *my* father about *my Heavenly* Father, my Abba – the one who lived and died for me, the one to whom I had given my life so that I could live, the one that changed my life forever. Daddy had looked me in the eye and told me it was "hogwash." All of it.

...Fast forward a few years, and there he was – dying. Every day of those six weeks, I witnessed the deterioration of his physical body. But I also witnessed the transformation of his spirit. Everything within me wanted him to get better so that I could have more time with this "new" daddy that I was just getting to know for the first time. This new daddy apologized, and he asked me for forgiveness over his being absent most of my life. This new daddy invited me to pray over him. This new daddy didn't object to, but rather welcomed, our daily scripture reading and devotional time.

Hope: The hope of all his doctors to get him into a "new study" was futile. The Lord did not give us more time. But His timing was, and always is, perfect. On December 31, 2002, Daddy went to be with Jesus. His "butterfly" had given him something far better than temporary healing and new life here. It had given him complete healing and eternal life – *that would never end.*

Two weeks prior to his death, the Lord graciously allowed me to witness Daddy recognizing his need for a Savior. This time it was not hogwash. This time it was real and wonderful, and he embraced it.

Hope.

That Christmas, without Eden Hannah, the word "hope" made me think of Daddy immediately, and it even became the word I used when I was asked about Eden Hannah. I was without her, yet I was full of hope.

Deep down, I had known Daddy was not going to make it, but I also believed the Lord would use it for His glory. And he did – those few weeks with him were used to change his life for eternity.

Deep down, I knew and believed that Eden Hannah would be home one day. I was hopeful that Christmas. Hopeful as 2011 became 2012. I was hopeful, and I waited in confident expectation on the Lord's perfect timing. My hands were open, as I placed my hope in my glorious Heavenly Father.

Therefore, since we have been justified through faith, we have peace with God through our Lord Jesus Christ, through whom we have gained access by faith into this grace in which we now stand. And we boast in the hope of the glory of God. Not only so, but we also glory in our sufferings, because we know that suffering produces perseverance; perseverance, character; and character; hope. And hope does not disappoint us, because God's love has been poured out into our hearts, through the Holy Spirit, who has been given to us.

Romans 5: 1-5

In late December, we received an email from the senator's office that was fighting for us to bring Eden Hannah home. "CONGRATULATIONS!!! YOU HAVE BEEN AWARDED A TEMPORARY VISA TO BRING EDEN HOME!!!" What a Christmas present!

Tears were streaming down my face, and I was shaking in thanksgiving. She was coming home... SHE WAS COMING HOME! We told Noah, Bella, Emma Lynn, and Judah. We were all jumping up and down together - it was time!

Several days later, I got another email that said the paperwork would be completed on January 3, so we should get ready. We began searching for flights and making preparations, and we would not even have to miss Leah's wedding on December 31, 2011, the same day my daddy passed away in 2002.

We drove to the beach to watch Leah get married. Leah, who agreed to bring Eden home and start caring for her; Leah, who for months, spent most nights up walking and patting Eden as she screamed in her illness; Leah, who knew Eden better than anyone in this world. It was Leah's day.

Outside the barn where she married her beloved, the Gallagher's twins from Uganda led the way. Eli and Ellie were 2 of the 7 that Leah had fostered with Abigail, and they came down the aisle first as if saying, "Look! This is one of the two whom God chose to rescue us. We love her! And she is getting married!"

Leah then came down the aisle, stunning and radiant with joy. A charm was wrapped around her bouquet with the word "EDEN." It was such a sweet reminder of the baby girl that she and I love so much. It was an honor to watch and support this woman who blessed our lives in every way.

It was Leah's day, the day that God brought her to the man He had intended for her from the beginning of time. It was the day he sealed them together in the celebration of marriage. Even this day was a reminder that *our* day was coming too, very soon in the future – in God's perfect plans and in His perfect time. On that day, we did not know how, but we knew God would bring Eden Hannah to us soon and us to her – forever – and seal us together in family. Another celebration was just around the corner. Another day was coming. Very soon, we thought.

Relent, Lord! How long will it be? Have compassion on your servants. Satisfy us in the morning with your unfailing love, that we may sing for joy and be glad all our days. Make us glad for as many days as you have afflicted us, for as many years as we have seen trouble. May your deeds be shown to your servants, your splendor to their children.

Psalm 90: 13-16

After returning from our beach trip, we got more information from the senator's office. We found out that there were two orphans with the same name. Two girls awaiting adoption, both with the name "Eden," and both stuck in Nairobi – in terms of their paperwork. There had been a mix-up.

It was not our Eden Hannah who was awarded the visa. It seemed that the Lord had allowed us to help bring another Eden home instead. We found out on January 10, 2012, that *our* Eden wasn't coming home, after all.

January 10 was also my daddy's birthday. Maybe God was giving us more hope, despite a horrible let down. But, we had been so close. I wasn't sure if my heart could take another blow.

I wondered if maybe this other Eden, in the end, would not have received a favorable visa without our fighting for her. I wondered if maybe this other Eden was not being cared for with such compassion and love as Gracie was giving our Eden Hannah. I didn't know the answer, and I probably will never know. But I questioned God again, "How can this be? How can there be two Edens?"

I cried from the depth of my soul, "How can there be two!?!" Two baby girls with the same name. Two families longing just to hold and kiss their child. Yet I knew and believed that it was not by chance that these two girls shared a name.

I wanted it to be us, but it wasn't. Still, I knew the Lord was sovereign. Our family began praying for this other family, this other family that must have been rejoicing, this other family that would be bringing their Eden home within the space of a week.

The Lord will surely comfort Zion and will look with compassion on all her ruins; he will make her deserts like Eden, her wastelands like the garden of the Lord. Joy and gladness will be found in her, thanksgiving and the sound of singing. "Listen to me, my people; hear me, my nation: Instruction will go out from me; my justice will become like a light to the nations. My righteousness draws near speedily, my salvation is on the way, and my arm will bring justice to the nations. The islands will look to me and wait in hope for my arm."

Isaiah 51: 3-5

In the midst of my journey with the Lord, He is always renewing me and always teaching me. He wants my whole heart – *the whole thing*. The same was true in *each* trial we faced in the guardianship process. The same was true in *this* trial as well.

He asked me, "What is your greatest longing, your greatest desire?"

And I had to confess, then, that somewhere along the journey, Eden Hannah became my greatest longing and my greatest desire. In the pursuit of getting her home, I lost the pursuit of my first love – Jesus. I became consumed with getting papers for our three lawyers. I would repeatedly look at my phone in hopes for news from Nairobi. How quickly I forgot that He already knew the outcome!

I started praying for the joy of the Lord to be my strength. That was it. "Lord, be my strength and be my joy. Take my whole heart."

The night I began praying this, He woke me up to pray for both Gracie and Eden Hannah. It was so overwhelming that I decided to text Gracie. Her immediate response was, "EDEN JUST CRAWLED! JUST NOW!" I *was* overjoyed, and it *did* strengthen me!

He cared enough to wake me in the middle of the night to let me know that she was crawling for the first time. He cared enough to fight for my whole heart. He cared enough when he died upon the cross, for me, for Eden

Hannah, *and* for the other Eden.

Do not grieve, for the joy of the Lord is your strength.

Nehemiah 8: 10b

Time wore on, but His provision continued to humble me. People were fighting for us on every side, simply because He had provided them for our encouragement and support.

Still, I tried not to let my little ones see just how much my heart ached for Eden Hannah. One night in late January, I had a moment of weakness. I thought that all four of our children were in bed, but Bella crept in the kitchen and saw me crying. "Mommy, why are you crying?" She asked with her big inquisitive eyes and her raspy little voice.

"I just miss Eden Hannah, that is all," I said, trying to smile really big. Probably too big.

Bella responded, "Oh, I understand. When you were in Africa with her, I cried a lot because I missed you." Little Bella cupped my face in her tiny little hands. Then she lifted up the cross necklace I was wearing, a gift my mom had given me. "Mommy, keep looking at this. It will help you." What a precious reminder from one of my baby girls. Bella turned eight the next Friday, and Emma Lynn turned seven the next Wednesday. Two days before Bella's first birthday I gave birth to little her sister, Emma Lynn. We actually brought Emma Lynn home from the hospital on Bella's big day. I remember placing Emma Lynn in Bella's arms, "Happy birthday, little one. Now you have a baby sister."

The girls are "Irish twins," the name given for siblings born within the same calendar year. Several times I asked the girls what they wanted for their birthdays. Can you guess what their answer was? Both girls just wanted their new sister.

Bella's first birthday present ever was Emma Lynn. But the spring of 2012 the girls were 7 and 8, respectively, and they both just longed for "their baby" to come home.

Let your eyes look straight ahead; fix your gaze directly before you.

Proverbs 4: 25

Things were moving forward. Not as quickly as I would have hoped, but they *were* moving forward. The Lord used so many people to spur us on. He had people that did not even know us offer to help; they simply heard our story and made offers to assist in any way.

Several friends ran errands for us in Kampala while we continued waiting in Nashville. We received so many gifts that blessed us in so many ways; we were continuously shocked and completely humbled. He is the One – The Great Provider - He laid it upon people's hearts to bless us. Yahweh, whose very nature is provision, the author of good and perfect gifts.

At one point, Gracie emailed that Eden was getting bigger, and she was about to outgrow the few clothes that I left in Africa. (When we went in November to bring her home, we thought we were only going to be gone for two weeks at the most.) So, I went to grab some outfits from her little drawers, where all of her clothes were neatly folded and smelling so clean… where they had been in anticipation of her homecoming. I was going to send Gracie what I had on hand for Eden Hannah, but I quickly realized that most everything I had wasn't going to fit her anymore.

I had size 6 months clothes, but those were finally too small. In God's provision, that same night at church, a dear friend who had adopted two little girls from China asked me if I needed anything for Eden. Her little girl was a few years older than Eden. She told me to come by the next day and pick up some of the clothes her daughter had outgrown.

The next morning when I arrived at her house, I was simply floored. She gave me bags and bags full: baby spoons, bibs, sippy cups, shoes in just about every color, a high chair, a pack and play – and, of course, a pile of clothes to send to Uganda! God had done this. He provided for a need, that twenty-four hours before, I hadn't even known that I had. I had a single need, He provided in overflow.

He did this monetarily too. Our adoption cost us way more than we anticipated as it wore on, but He knew. And He provided. He is "Jehovah Jireh" – The God who Provides. There were many days that He blessed us with a gift the very day we needed it.

And why would we have expected anything else? He gave Eden Hannah two nurses to care for her when she was extremely sick. He gave her Gracie's arms, and he gave her Gracie's other children, to play with her and care for her in my absence. He did that. He used every person along the way to show her – and us – the deep, overflowing love of Jesus.

And God provided a family for Eden – our family. He placed her in a family that would love her all the days of her life, even before she came home. She had a family. She had a home. He did that. And we had a new daughter. The kids had a new sister. We would be part of His overflow for her, and she would be part of His overflow for us.

She didn't make it home for her sisters' birthdays in January, but, oh, how we prayed that she would be home for her own birthday, her first birthday, in March. I dreamed of giving her a birthday cake with one little candle on it. I dreamed of us - her forever family – right beside her. I hoped we could sing and celebrate the life that Jesus gave her and the daughter that He, Jehovah Jireh, had given us.

And Abraham called the name of that place Jehovahjireh: as it is said to this day, in the mount of the Lord It shall be seen.

Genesis 22: 14 KJV

So Abraham called that place 'The Lord will Provide.' And to this day it is said, "On the mountain of the Lord it will be provided."

Genesis 22: 14 NIV

Another page flipped on the calendar. In February, I attended a mother and son skate party with my two boys. While trying to manage and minimize the wipeouts of 6-year-old Judah, the kids' computer teacher approached me. (Just 2 years later, this teacher adopted her own son from Uganda.) Though she taught all of my four children at that time, she began telling me a story about Emma Lynn – cuddler, singer, pleaser.

Her first grade class was learning about the Internet. The teacher explained how you could use a search engine to type in any question and wait for your computer to give an answer. The first little boy to raise his hand asked, "Who is the fastest person in the world?" So the class typed in the question, and they immediately got the answer.

Emma Lynn was second to raise her hand. She tentatively asked, "Will you ask the computer the day that Eden Hannah gets to come home?"

How many times did I ask the Lord this very question, "Lord Jesus, when will she get to come home?"

"*Will* she even get to come home? When will we get to be a family all together?"

The answer to my yearning was simply – step-by-step, moment-by-moment – "Walk with me."

Ryan and I were constantly challenged to look at our story from every different side. We knew and believed that the Lord had asked us to care for and to love this little one that He had given to us, and, even then, we could see how He had provided for her at every turn. Nothing had been an accident or a coincidence.

136

My frame was not hidden from you in the secret place, when I was woven together in the depths of the earth. Your eyes saw my unformed body; all the days ordained for me were written in your book before one of them came to be. How precious to me are your thoughts God! How vast is the sum of them! Were I to count them they would outnumber the grains of sand – when I awake I am still with you.

Psalm 139: 15-18

When spring came in Nashville, the kids were running outside at the first sign of warm weather. One day, they were chasing snowflakes, days later it was sixty degrees. It brought us laughter and games, loud noises and a flurry of outdoor activities. We prayed, as the spring flowers burst out of the ground in new life, that Eden Hannah would bring new life into our house – that she would get to experience spring with us. I dreamt of strolling her on walks and pushing her on the swing. Soon enough, it was March.

Deep within me, I experienced the familiar stirring of the Holy Spirit. I felt as if Ryan and I were about to hear big news and that we needed to pray throughout the entire night. I emailed friends, who had been in Uganda with us, to also be in prayer that evening. I had not felt the calling to pray all night before that point, but it was so strongly on my heart. Ryan and I listened to worship music and prayed throughout the night.

At exactly 6:49 am the following morning, I was finishing putting breakfast on the table, when my phone chimed. Was it the news that we had prayed for? Was it the news that we had been anticipating for the past 3 months? Was it the news that we had counted on every day of the 108 days that we were apart. I thought, "Yes... we prayed all night, this will be the email we have been waiting on."

I picked up my phone, and there it was, "ADOPTIONS, NBO." ("NBO," meaning that it had come from the US embassy in Nairobi.) My heart was beating like crazy, and I wanted to jump up and down with joy. I opened the email on my phone, and I saw the words, "Notice of intent to deny."

My legs felt like they were crumpling beneath me, and I grabbed my stomach as if I would be sick. I looked up and realized our four little ones were looking at me. I smiled a very weak smile, and told them I needed to go talk to Daddy. I shut our bedroom door, gave Ryan the phone, and collapsed.

It is called a "N.O.I.D." Say it. "A NOID." Yes, it sounds like, "annoyed."

In international adoption, you are allowed 3 total NOID's. A third NOID would be our final – and we would never again be able to apply for a visa to bring Eden home. This was our second, and we were advised to hire yet another attorney. So, in addition to the 4 lawyers we already had, we hired a second immigration lawyer. At that point, we had 28 days left to answer the final "request for (more) evidence" (RFE) and have our last shot in Nairobi. That was it.

"You intended to harm me, but God intended it for good to accomplish what is now being done, the saving of many lives. So then, don't be afraid. I will provide for you and your children." And he reassured them and spoke kindly to them.
Genesis 50: 20-21

Friends began taking different times to pray so that we had prayer warriors petitioning on our behalf around the clock. They prayed for our family, the lawyers, and those who would make the decision. They prayed for Gracie, who loved Eden so faithfully, and ultimately we all prayed for a visa to bring our daughter home. We had the body of Christ fighting for us in the valley. They came alongside us and lifted us up. They reminded us to walk by faith and not by sight.

It would have been easy to give up hope and stop fighting. I will be honest – I was weary. But I kept remembering the Mighty God we serve, a Mighty God who could move mountains. A Mighty God who wasted nothing, and who used every tear that I cried for Eden. He used every prayer from my little ones, as they begged Him for us to be a family. He used people that we did not even know to sustain us as we walked the journey. It was as if he were continually saying, "Keep going. Don't give up. I am here." We had only 28 days left, but we were trusting in the God who saves.

Our prayer from the beginning was always that God would be exalted through our adoption. I also always felt that He was doing something, something I could not see, and I felt as if it were something big. I knew in my heart that He would never leave us. I knew that our journey was much bigger than our family, and all I knew to do at that point was to continue trusting Him. He had called us to our daughter, Eden Hannah, and we knew that would never change, even at day 28.

The Lord is a stronghold for the oppressed, a stronghold in times of trouble. Those who know your name, put their trust in you, for you, O LORD, have never forsaken those who seek you.

Psalm 9: 9-10

Eden's birthday was fast approaching. We had hoped she would be home to celebrate, but it was not to be. In Gracie's "spare time," she was going to have a pink celebration for our one-year-old. Gracie, who loved and cared for her husband and her own children, who served hundreds of other children in Uganda, who ministered to many others there by being the hands and feet of Jesus... and she was planning a birthday celebration for Eden.

I had found Eden the perfect birthday dress, purchased weeks earlier in the hopes of having a celebration at home. However, like so many of our hopes, God filled them, in His way and His timing. Though Eden wouldn't be home for her birthday, the Lord provided a way for her to wear her birthday dress – I had a friend leaving for Uganda the week before Eden Hannah's birthday. She was not only going to bring the dress to Eden, but the baby doll we had gotten her and cards from everyone in our family.

Then, three days before her birthday, Eden Hannah contracted the measles. If you do not know the seriousness of an infant with measles, consult the Internet. It was more than I could bear.

I wanted nothing more than to hold her. I knew that He held her. I knew that Gracie held her. But, "What if?" Here I was yet again, "What if?"

I thought my dependence on my Savior had been tested through this journey. I thought I had already been stretched thin. I thought I had already surrendered it all. Was He now asking me to surrender her very life?

We had surrendered our plans for our family, and He brought us on a second adoption journey with Eden. We surrendered our plans for what that journey would look like, and the Lord continued to provide for and sustain us, though the battle kept escalating. We finally surrendered our home and our community. We had decided, at this point, to move to Uganda if her visa was denied the last time.

We wondered if this was to be the final surrender. Three years in Uganda would give us her visa – as Ugandan citizens. The American visa would no longer matter. Despite that our lives were in Nashville – our church, our jobs, our kids' school, their friends and all of ours – we would surrender it all, if that's what it would take.

Surrender is a hard word. All our plans gave way to His plans for us. All our questions found answers only in Him. All of our waiting would soon be over, one way or the other. The judge had ruled in our favor – we were her legal guardians in Uganda, and just as Jesus says in John 14: 18, we would not leave her as an orphan... even if it meant moving our life and our family to Uganda.

But then Eden got the measles.

She was *really* sick. She was on an IV to keep her hydrated. Her fever was so high she had begun seizing. We worried about brain damage and other complications. All through her worst night, we prayed for her health, but we prayed also for the ability to surrender – even her life. There was nothing we could do except pray and lift our daughter to the Lord. I have never felt so helpless.

We knew surrender would bring freedom, so we prayed all night to have open hands, because the story was not about us, not about her – it was about God. The God of freedom, the God of surrender, and the God of healing. Was He asking us to give her back, that she would be healed in Heaven?

He was not, and He made it evident that He planned to heal her here on earth – she made it through the night, to the day before her first birthday. And not only was it to be her birthday, but also a critical final meeting regarding her visa. It was basically a last shot… a last attempt to bring her home – into America and into our arms.

Even now my witness is in heaven; my advocate is on high. My intercessor is my friend as my eyes pour out tears to God; on behalf of a man he pleads with God as one pleads for a friend.

Job 16: 19-21

While our dear friend, Gracie, was making Eden a pink birthday cake for her first birthday, our lawyers in Washington were hard at work on a final packet to respond to the second "Notice of Intent to Deny." The most vital document in this file would be a new ruling from our judge in Masindi, but this would also be tricky. He had *already* ruled in our favor! Wouldn't he surely see a second request as a bother at best, or as an insult at worst?

The Lord provided an advocate for us, to explain our complicated case to the judge, for the second time. An American go-between stepped into our case in Uganda, so that our judge could use the necessary American wording for the American Embassy in Nairobi. More times than I can count, God made the impossible possible. Our second ruling, and the documents explaining it, were no exception.

Another miracle occurred when the judge who awarded us legal guardianship in November 2011, ruled for us *again* in April of 2012. This judge did not have to hear our case the first time, much less a second. But he did so, favorably, both times. He went above and beyond even our first ruling, because he is a man of integrity, a man of the law, *and* a man who follows Jesus.

It wasn't by chance that we were to receive our last response from Nairobi on Good Friday.

Pastor Scotty Smith wrote this prayer for Good Friday:

> *Lord Jesus, it's the day in Holy Week we call "Good Friday." I've always felt conflicted about calling the day of your crucifixion "good..." That there had to be a day when you, the God who made us for yourself, would be made sin for us, is not good at all. But on the other hand, that you would so freely and fully give yourself for us on the cross, is never-to-be surpassed goodness... For out of the same heart and the same mouth came these two cries from the cross: "Father forgive them..." (Luke 23: 24) and "My God, my God, why have you forsaken me?" (Matt. 27: 46) The first required the second. The second secured the first. Together they buckle my knees, still my heart, and loose my tongue... No one could ever take your life from you, and I could never find life on my own. Because you were fully forsaken, I am forever forgiven. Because you exhausted God's judgment against my foul sin, I now live by the gift of your perfect righteousness. Hallelujah! Hallelujah! Hallelujah![4]*

Then I heard what sounded like a great multitude, like the roar of rushing waters and like loud peals of thunder, shouting: "Hallelujah! For our Lord God Almighty reigns."

Revelation 19: 6

By mid-April, I was in Uganda for the third time. We knew our final 28-day period would soon come to a close, one way or the other: If we were awarded a visa, I would take Eden home. If we were denied a visa for the third time, I would stay a bit longer to begin making arrangements for our new life in Uganda.

I was walking the dirt roads of Jinja with a friend, winding and wandering, looking at homes that could potentially hold our family for 3 years. When we returned, I decided to check my email on a whim, not thinking there would be any news. I was wrong. There were the words again: "Decision Regarding Visa." Oh, how my stomach turned from having been there too many times before. I thought, "Here we go again..."

Though Eden Hannah had been glued to my hip since our reunion, I set her down on the floor to give my attention to the message from the Embassy. She screamed, "Mom-my!" as she had been doing ever since my return, panicking even when I would walk into another room. So, I tried to settle her and open the email, both at the same time...

I tried and tried *and tried* to open the email. No luck. It was in a zip file. I am completely unskilled when it comes to computer, egregiously so. So I sent the email to three out of the six lawyers, to my mother, and of course, to Ryan. (He left Uganda after being with me initially, to care for our other children.)

But waiting on a response without further effort on my part just would not do. I had already waited so long! So, I called my mother, who is brilliant with technology. She opened the email and began reading it to me, word for word. "The U.S. Embassy in Nairobi has approved your visa."

That means: IT IS A YES. Yes, we can bring our baby girl home. Yes, it is time. Yes. Yes! YES!

My mom transferred the zip file into a PDF file (don't even ask), and she sent it to me. I then immediately called Ryan and tried to get the words from the email out of my mouth when the only words in my head were, "It is time! Thank you Jesus! Thank you. It is time."

I was in shock. The tears that had flowed for so many months wouldn't even come. It was as if I were afraid to believe the incredible news. News I had longed for, dreamed about, and for which I had begged the Lord daily. But this time, it was real. Our visa was approved. I looked down at Eden, who was playing with my shoe, and my gratitude completely overwhelmed me.

We would all be a family now. One family, all together, on one continent. Yes. It was time.

How lovely is your dwelling place, Lord Almighty! My soul yearns, even faints, for the courts of the Lord; my heart and my flesh cry out for the living God. Even the sparrow has found a home, and the swallow a nest for herself, where she may have her young – a place near your altar, Lord Almighty, my King and my God. Blessed are those who dwell in your house; they are ever praising you.

Psalm 84: 1-4

Chapter 7 | "Dees Ees Aah-free-kah": The Second Trip

Before the end of our first trip to Africa with the Morrows and the Doyles, I was plotting my return. Ryan and Nate began planning a summer trip with a team of high school students in June 2012, and there was no way I could miss out! I would be the first to volunteer as a chaperone for such a trip. Or I would fill any other role that would just get me back on that plane!

I cannot remember what possessed me to ask Adam about Hannah Whit coming, and I cannot remember what made her so eager to come with me either, but no sooner did I return to the states than I was making appointments for her passport and shots. I think the presence of God I felt in the country and the people of Uganda, the love I gave and received from the kids... I think that is what motivated me to return as soon as possible, and I wanted my kids to know this love as well.

I guess I understood then that God was giving me forever relationships. And if it was to be a lifetime, it would include my family. Another pipeline to God's overflowing well had been laid, and I knew it would come pouring out of my heart.

I have always wanted my children to see how the Lord provides for his people through mission work, and honestly, I wanted to see God's provision too. I went on only one mission trip before Africa. Right after I became a follower of Christ, I went to Costa Rica, and mainly, my parents and grandparents footed the bill. But it was going to take a lot more dinero to get two people to Africa than to get one person to Central America.

No better time than the present to take God at his word on provision, with my oldest child watching, I thought. We definitely could not afford to fund another 2-person trip across the globe, so we raised support for my second trip. In the end, we had to contribute very little of our income for the summer trip with Hannah Whit.

145

The Lord provided very generously through so many friends and family members.[1] Our "senders" were as much a part of God's eternal work in Masindi as anyone else who has actually gone. Our supporters mean the world to me, and I know they mean even more to the children at Family Spirit. Only God knew then how far into the future their investment would reap rewards, not only for us, but especially for the children. How deep His roots of love would reach into our souls and how binding the heartstrings of our relationships would be!

I think many people fail to realize that sending, *truly*, is as important as going. And in our short sightedness, we often fail to think beyond the scope of the present. We even fail to think beyond the scope of the one individual going. I am no less guilty, as Adam and I often *discuss with each other* how to give our money and in what amount – INSTEAD OF ASKING GOD!!

We are too weak, limited and incompetent to make such decisions! We are prone to think, "What difference can one person or one trip make?" So, we fail to be "senders" by failing to give at all or failing to give as we should. Instead, we think, "I can only give so much – it could not possibly make an impact." We fail to see the far-reaching effects that our giving has in God's eyes, on the people reached in mission work, on the future plans God has, and definitely, we often miss the impact God plans to make on the person who is going.

I made a prayer sign-up sheet for our trip, also, so that one or more person would be praying for us each day while we were away. Many of the people who supported us financially supported us in prayer as well. I wanted Hannah Whit to see and know the reality of prayer on our behalf for God's power, protection, and provision. More than that – I knew it was critical for us!

We have different gifts, according to the grace given us. If a man's gift is prophesying, let him use it in proportion to his faith. If it is serving, let him serve; if it is teaching, let him teach; if it is encouraging, let him encourage; if it is contributing to the needs of others, let him give generously; if it is leadership, let him govern diligently; if it is showing mercy, let him do it cheerfully.

Romans 12: 6-7

When I left for this second trip for Africa with Hannah Whit, I was praying through Luke 10: 1-24 in my personal prayer times. "The harvest is plentiful, but the workers are few. Ask the Lord of the harvest, therefore, to send out workers into his harvest field… Go! I am sending you out like lambs among wolves" (v. 2-3).

As I studied this passage in Luke, God fostered my personal beliefs about missions. Since Family Spirit was quickly becoming a lifetime commitment for me, I desired to grapple through cultural objections to arrive at God's larger perspective for my future. At the risk of grossly oversimplifying many things, I will share a few of my own thoughts, as I spent time processing these words in prayer.

There are many "wolves" in Africa: diseases like HIV/AIDS, Tuberculosis, and Malaria. There are other predators, such as lack of healthcare and medicine. There is also an entire generation of parents that is missing (because disease has wiped them out), and they are leaving a new generation of orphans.

Like America, they also face the "wolves" of parents who won't parent. Of sexual immorality and adultery. Of physical violence and sexual abuse. Of political corruption. Of poverty, homelessness and hunger. Of witchcraft, which seems far more rampant in Uganda (but may just have a greater public display there.) There are many "wolves" that we face, since we live in a fallen world.

Unlike America, however, these wolves have a darker face because Uganda does not have the law enforcement infrastructure or military capabilities that we have, something we often take for granted here. In addition, they have Kony, and other rebel maniacs who have thus far managed to escape capture. The widespread and devastating lack of clean drinking water and sanitation make the sick even sicker. And long-term oppression makes the poor even poorer.

Just the same, it would be a horrible mistake to think that darkness is only in the faraway continent of Africa. God impressed on my heart, through this passage in Luke, that the evils in America are equally destructive to faith and missions. Satan is opposed to the Gospel of hope and love being spread in *all* places.

The enemy will use the evil that is rampant in Africa to try to stop the spread of his Good News. Likewise, he will use complacency, cost or difficulty of travel to keep Americans from going to share His message. Regardless of the form, it is still Satan working to keep the message of love, hope and healing from helping and saving the ones who need it most.

There is an intricate backlash happening in America, I think, crafted by the serpent who twists and distorts Truth. Some Christians argue, rightfully, that it is cheaper to send money than people. However, many conclude wrongly, I believe, that we shouldn't send people at all. The God who created the galaxies and the universe, and every one of us, journeyed his own cosmic highway to bridge heaven and earth, natural and supernatural. Why shouldn't we, too, *go*?

He left everything to come to us, who have nothing, to rescue and redeem us. He left the unimaginable comforts of Heaven that we might take comfort in Him. He forfeited relationship and intimacy with His Father so that *we* might have relationship with His Father. And the darkest evil of hell consumed Him temporarily, that we might be saved from hell eternally. He humbled Himself continually and ultimately, that we might have fullness of life here.

If He can (*and He will*) use any of us to provide a taste of any of *that*, in any continent or capacity, shouldn't we surrender ourselves to His purposes and plans, whatever those might be?

How, then, can they call on the one they have not believed in? And how can they believe in the one of whom they have not heard? And how can they hear without someone preaching to them? And how can anyone preach unless they are sent? As it is written: "How beautiful are the feet of those who bring good news!"

Romans 10: 14-15

In addition to the general objections I have heard about missions to other continents, people have asked me questions regarding the specifics about the country of Uganda. Why couldn't I choose a country that is easier to reach, cheaper in travel and closer in distance? I'm not sure I know the answer, but I am pretty sure God, who continues to lead me to Africa, *does* know the answer. So for now, I will trust God to send others near and far, here and beyond, while I trust Him *personally* to take me to Africa, for as long and as often as He wants me to go.[2]

Finally, I think there are some who believe that what I am doing is just plain crazy – *too* radical. Beyond the money and the distance, a few have voiced questions of my personal well-being. I've heard doubts about my sanity, yes, but far more so I've listened to fears about putting my life in danger: "What about rebel troops and terrorists? What about HIV/AIDS or other diseases?" [3]

Because God has given me a crazy kind of love—giving His only Son—I want to share it with others! God is sending me, and I want to go in full obedience! And if that is not reason enough, I plead childishness as my excuse…

For in the end of that very same passage in Luke, Jesus says this, "At that time Jesus, full of joy through the Holy Spirit, said, 'I praise you Father, Lord of heaven and earth, because you have hidden these things from the wise and learned, and revealed them to little children. Yes, Father, for this is what you were pleased to do' "(v. 21).

I am in the habit of asking God to use me, in any way he pleases, for the glory of His Kingdom. I got involved in this Africa business because I asked God to send me on a short-term mission trip. I tried to lay out my plans for Him as *little* as possible, and listen to what His answer was as *much* as possible. He is my Abba Father, and I am his child. And yes, that may seem crazy to some. I'm OK with that.

Paul Miller writes in *A Praying Life*,

> *Let's do a quick analysis on how little children ask. What do they ask for? Everything and anything. If they hear about Disneyland, they want to go there tomorrow. How often do little children ask? Repeatedly. Over and over again. They wear us out. Sometimes we give in just to shut them up. How do little children ask? Without guile. They just say what is on their minds. They have no awareness of what is appropriate or inappropriate.[4]*

God wants us to ask like children, whether it seems appropriate or not. Jesus says in Mark 10:14, "Let the little children come to me, and do not hinder them, for the kingdom of heaven belongs to such as these," and He tells us that we should change and become like children... in child-like faith, awesome belief, bold expectation and unequivocal trust.

I may seem crazy, but I am resting in my Father's arms, even when I cannot feel them around me. I am trusting, often like a foolish child, that He has the answers when I do not, and that He will provide the way down the path to which He has called me. He did it through my husband, on our first trip to Africa, and He did it through our friends and family when he called me – with my daughter – back for the second time.

If our imperfect earthly fathers will provide for the needs of their children (and mine certainly provided much for us to go!), "...how much more will your Father in heaven give the Holy Spirit to those who ask him" (Luke 11: 13b)!

God used Luke 10 along with my personal experiences, to grow my foundational beliefs about international missions. He helped me to deal with some of my own questions and fears about how He could use me in another continent. It is my position that we should fight the "wolves" in America, that would prevent us from being sent amongst the "wolves" in Africa, so that we may lavish His love on His lambs in both places and be made more like Him as we go!

Know that the Lord is God. It is he who made us, and we are his; we are his people, the sheep of his pasture.

Psalm 100: 3

In the months following our trip with the Doyles and the Morrows, Ryan was able to redirect the high school summer mission plans at Christ Presbyterian Church where he was youth pastor. He began gathering a team of students and adult chaperones, which would include himself and Nate Morrow, Janie Omer and Angie Gage. Ever since returning from the first summer trip, these two women and their husbands, Chris Omer and Rob Gage, have been a part of our Nashville group, which would ultimately include 8 families total.

Our group banded together in every effort to partner with Family Spirit for life. We desired (and still desire) to assist them in any way that will further their progress toward a self-sustaining school and home for the children: through farming and local business relationships, utilizing a feeding program immediately and building a child sponsorship list eventually. Nate Morrow came home lobbying for West End Community Church kids to join Ryan's team from Christ Presbyterian on this first summer trip. And Bobby Freeman, our youth pastor, was nothing but inclined to do so – he and his wife, Adrienne, were as equally and instantly tied to Family Spirit as the Morrows, Doyles and Adam and I were.

The Freemans made a special visit to Family Spirit to check on the kids on our behalf during a 3-week mission trip with Visiting Orphans[5] in April of

2012. The purpose of their trip was to serve orphans in various countries in Africa, but they extended their trip to include Masindi.

Bobby was an instant hit with the Family Spirit children – as he is with most people, especially those 18 and under. Gregarious and outgoing, his personality fills up any room he enters, just like his 6'4" stature and his beaming smile. Adrienne was in love with the kids, as well. Cords tied her maternal heart instantly to the kids, and her kind and gentle nature strengthened her bond with them.

Adrienne was hooked and smitten, like the rest of us, and her educational background and career as a Pediatric Physician's Assistant have made her an invaluable asset to our team as well. She has consulted with Susan about treatment for Jacob who has a lazy eye, and with Isaac about nutritional goals for the future of all the children. Adrienne also eventually became our group leader and point person for most matters in The Masindi Project. She has served as a diligent liaison between Masindi and Nashville in finances and budget, prayer and other communication, marketing and publicity.

Though Bobby and Adrienne were certainly on board with all efforts to assist Family Spirit, Bobby was unable to change the West End Community Church youth mission plans that first summer. They would continue to be involved in Nashville, and Bobby would return later with another group.

For the time being, however, Janie and Ryan charged full steam ahead with Christ Presbyterian Church. And so, in June of 2012, I was on my way to back to Uganda in a team of 6 adults (including one intern, Zack Wise), 19 high school students, and one 8-year old Hannah Whit.

But the Lord said to me, "Do not say, 'I am too young.' You must go to everyone I send you to and say whatever I command you.

Jeremiah 1: 7

We flew Delta from Detroit and connected in Amsterdam to a KLM flight to Entebbe. We were travel-weary but everyone was excited to land. Understatement. Mustafa was excited for us to land also. Bigger understatement.

Mustafa is our liaison on the ground for every trip to Uganda. He has been in charge of getting us where we need to be, in addition to so many other things. He is from Masindi, so he helps us with all details regarding Family Spirit as well.

He was there at the airport to pick us up with a couple of busses and drivers. He embraced Ryan and Nate, then practically picked me up off the ground. He was excited to meet Hannah Whit, and she was thrilled to meet him as well.

One of the most pronounced memories I have from this second trip was Mustafa circling the parking lot in front of Masindi Hotel with Hannah Whit on the back of his boda. He instructed Hannah Whit, "Say, 'Hi, Mom,' " and the image of them both smiling is not only recorded on video, but also emblazoned in my mind. Her hand waving excitedly in the air, giggling and grinning at me, in response to Mustafa, she shouted, "HI, MOM!"

Abigail and Leah befriended Mustafa while they lived in Masindi, and Abigail introduced us all on the first trip. Mustafa is too friendly, too loving, too happy, and too funny to adequately explain here[6]. Words do not do justice, anyway. A whole book could be written on his life and his demeanor, his role and his help. Although I have known Mustafa since my first trip to Uganda, our friendship and my appreciation of him has continued to grow, whether I am here in the States or in Masindi.
I will start with this, and it should read like a title or a headline, fitting to his stand-out character and personality:

**Mustafa - a Muslim man from Masindi
with a motorcycle and a mission to help the mzungus[7]**

A boda driver by trade, he has also become our local ambassador on the ground in Uganda. He wore a black t-shirt on my second trip that reads, "Do I look like your therapist?" And yes, in Africa, he does. So much so that I have requested he wear the shirt as often as possible. He has been our tour guide, travel guide, translator extraordinaire, while in Uganda, and our point person with Family Spirit. All things to all people at all times. Now he is on staff.

He loves Kit Kats and Nature Valley Granola Bars, which we never forget to bring him when we travel. He loves the American song, "Good Morning Beautiful," by Steve Holy[8], but also taught us that the local women in Masindi have taken popular American lyrics, "All the single ladies" by Beyoncé[9], and made them completely their own, "All Masindi Ladies…" That is certainly something I put *my* hands up for!

Mustafa has never met a stranger and never been ruffled, upset or concerned in the least by long waits, last-minutes changes in plans, broken down vehicles, stops by the intimidating Ugandan police, or getting oneself stuck – quite literally – in the lion's den.

Have a problem? Mustafa has the solution. Have a question? Mustafa has the answer or knows whom to ask. Need help? Mustafa knows the person to provide assistance if he himself, jack-of-all-trades, cannot give it.

We love Mustafa like a brother. He is not only instrumental in our travels to Uganda and our care for Family Spirit – he is a dear friend. He has become family to ALL of us, and even now refers to Jessie Omer as his sister and Janie as his American mother. He calls her, "Mom," (Maaa-hm) with the same thick African-accented southern twang he attempted when Hannah Whit rode on the back of his boda.

I missed him in the six months I was gone, and not only that, but I prayed fervently for him in the time between those visits. I had a vision, and I told him about it, that one day he would follow Christ and be baptized in the Nile. I pictured him in a white gown, like I picture Gabriel in the Gospels – *glowing*. His dark skin glowing even brighter, and his white smile brighter still. The water dazzled like it would in the scene of a movie. I want to be there for his baptism one day. One Day.

I mentioned my prayers and our collective affection for Mustafa to the former missions director at our church, Shane Bowen. He recommended I read *Miraculous Movements* about Muslims coming to Christ around the world. It has given weight, as well as new motivation and hope, to my prayers. The day has not yet come, but it hasn't changed our love for Mustafa, nor his love for us.

One subtitle in this book reads, "Behind every dramatic story is much prayer." I could not agree more, both in practice and in theory. Trousdale writes,

> *Why and how are entire mosques of Muslims becoming followers of Christ? The final answer, of course, is this: God has chosen to do so at this time. But on a human level, there is one constant theme that keeps coming up in the interviews we have conducted with Christ followers from a Muslim background: abundant prayer. Prayer is the greatest weapon that any disciple maker can wield, and God's people are using it effectively around the world at this very minute. Prayer takes the spiritual battle out of the human realm and puts it fully into God's hands, and not even the powers of hell itself can stand against His mighty Spirit.* [10]

Reading the book certainly fanned the flame of my prayer life in Mustafa's direction more than ever before. As I began nearing the completion of writing for this book, I asked my prayer partner (and member of our Masindi Fellowship), Stephanie Edwards, to hold me accountable to writing for at least one hour a day. (You might laugh at that effort, but I was trying my best, amidst the life of a busy homeschooling mom, to drive this thing home!)

Reading about Muslim movement toward Christ, and being encouraged about prayer beyond that, I upped the ante of my accountability. Pray for

Mustafa every day, every time I sat down to write. What could be more important for one we love like a brother?!?

Though he doesn't have a relationship with Jesus, he has a deep longing to know God. He shared his heart's desires with us on that trip, in our nightly group times of prayer and study. He listened intently, as well, and often with tears in his eyes, as our students and leaders shared their own hearts.

Mustafa even worshipped with us. He loves singing hymns and praise songs with us – his favorite is "Amazing Grace."[11] He is getting to know the God who finds those once lost and opens the eyes of those once blind. And I see, through Mustafa, the God who so recklessly pursues our hearts. Heaven is after the Muslim man from Masindi.

For even if there are so-called gods, whether in heaven or on earth (as indeed there are many "gods" and many lords"), yet there is but one God, the Father, from whom all things came and through whom we live.

I Corinthians 8: 5-6

When we loaded the buses at the airport, we needed almost as much room for our luggage as we did for our bodies. (And after our luggage was accounted for, there wasn't much room for the bodies!) Each member of our team brought 1 carry-on bag for themselves, and checked 1-2 bags filled with humanitarian aid goods: deflated soccer balls and pumps, soccer nets, clothing and shoes, first aid items, and things for the Vacation Bible School we hosted. Among the checked luggage was a non-descript black trunk.

When we landed, we got all of our bags and our single black trunk. We found out the next morning, however, that the trunk we carried from the airport was not ours. After a few calls, we discovered that the black trunk in our possession belonged to an American family, also from Tennessee (Memphis), also traveling to Uganda for mission work! We had their trunk and they had ours, but swapping these 2 trunks was somehow proving to be impossible.

Their driver was very protective of their luggage, and two other obstacles stood in the way of our rendezvous: the language barrier and the geography. Not only is Kampala roughly 75 square miles (the largest city in Uganda, which encompasses more land than Washington D.C.), but also, all of it – every square mile, was unfamiliar to all of us. These things combined were making our hook up more difficult, even after calls from our driver, Lawrence (Lawrence of Masindi, we called him), and from Mustafa – the Renaissance man.

We made as many calls and attempts as we could that first morning in Kampala. And we prayed! We wanted our trunk, and we were sure that they wanted theirs! But we had only that one morning in Kampala before we loaded the buses and headed northwest to Masindi, three hours away.

Our one and only stop, which would take the better part of the morning because of our numbers, was at Nakumat (a strip mall) – where we planned to visit the grocery store, the bank and a local eatery for lunch before journeying on. We purchased food and other incidentals for Family Spirit at the store, along with giant water jugs for our team. We traded our crisp, unmarked and unwrinkled, 2006 issue or newer, $100.00 bills at the bank giving the best exchange rate for Ugandan Shillings.

Our last stop was for lunch in the western-style restaurant Café Java. Our calls and communication over the trunk had been unsuccessful all morning. It appeared that we would have to leave the black trunk belonging to the other team where we spent the first night, Adonai House. We hoped the other family would be able to pick it up at some point. As for our black trunk, it was looking like we would have no choice but to travel on to Masindi without it.

After an hour and a half, our lengthy lunch was over, and our large group was straggling out of the restaurant in several smaller clusters. One of those clusters overheard other Americans talking about missions and approached them, because the students realized they had been talking to these people on our plane ride the night before. We soon discovered – *this was the family from Memphis*, the owners of the black trunk and holders of our *matching* black trunk!

The God who numbers hairs on our heads and grains of sand on the seashore had brought two groups from Tennessee together on the other side of the globe, in a city of over one million, with no effort whatsoever on our behalf! If He can "find" us, His lost sheep, certainly he can help two groups, with two lost trunks, find their way back to one another! It left an instant impression on leaders and students alike – God was in charge and He would show up continuously in provision and details, just as He had done on our first trip to Uganda.

Then Jesus told them this parable: "Suppose one of you has a hundred sheep and loses one of them. Doesn't he leave the ninety-nine in the open country and go after the lost sheep until he finds it? And when he finds it, he joyfully puts it on his shoulders and goes home. Then he calls his friends and neighbors together and says, 'Rejoice with me; I have found my lost sheep.'"

Luke 15: 3-6

"Why," I have asked myself so many times, "does God seem everywhere in Uganda?"

"Why does He do these crazy miracles recurrently in Africa?"

The answer I have come up with is truth – God is doing the same things every day in America, but we are often too comfortable, too busy, too self-sufficient, too distracted and too deceived-about-our-helpless-condition to notice. We need God's intervention and provision just as much here as we do in Africa, but we too often deceive ourselves into thinking we are fine on our own.

In Africa, I have to pray for everything, because everything is out of my control. In America, the same is true, though the reality of my lack of control is veiled, due to the comforts I enjoy. I have my plans and my schedule to maintain. I know the roads to take to get to the places I think I need to go. If I have a problem, I know plenty of people to help me find a solution, and I know the language in which to communicate my issue.

I hold tightly to my sense of control, my sense of ownership, my entitlement and my rights. Though I have control of NOTHING, I can, unconsciously almost, live under the distortion that I control many things. This is because in America, there is money in the bank, a hospital on every corner (and in the South, a church on every corner, as well), and a routine and rhythm (often man-made), to every day and week.

In Africa, there are no such false pretenses. I feel out of control because I am out of control. But oddly, I am also more at rest because I am more *dependent* – and the Object of my dependence *is truly in control*. That has been part of the beauty I have found walking with God in Africa – I see His intricate control so clearly... along with His gracious goodness, perfect provision, and lavish love.

My heart seems more at rest in Africa.

When I don't have immediate access to a checking account, and I'm using a different currency, I have to trust God more. When I don't speak the language, but I hear its beauty all around me, I have to trust God more. When there aren't grocery stores, restaurants or bathrooms, I have to trust God more. When there are more dirt roads than streets, and there is more gravel than pavement, I have to trust God more. When I don't carry a calendar and a to-do list, I have to trust God more. When it seems the sun is a better clock than my wristwatch, I have to trust God more. When the nearest first-aid is likely the small travel kit I carry in my backpack, I have to trust God more. When security guards carry semi-automatic assault rifles, I have to trust God more. And when the "local zoo" doesn't cage the animals, I have to trust God more.

God becomes very big to me when He is all I have!

Do you want to know how hard it is when someone steals your credit card in a foreign country – especially a *really* foreign country like Uganda, where even obtaining a cellular connection can be challenging? Where even the little English that is spoken is a very heavily African-accented, British English? Ask Lindsey Doyle, because it happened to her our first trip.

Do you want to know what it is like to have a severe stomach virus in a place that is vastly unfamiliar, completely deprived of a clean bathroom floor upon which to lie prostrate in misery? Ask Elizabeth Patton, because it happened to her on this, my second trip.

And I've already given a frame of reference for lost luggage.

So why does my heart seem more at rest there, in a third-world country, on the other side of this planet? Maybe because when I have to trust Him more, He seems bigger. And when He seems bigger, my heart seems more at rest.

Is God bigger in Africa? A resounding, "No." Absolutely not. God is the same yesterday, today and forever (Heb. 13: 8). The same in Africa as in America. The unchanging, Almighty, Everlasting King of Kings, Creator of *all* Continents.

But in Africa, *maybe*, *I* am different... without my American trimmings. *Perhaps,* I am smaller... Without my plans, my schedules, and my agendas. Smaller, without my appliances and conveniences. Smaller, without television, email, social media, and functioning Internet service. Smaller, without toilets and trash service and running water in local hospitals. Smaller, without the Army, Navy, Air Force and Marines.

Smaller. Relying on the Same Big God. And without surprise, more at rest.

I started to ponder these things on my second trip. My dependence on God certainly creates a new kind of beauty: it is called Relationship. Walking with God in Africa gives me a closer glimpse of what walking with God must have been like in the Garden, in the cool of the day. More peaceful, more intimate, slower and simpler – more being and less doing.

I've often said that there exists in Africa a beautiful simplicity. If this ease evokes new levels of depth in my relationship with God, it certainly does the same for my sense of fellowship. If I want to talk to someone in Africa, I have a conversation – a *real* conversation, *face-to-face.* We had plenty of time for it: lots of time travelling in busses, walking along roads, and (hold your breath) sitting. My friend Brooke Edging, who is a missionary in Kampala together with her husband Steven, has said, "Americans are task-oriented people. Ugandans are relationship-oriented people."[12]

I certainly found this to be true, and it engendered a more pronounced proclivity for fellowship within our group as well. I didn't know Angie Gage before we left America, but by the time we returned home, we might as well have been friends forever. My childlike heart connected with the youthful spirit that she, too, possessed. It seemed we always found a place next to each other at the table or on the bus. Our conversations were as natural as if we had known one another for years. God knit our hearts together… He had all of the necessary time and *none* of the usual distractions.

The service is slower in Uganda, too – even the hotel and restaurant staffs were more interested in knowing us, truly serving us, than they were in "processing us" down some customer-needs assembly line. No one seems to be in a hurry, and there aren't flat-screens plastering the walls of every establishment, so the group lingered over meals. Quite literally, due to less-than-dependable electricity, candlelight saw us through many dinners.

Call me sentimental, but there is something different – and slower, and simpler, and more beautiful – about candlelight in the warm, open, African night air (even when highly concentrated amounts of deet are involved), than dinner in a busy, over-stuffed American restaurant where the servers move at a frenetic pace and the patrons are paying homage to the cable on the walls or the electronic devices in their hands. The difference between the travel-services industry in Uganda and America are like those between night and day, or perhaps between Martha and Mary, especially at the Adonai Guest House in Kampala and at Masindi hotel, where we have stayed the most frequently. They *both* always go over and above our expectations in the hospitality, kindness and friendship they show us.

As Jesus and his disciples were on their way, he came to a village where a woman named Martha opened her home to him. She had a sister called Mary, who sat at the Lord's feet listening to what he said. But Martha was distracted by all the preparations that had to be made. She came to him and asked, "Lord, don't you care that my sister has left me to do the work by myself? Tell her to help me!"

"Martha, Martha," the Lord answered, "you are worried and upset about many things, but few things are needed- or indeed only one. Mary has chosen what is better, and it will not be taken away from her."

Luke 10: 38-42

The added benefit of our bona fide summer mission trip was the number of people we had there. And the largest portion of our team was under age 20. With so many high school students, it seemed there was an inexhaustible store of energy in our group. We started early in the day at Family Spirit and only left when dusk approached. We ate breakfast, loaded our stomachs with eggs and peanut butter to last as long as possible, and we didn't eat another meal until we finally sat down for a very late dinner.

A set of twins, James and Matthew Wilson, played soccer with the boys literally all day, always in direct sunlight and always in the dirt (unless it

162

was pouring rain, in which case the "pitch" turned into a mud bath and kicked the exertion up a few more notches, turning an already exhausting sport into a veritable battle zone). They stopped like the rest of us, only occasionally, for a drink of water from the barrel we brought or a quick protein bar. I lost 5 pounds on this trip – I can't imagine these guys lost less than 10, as their physical output far exceeded their caloric intake.

The guys spent every reserve of energy in sport or construction. They built a wall of rudimentary cement blocks that would help divide the Family Spirit from their neighbors, who often complained about those stray soccer balls, for one. The girls held hands, held hearts and hosted a Vacation Bible School for all the kids. They led the children in different lessons, songs and crafts each day.

Most American Christians have seen the Gospel bracelet before: a strand of yarn with 6 different colored beads. But this simple exercise was entirely new and exciting for over 200 kids at Family Spirit, regardless of age or gender. They placed the black bead on for our sin, which separates us from a perfect and Holy God, followed by the red bead, which represents Christ's blood and the sacrifice that he made on our behalf.

Next, the white bead stands for purity that we have before God when we place our faith in Christ. God no longer sees our guilt, and he takes away our shame, seeing us anew through Christ's perfection. The blue bead represents the water of baptism, an outward display of the new inner purity God gives us in Jesus. Finally, the green and gold beads: our growth in Christ and the promise of our future and eternal home.

Again, simple. But how lovely, powerful and descriptive! I, too, beheld the inestimable worth of the Gospel with new eyes.

Jesus' gifts to us on the Cross, redemption and faith, are more valuable than gold, and thanks to scores of high school girls from Nashville, the kids saw this too. Not only that, they treated the bracelets themselves like they were precious stones and metals from Tiffany's. It didn't matter that the jewelry was made from string and plastic – it was *their* string and plastic.

And it represented *their* God, El Roi, the God who sees *their* lives, each little face and each broken heart. They placed this reminder on their wrists: God's heart was broken for them too.

Praise be to the God and Father of our Lord Jesus Christ! In his great mercy he has given us new birth into a living hope through the resurrection of Jesus Christ from the dead, and into an inheritance that can never perish, spoil or fade. This inheritance is kept in heaven for you, who through faith are shielded by God's power until the coming of the salvation that is ready to be revealed in the last time. In all this you greatly rejoice, though now for a little while you may have had to suffer grief in all kinds of trials. These have come so that the proven genuineness of your faith – of greater worth than gold, which perishes even though refined by fire – may result in praise, glory and honor when Jesus Christ is revealed. Though you have not seen him, you love him; and even though you do not see him now, you believe in him and are filled with an inexpressible and glorious joy, for you are receiving the end result of your faith, the salvation of your souls.

I Peter 1: 3-9

After five full days with the kids at Family Spirit, we crossed the Nile by ferry for a game drive at Murchison Falls Reserve, the same as we did on my first trip. Goodbye was exceedingly difficult, but there remained one shimmer of hope- we would have just a few more hours with the kids when we passed back by the orphanage the next day. The route we would travel to Eastern Uganda, for the remainder of our trip, required us to travel back through Masindi.

But for now: safari! Many students, including Hannah Whit, geared up for their first interaction with African wildlife, and the van ride was actually inviting in our general state of group exhaustion. The tsetse flies were every bit as bothersome on the way in as on the first trip, but a new sight for us all: a gigantic river crocodile. Rainy season did not end as soon as expected, and the swollen tributary we passed over before we entered the reserve made the perfect home for the croc. What a welcome!

We did not have the powerful lion sightings that we had previously, but our van came to a stop as we were entering the savannah. We were greeted by a very playful band of giraffes. The other big game score- hippos. We happened upon many more hippos than on my first trip, and all were very close up. In fact, they were too close up for my personal comfort!

The hippopotamus is Greek for "river horse," and it is generally considered the most dangerous animal in Africa. Its behavior is unpredictable, and its large body is surprisingly efficient in the water. Despite the fact that they kill more humans than any other African animal, that they can weigh up to 9000 pounds, and that their teeth are razor sharp, our drivers decided to park our vans and buses right next to the Nile River bank where large herds of them were feeding and fighting.

I stayed on the bus for this one, and I made Hannah Whit stay right next to me. Hippos may be very protective of their territory and their young, but I happen to be fairly protective of my young as well! Needless to say, everyone survived our trip into the wilds.

When we left the reserve, we would travel on to Jinja to work for a day with Ekisa[13], a small special needs orphanage. We would take their kids to a swimming pool at the Nile River Resort. And we would visit Nashville's own Katie Davis (Majors) to help with her feeding program for a day. Finally, we would move a home for babies from one location to another, guys carrying beds and cribs down the road and girls carrying, *well*-babies!

Forget about "Two Men and a Truck."[14] There aren't exactly any moving services available in rural Uganda. Plus, who needs a truck when you have not 2, but 12 total men! Our moving services included picking up what we could (an infant chair- or an infant) and walking down the dirt road to the new location.

But in order to begin our mission work in Jinja, we had to travel a reverse route, straight back through Masindi. And everyone felt the same – we couldn't drive back through without visiting the kids one last time. We soaked up those last moments in our final 5 hours at Family Spirit. None of us knew when, if ever, we would see the kids again. I felt sure I would continue to return to Uganda... but considering the high price to travel there, how long would it be?

When it was, at last, *really* time to leave (for *truly* the last time), we sang "We Fall Down" [15] in worship together. Ryan Doyle had worked with one of the older kids, Charles, to translate the entire song to the local language, Runyoro, so that we could all learn the chorus in the local tongue. Ryan has also been teaching him guitar, a little more musical education on each successive trip.

Our departure was eminent, and terrible grief was penetrating us to the very core. The tears started again, this time both for me and for Hannah Whit. We were among the last, most of us weeping, to load the bus. My feet felt leaden and planted, and for a while, I thought one of the guys was going have to physically pick me up to remove me.

Margaret was crying; she had leaned over herself standing. Hope wept aloud, moaning between sobs. Calla embraced Hannah Whit for a long, long while, both girls were crying again, but she raced to me instead, at the last minute. Calla put her head in the pit of my stomach which was the only available surface area... It was as if she realized that clenching Hannah Whit might not be as good as laying hold of her mom.

Upon seeing Calla with me, a younger girl (named Emma) kneeled at my feet also. She put her hands in my lap and quietly asked, "Are you going to take Calla with you?"

While I fumbled with her question, she waited stoically, her eyes pleading for my answer. It seemed her little heart was split in two – part of her wondering if we were actually going to take Hannah Whit's new best friend and maybe even petitioning on Calla's behalf. The other part of her was possibly wondering if our taking Calla meant us leaving *her* behind.

Surely Hannah Whit could have taken Calla's hand and led her onto the bus with us. Surely, she could grab a few belongings and be gone. And yet, that had not happened. So Calla had darted for me with beautiful, pleading eyes… filled with tears and longing. That her remarkable friendship with Hannah Whit could morph into sisterhood. That her loneliness as an only child, who had lost both parents to disease, could be healed by finding a forever family. I'll never know exactly, but I wondered if maybe she, too, thought I could just take her home.

One thing I do know is that both of us, many of us, were feeling that if we just gripped a little tighter, our goodbye would never come to pass.

Like with Aaron – at first, he ran away. I didn't know what he was doing. I didn't know what to think. We had spent most of our time together, some talking of his family, some talking of mine. He was especially interested in our boys, what it was like to be an American son. Just as often, he and I were together, comfortably quiet, simply content to remain in each other's presence. So when he ran, I didn't understand. I thought maybe he was going to retrieve something to give me, because many of the children handed us parting letters throughout that last day. (And Hannah Whit, I am sure, received the greatest number of these tokens of affection by far, written forget-me-nots, scores of homemade envelopes, of letters and artwork.)

I soon realized that Aaron had fled the scene for one reason alone, because he had started to cry. And the crushing weight of this realization, the teenage humanity in his tears, made me cry all the more. He was just a boy, a 13 year-old boy, who needed to save face. When he returned, he was discreetly wiping tears underneath my sunglasses. The sunglasses I had loaned him earlier to shade the bright African ball of fire that burned in the sky, they were now shading his tears from on-looking friends.

But not five minutes later, and almost as if he could no longer help himself or no longer cared, he stood in front of my shoulders and buried his face in my chest, heaving and sobbing. I wrapped my arms around him for at least 10 minutes. Our embrace was a temporary shield from the sinking reality that we were leaving.

Finally, I found my voice and told him to keep the sunglasses, so he could salvage whatever was left of his male pride. Then, I held his face in my hands and spoke into his eyes, his eyes that were somewhere behind dark lenses, "You are a special and strong young man, and God has great plans for your life," because I believe it immensely.

He asked again about Austin, my oldest son. He reminded me to tell him hello. He promised (again) to pray for us. To pray that we could return soon. (He offered that we should return that November, as he knew we had last come the past November.)

And I promised him that I would pray for the Lords plan's for his life. The remarkable plans that God has for Aaron, the incredibly smart and well-spoken young man, with the knowing smile, wearing the black Star Wars shirt.

You number my wanderings; Put my tears into your bottle; Are they not in your book?

Psalm 56: 8 NKJV

It was late afternoon when we finally pulled away, and everyone was exhausted, both physically and emotionally. An atypical hush fell over our bus, which was usually full of talkative and boisterous teens. While I nursed my heart in prayer and silence, I began to record in ink the stories of many of the children.

Bus rolling across miles of green, low-lying, jungly fields. Plenty of red dirt everywhere too. All windows rolled down, wind flying everywhere, the air was unbelievably cool for Uganda. I breathed slowly and deeply.

I tried to make myself laugh and take heart, even as the tears began to fall. On my blue shirt, red stains were still visibly present. I was caked and covered from our final afternoon – from kids crawling on me, from sitting in the dirt, from the tears and the sweat. It would be hours before I would see a shower.

Hannah Whit was right in front of me, already passed out from exhaustion, and there was mud painted quite unintentionally on both of her cheeks below her droopy eyes. In a matter of days, she would return to her own warm bed, her own welcoming home, and the arms of her waiting family.

But what about Hope? Where would she sleep? There would be others crammed next to her on her bunk, and tacked three high, but would loneliness linger in her heart? What about Asher, who had only known one home before Family Spirit...and it was a home he was never allowed to enter. He slept with the pigs outside. Rejected by everyone, would he ever find anyone to welcome him in?

And what about siblings, like Grace and Peace? They had no family at all, except each other. Abandoned together. They walk arm in arm, but whose arms will embrace them both?

So many bellies waiting for food and bodies waiting for medicine. So many hands longing to be held and hearts longing to be heard. So many stories hungry for purpose; so many lives craving ears who will hear and eyes who will see...

Then the eyes of those who see will no longer be closed, and the ears of those who hear will listen.

Isaiah 32: 3

Chapter 8 | The Display of His Splendor: The Children of Family Spirit

At Family Spirit, that final day of our second trip, I spent the majority of the time sitting with children on my lap, kneeled at my feet, and latched onto each arm and shoulder, beside me and behind. Susan sat next to me, and I asked her about the specific stories of the children, "her" children, whom I had come to love so much.

I gave up trying to keep a strong face. I wept openly as I listened to her speak of them, even though some of whom we spoke were sitting within ear shot. Though I asked gently, quietly, in complete respect, and she answered and offered more than I asked, the kids were listening and watching.

They are far more familiar with the vocabulary of broken hearts and broken lives than any child should be. It was a depth of pain that could fill the Grand Canyon. I can only hope that my tears lifted some of the burden from their own shoulders, but quite honestly, they looked possibly shocked that anyone would weep over what were their "obscure" stories.

They stared at me as I listened to Susan, their eyes silent and still as saucers, watching my emotion in disbelief.

My sacrifice, O God, is a broken spirit; a broken and contrite heart you, God, will not despise.

Psalm 51:17

Timothy

I begin with Timothy's story, because he was the first child placed into my arms on the first trip. He was around age 5. His legs were hardly bigger around than Adam's finger. He was severely malnourished, and his body wore the effects of the disease he had – Sickle Cell Anemia, a rare blood disease where pain and fatigue are common.

Normal red blood cells live 90 – 120 days; sickle cells live only 10-20 days. Sickle Cell is a "long-life illness," but only for people who receive treatment. Early diagnosis and medical care are crucial. He needed medications and transfusions, but as an orphan in Uganda, that was simply out of the question.

Abigail would frequently hold Timothy, so when we arrived on that first trip, she asked if I could hold him for a while. It comforted him to sit still, protected him from the many other children running around, and it ensured that he got the first of any food that was distributed.

We bought several bunches of bananas available at a roadside stand the first day we ever visited Family Spirit. The bunches are much larger than what we think of in America – they are taken straight from the tree and sometimes are attached to a small part of the branch. Though we bought all we could, we still needed to slice them into halves to be sure there were enough to go around.

We distributed the banana halves to all of the children, but Timothy was first, since his medical needs dictated he receive ample nutrition- as many vitamins and minerals as he could get. His one whole banana was far from ample, but it was more than the half piece that every other child would get.

We brought bags of mismatched garments with us, outgrown by our own kids. There were certainly not enough to clothe over 200 children, so we couldn't give every child something on the spot. Susan and Isaac would keep them and later distribute them to the children, as needed. However, I took Timothy aside to find something that could be just for him, again to guarantee he was not overlooked.

He picked out a striped shirt that had belonged to one of our boys. It didn't matter that it was a long-sleeved pajama top. This was what he wanted – so, this was what he got! We helped him put it on immediately.

As a 5-year old, he should've worn roughly a size 5. This shirt was a size 2.

Timothy's story has a happy ending, though. When I returned to Uganda the second time, during the summer of 2012, I noticed a little boy running around. He was active, playing, running and laughing. I was sure I had never seen him before.

I asked Susan what his name was. It was Timothy.

I absolutely couldn't believe it was the same child. He had grown slightly taller, and he must have doubled his weight. His adoptive family was now paying for food and medicine. (Imagine what Family Spirit could be with *each* child receiving adequate nutrition and care!)

When I returned for the third time, Christmas of 2012, Timothy was not there anymore. He was in his new home, with his new family.

God sets the lonely in families...

Psalm 68: 6 a

Asher

In Uganda, programs that teach about "living positively" help reduce the stigma of HIV/AIDS, while education and healthcare have slowed the spread of the disease and worked against the widespread social out-casting that is far more rampant in other African countries. Uganda is among the countries that offer free anti-retroviral drugs, as well as social-support campaigns driven by catchy slogans. In *28 Stories of AIDS in Africa,*[1] Uganda is hailed as "Africa's great AIDS success story."

Asher's childhood story is not one of those successes.

Asher is 13 and has no siblings, at least none at Family Spirit. He was born with HIV, and his mother died of HIV when he was a baby. He was left to the care of relatives, and he was grossly stigmatized in their village simply because he had this disease.

He was outcast as a newborn, rejected as a baby... for being born with a disease his mother passed to him at birth. His whole reason for being, as his relatives defined it, was to feed the family pigs. I guess that is the only reason they kept him around as long as they did.

Asher also slept outside – with the pigs. The village called him "madman." A neighbor rescued him when he was around 10, and brought him to Family Spirit. He is quiet but strong, and is a respected leader and helper among the children.

Handing out clothes at Family Spirit is exciting... it is fun to see the children's faces light up. The second trip, we had giant garbage bags full of various t-shirts. We distributed these shirts, one classroom full of kids at a time, to minimize the mayhem. We had enough t-shirts to allow one for each child.

Handing out shoes this way would've been pure chaos, because there were more children who needed shoes... and fewer shoes to go around. Shoes weigh so much more than articles of clothing, so we are never able to bring as many with us.

When we handed out the prized shoes, we were very careful about the timing, pulling children aside into Isaac's office one by one, when and where we saw the greatest need. We were also calculated about the assignments, based on size. If we knew we had a certain sized pair of shoes, we would look, maybe for an entire day, to find a kid who not only needed shoes, but also whose feet we guessed would fit into that pair.

I got very good about gauging shoe size, and I was very sneaky about looking at feet! All week, that second trip, I kept looking for a pair of shoes for Asher. As an older boy, I wanted to be sure he received a much-coveted pair of "trainers": athletic shoes. Plus he was not one to speak up and demand something for himself.

Near the end of the trip, I finally matched Asher's feet with a pair of cleats that would work. I will never forget his proud smile when he put those red shoes on his calloused, bare feet.

How beautiful on the mountains are the feet of those who bring good news, who proclaim peace, who bring good tidings, who proclaim salvation, who say to Zion, "Your God reigns!"

Isaiah 52: 7

Grace and Peace

These sisters, 8 and 6, arrived as babies, 3 years and 8 months old. Their father beat their mother to death with an iron pipe. He is wanted by the government. Their maternal grandmother, who is in her mid-60's, brought them to Family Spirit. Her husband (not the biological grandfather) never liked them, and he was violent toward them.

To know both of these girls is to know smiles and laughter, cuddles and giggles. These two are often seen hand in hand, arm in arm. They have only ever remembered having each other in the world, and they are thick as thieves.

Neither likes to share, like some children I know in *our* home, most of all Peace. However, Grace can cry more easily about being asked to share. Cute as buttons, and their names bestow something about their personalities, as well as God's character.

On our most recent trip, Grace had grown what seemed like 4 inches! Too much, too soon, in just 6 months time. A seriously sassy "Miss Priss," she is often seem with her hand propped on her hip, which is cocked to one side. This girl has obvious rhythm in her dance moves, too.

Grace likes sweets. She is good at Math and English. She wants a good home for herself and her younger sister. Peace likes cookies and car rides and says she wants to live in the U.S.

Please don't hear me say that I think I know what is best for these girls, or for any of the children. I am simply conveying *their* hearts unfiltered…

Many children have hopes and dreams of Europe or America from things they have heard. The Western world supplies them with visitors who love them and care for them. It certainly isn't the answer to their pain and their wounds, their loneliness and longing – we know that. But they do not. They are just children, longing for love, hoping for a leg up and a way out.

Many of them have idealized notions about a land far away from the pain they have known; a land where there is an overabundance of food, where there are even sweets to eat; a land where beds are cozy and homes are cozier; and a land where people give hugs, and affection, and attention, and often times special gifts- for birthdays, holidays, or for no reason at all; a land where there are sometimes families with moms and dads and siblings, and maybe pets - all living under the same roof.

It's not all true, especially not all of the time, but a lot of it *is true*. And for a child who has suffered abandonment or abuse, hurting and hunger, filth and poverty… For a child who doesn't own shoes, who can't afford school fees, who cannot conceptualize the wealth in much of the West… why wouldn't she dream about these things?

Many of the children long to be adopted because they all long for family and for home. Adoption isn't always the answer either – I know that. But try telling that to a child who has never had a family.

There are wonderful ministries in Uganda that fight to get children back in their homes, or at least back with relatives. It is a joyous occasion (and I believe, a best-case scenario) when a child can be reunited with family, when parents can learn to parent and are given the skills and support they need. But again, these are just two little girls, who don't understand why they were abandoned to begin with.

…as when a hungry person dreams of eating, but awakens hungry still; as when a thirsty person dreams of drinking, but awakens faint and thirsty still…

Isaiah 29: 8a

Philip

Philip is five and has 3 other siblings at Family Spirit. His parents divorced. Neither parent wanted the children, because both parents remarried or re-coupled. This is confusing and crushing, but it happens all too frequently in Uganda. The new partners or spouses reject the children and will often abuse them if they stay in the home.

These kids are categorized as simply "abandoned" – like Philip and his siblings. He spent most of his time on one of the laps of our leaders on the second trip, and he silently stole her heart, also.

Though my father and mother forsake me, the Lord will receive me.

Psalm 27: 10

Johannah

Johannah is 13, but she is very small for her age. She has 2 younger brothers. Their mother died of HIV. Johannah is termed a "single orphan" because only one of her parents is dead. Her father is living, but he has abandoned Johannah and her brothers. He lives in Kampala now. He returns occasionally to Masindi for disease treatment. Very rarely when he is there will he visit his children.

This situation happens frequently also – a parent dies and the remaining parent abandons the child or rejects the children. The living parent chooses to leave the child at an orphanage, if one is available, because they feel they either cannot parent alone or they do not desire to do so. Johannah's father, however, will not sign papers releasing his legal rights to his children.

I find this situation unfathomable. He is willingly consigning them to the life of an orphan – deprived of his own care and, simultaneously, unable to be adopted by another family.

That being said, who knows what his personal childhood was like? I certainly have not faced loss like his, circumstances like his, failures like his- it is likely that society's failing him has preempted his failing his own children.

Praise be to God who has not rejected my prayer or withheld his love from me!
Psalm 66: 20

Simon

Simon is ten and has no siblings at Family Spirit. He has *the* biggest smile you have ever seen. He is friendly and outgoing, gregarious. Simon is termed a "double orphan" because both parents died (of HIV).

Hannah Whit taught him how to fly like an airplane – they spent an hour one afternoon, during a downpour, with their arm outstretched running circles in the mud. Many of the other children, who did not want to get their only clothing drenched, watched in fascination from underneath a metal eave. None of them had ever played "airplane" before, because most of them had absolutely no concept about what an airplane really is.

One of the children told me she was not surprised that Simon, a boy, would be running in the rain, but she was shocked that I let Hannah Whit do this –

in a dress, in the rain, and in the mud. She couldn't believe a mother would watch her daughter grow increasingly filthy and *not* intervene.

"Will you beat her later?" she asked me, as serious as she could be. A knife to my heart. I held this girl and assured her that I would not scold Hannah Whit for playing in the rain, but she seemed entirely unsure if I was being honest.

But those who wait upon God get fresh strength. They spread their wings and soar like eagles, they run and don't get tired, they walk and don't lag behind.

Isaiah 40: 31, The Message[2]

Margaret

Margaret is 14, and she has a younger half brother and sister who are 13 and 11. Her grandmother sent them away from their home in Kenya with a local pastor, because she could not care for them. The mother (to all) died. The father (to the younger 2) abandoned them. They have been at Family Spirit 3 years. Their grandmother has visited once.

Margaret has a strong personality. She can be an extremely helpful leader, but scowls at the little ones when they cross her path in the wrong direction.

Her younger half-brother is a handsome boy with a winsome smile! He has an infectious demeanor, and he wanted to be Facebook friends with everyone in our group. He has "33 friends" at last count – he probably has computer access at his secondary school.

"Truly I tell you," Jesus said to them, "no one who has left home or wife or brothers or sisters or parents for the sake of the kingdom of God will fail to receive many times as much in this age, and in the age to come eternal life."

Luke 18: 29-30

Kimberly

Kimberly, 13, is eldest of her sibling group of 5, and the youngest is just two. The sister closest to her in age is her spitting image, in miniature. Absolutely drop dead gorgeous, both of them. Their beauty is punctuated by their smiles, and they both have a dimple in each cheek. Their deep inward joy radiates externally.

Their mom left them "for a better life" in Kampala. She looks for work as a prostitute there.

The oldest three, all girls, have been at Family Spirit since the baby was born. At the time I learned of their story, the youngest 2, both boys, were too little to attend school. The girls would go to school during the day while the boys would sit or play just outside nearby.

When school was over, they walked "home," following Kimberly's lead. One of the older girls carried the baby piggyback. Kimberly is "mom" to all of her younger siblings.

Your beauty should not come from outward adornment, such as elaborate hairstyles and the wearing of gold jewelry or fine clothes. Rather, it should be that of your inner self, the unfading beauty of a gentle and quiet spirit, which is of great worth in God's sight.

I Peter 3: 3-4

Aaron

This young man of 13 sat with me whenever I could sit. He stood next to me much of the rest of the time. He is kind, helpful, steady, strong, and wise beyond his years. His eyes reveal depth and intelligence, and his words are carefully chosen and discerning. He is the perfect gentleman, too.

It became very evident that his parents, first, or his grandmother, currently, cared for this boy extremely well, and with exceeding love and attention. When I left, Aaron gave me a letter he had written me. I couldn't find the emotional strength to read it until I had been home a few days. When I finally got around to opening it, it didn't surprise me in the least that the letter was well written – and with perfect penmanship.

Aaron is respectful, bright and self-sacrificing. When it was clear to him that our team had some shoes to give away, he asked me if I thought that I could possibly get him a pair. I spent so much time with him, loved him so much after so few days. Plus, no one could have been more deserving, and so I answered, "I will do my absolute best to find your size. "

Aaron replied, "No, they are not for me. They are for my little brother (who is 6)."

I frequently found it a convenient thing at times like this that I almost always had sunglasses on my face. I started crying.

"Yes, Aaron, yes," I will find some shoes for your little brother. The six-year old sibling ended up in a pair of white leather New Balance shoes that Austin had just outgrown.

Aaron often wanted to hold my hand or arm, sit very near me, or walk with me. Every time I put my hand around his shoulder, he would lean closer still and linger as long as he could. Even though he was older, and a boy, not with any other child did I feel as strongly, somehow, that my presence soothed a place in his soul that was hurting for someone he had lost.

This fact, and my own heart that misses him so much, makes it even hard to write these words without crying. There are a handful of children I think about every day – Aaron is one of them.

I told Aaron that he was so much like my middle son: smart, gentle, compassionate, and deeply intuitive and feeling. For this reason, I left him with the life verse that we have long prayed over Austin: Jeremiah 1: 6-10, and I told him I truly believed God had great plans to use him in mighty ways. I missed him *before* we ever left.

I realized as soon as we landed in Atlanta, on our second trip, that I had a voicemail from someone in Uganda. I waited until we cleared customs and were waiting at our final gate. I sat down on the floor and listened to my messages – It was Aaron who had called. He had borrowed someone's phone – someone outside Family Spirit.

He said, "This is Aaron. When are you coming back?"

The emotional waterfall, which had been dammed up inside of me since we left Uganda in the dark of night, burst forth. There was no stopping the tears. I just put my sunglasses back over my eyes, in the middle of hordes of people in the airport, and lowered my face into my hands.

"Alas, Sovereign Lord," I said, "I do not know how to speak: I am too young."
But the Lord said to me, "Do not say, 'I am too young,' You must go to everyone I send you to and say whatever I command you. Do not be afraid of them, for I am with you and I will rescue you," declares the Lord.
Then the Lord reached out his hand and touched my mouth and said to me, "I have put my words in your mouth. See, today I appoint you over nations and kingdoms to uproot and tear down, to destroy and overthrow, to build and to plant."

Jeremiah 1: 6-10

Calla

Calla has two much older sisters whom she rarely sees. They both live in Kampala, one working, one in school. Both of her parents are dead. Her father died when she was 2 months old. Her mother passed HIV to her at birth and later died from AIDS, leaving Calla as an orphan at 6. She now lives with her grandmother, who is in her 80's.

Austin was 6 at the time of our second trip, and he is also very close with my mom – this made Calla's reality all the more real to me. God! What would it be like for Austin to be raised without the father he adores, then lose me when he was so young, only to be faced with losing his beloved grandmother next? I filed it away with so many other unanswerable and unfair questions.

At the time of my second trip, Hannah Whit was 8, and Calla was 12. I don't know why they gravitated to one another or how they so quickly became glued at the hip, but they spent every waking moment together. If Hannah Whit was following a flock of black children, Calla was right next to her, holding her hand, bringing up the rear. If Hannah Whit was the white spot at the front of the line, or had an audience of orphan eyes circled around her, teaching some new game or performing a dramatic comedy for them, Calla was up front or at center with her.

I didn't really get to know Calla that second trip. She and Hannah Whit were always in view, but rarely within earshot. Ever happy and always playing together each day... up until the day it was time for us to leave. Then, they were *still* inseparable, but also inconsolable.

So, on the third trip I made, I wanted to connect with Calla immediately. I wanted to get my own arms around her, but I also had a special delivery for her from Hannah Whit. I asked Susan and Isaac where she was as soon as I arrived. They told me she was at her grandmother's, because school was not in session over Christmas, and she was spending her days with her grandmother until school resumed.

However, word very quickly got to Calla that we were there.

The next day, I was seated, with the other 2 women on the trip. We were cataloguing all the children: getting their pictures, shoe sizes, and other information that might be necessary to know for a child sponsorship program in the future.

I was busy engaging with them, both to my hard left, when I felt someone fall in my lap... I looked down, and it was Calla. She had kneeled in front of me and rested her head on my knees. My chest fell over her, almost instinctually, my arms on the back of her head and my cheek resting on her back.

I was overtaken with emotion as I held her embrace... and then, as both of us looked up at each other, I held her face in my hands, laughing and crying, both at the same time. I was overjoyed to see her, and I cried for Hannah Whit, who couldn't be seeing and hugging her also.

Calla stayed mainly near me, most of the rest of our days there. And we took her home in our van at the end of each day, as her grandmother's house was right on our way back to our hotel. She certainly didn't need a ride – her grandmother lives a stone's throw away on the same dirt road as Family Spirit, but we offered her a lift so that I could have a little more time with her each afternoon... a few more minutes for her to sit next to me, and another hug before parting.

I also waited to give her Hannah Whit's special present until she was in the car with us one afternoon. I knew it would go with her directly back to her grandmother's home, without a chance of another child taking anything that had been intended for her. I also knew no one would be looking on with hurt feelings for not having received anything.

Hannah Whit had packed one of her backpacks full of things for her friend – all from our home, all from her own room. The bag was a pre-school sized Pottery Barn standard issue, pink with brown polka dots. It included a stuffed, pink, miniature poodle, a tiny Madame Alexander Doll (that had come as a kid's meal toy from McDonald's), a letter from Hannah Whit in which she reminded Calla that "God would not leave her as an orphan" (John 14:18), and finally, a Webster's child's first dictionary.

Most of these things were far too elementary for Calla, because they had become even too juvenile for Hannah Whit. However, Hannah Whit had carefully chosen each item and placed them with love and care, not thinking a thing about the childishness of the gifts she was giving, and Calla treasured every gift as she slowly pulled each thing from the bag.
And I was sure to point out to her something I had, only the day before, discovered myself…

Hannah Whit had made Calla a bookmark to go in the dictionary she had chosen for her. It was a clear piece of plastic that she designed and colored to look like a stained glass window. I initially assumed that Hannah Whit had randomly placed it in the dictionary, opening and inserting without looking, because the bookmark held a place near the middle.

It held that same place from September until December, from the time Hannah Whit packed it, until the day Calla took it from me. She clutched the backpack in her lap while sitting next to me in the van, and then against her chest when she got out walked up the little hill to her grandmother's home.

My friend Lindsey, on this trip with us, had called me over the day before, as she peeked at all of the sweet gifts from Hannah Whit: "Allison, look at this! Did you see this?"

Hannah Whit had placed the bookmark between two pages in the dictionary where the word "love" fell. She had underlined the word with a black marker and written, "I love you, Calla."

I gasped for breath and choked back tears, as I still do now, when I think about it. Hannah Whit loves Calla purely and truly, as God loves us – orchestrating every detail, every blessing, every gift. I made sure Calla saw this additional note from Hannah Whit, this piercing gesture of *love*.

184

How great is the love the Father has lavished on us, that we should be called children of God! And that is what we are! …This is how we know what love is: Jesus Christ laid down his life for us. And we ought to lay down our lives for our brothers and sisters. If anyone has material possessions and sees and brother or sister in need but has no pity on them, how can the love of God be in that person? Dear children, let us not love with words or speech, but in actions and in truth.

I John 3: 1a, 16-18

These are not only the stories.   What about adorable Luke? What about Francis with the funny poses? What about Martha or Kelly? Or Anthony whom you could just eat up, yummy handsome little Ugandan character that he is?

If you asked any member of our summer team, or any member of a subsequent team, thcy would give you more names, more stories.
I left a second time, came home from another trip, only longing to return again.

How can we thank God enough for you in return for all the joy we have in the presence of our God because of you?

1 Thessalonians 3: 9

"Return home and tell how much God has done for you." So the man went away and told all over town how much Jesus had done for him.

Luke 8: 39

185

Chapter 9 | The Road Traveled by The King : The Third Trip

Not a year had passed, and I had been to Africa twice.

In the fall of 2012, Adam and I were going on a short weekend trip to Las Vegas for his job. We were flying out around 5:00 p.m. on a Thursday in mid-September. My parents were already in town to keep the kids while we were away.

Just before 2 p.m. on the afternoon that we would leave, I was pulling together the final details for our trip and picking up Liam from preschool. When I sat in the hook-up line, the craziest idea "came to me."

I raced home to share it. Liam and I pulled into the driveway. Adam pulled in right behind us, so that he and I could leave for the airport. I bolted up the stairs to capitalize on the short time I had before leaving. My parents stood precariously balanced on a step stool in Hannah Whit's room, fixing the shade over her window.

I called Adam up to her bedroom, cornered them all there together and blurted out, "I had an idea in the hook-up line. It could be the Lord speaking, you never know... I think we should all go to Africa in lieu of 'doing' Christmas this year." I longed to return for my third time, but it wasn't only that – I felt God might be initiating the trip.

I made my dad promise to pray about it over the weekend, instead of shooting me down outright. (Small detail – Dad does not fly.) Then, Adam and I left for the airport. When we boarded the 4-hour flight to Nevada, I began to journal, pray and read my Bible, which I did for most of the trip, about Christmas... *in Africa*.

When we arrived in the City of Lights, I still had only one thing on my mind. We quickly checked into our hotel, left our bags in our room, and we went straight back out the door for dinner. From there, we headed directly on to a 10:30 p.m. performance of "O" at the Bellagio[1]. I was not feeling so hot all during the show, and I was ready to collapse at around 1 a.m.

Collapse, I did, but not for long. At 1:30 a.m., I was up dry heaving. This was my first-ever bout with food poisoning, and I spent the next 24 hours feeling worse than I have in my whole life. Friday, I could not turn on the lights. I could not even turn on the TV. I consumed only 4 crackers and half a bottle of electrolytes over the course of the entire day.

Saturday mid-day, after hours on the cold bathroom floor, I stood for the first time. Late in the afternoon, I was able to watch football on TV, and by evening, I left the room for the first time in two days.

Adam and I went out to dinner Saturday night (at a different restaurant!), and we got up Sunday morning around 5 a.m. to catch our flight home. That was the extent of my time in Vegas. On the flight home, I prayed with even more resolve about what God wanted regarding another trip to Africa.

I was beginning to suspect that he *did* want us to go, since the enemy had slapped me so quickly with a back handed compliment. Satan was clearly driven to take me down, after my "mini-revelation" in the hook-up line and my hours of praying that followed. Usually when evil is raging in a big way, God is up to something even bigger.

I wrote my dad a letter on the plane home as well, telling him of my heart for Africa, and of my heart to hear the Lord. I told him I didn't want him to think of the letter as a ploy to persuade him. Rather, I wanted him to know that I believed nothing could convince him, save the Holy Spirit. I only begged him to be open to hearing from the Lord himself.

My parents left for Birmingham within the hour we returned. My mom read the letter to my dad, as he drove home. That Sunday night, on the way into town, Dad called my brother (who lives in Birmingham also) to ask him to come over for dinner and discuss Africa.

These were miracles in my mind – not only that my dad would *consider* the trip, but also that he would ask my brother so quickly. And not just quickly, but immediately upon their return from Nashville. Miracles.

The following day, however, on Monday, Sept. 17, Dad texted me:

> *Thanks for the very sweet letter. You and Mom have the biggest hearts, and I love you more than anything! Justin came over last night, and we talked it over with him. He said there is no way he can get off. So for this year, it's probably not possible. We'll reconsider at some future date.*

I was beyond sad that Monday night, and not without tears, thinking of the missed chance to see the kids at Family Spirit. However, as I had first told my dad, I truly did have a peace that the Lord was in charge and that He would bring about our next Africa trip in His perfect timing. So, I went on to bed.

As I slept that night, however, I got an email. It came in at 3:30 a.m. on Tuesday, Sept. 18. It was from Susan (from Family Spirit), *of all people,* "out of the blue." (I had last emailed her on August 7th – and only to send her some pictures from our summer trip.) I saw only one option: go back to God again in prayer.

> *What a friend we have in Jesus, All our sins and grief's to bear!*
> *What a privilege to carry, Everything to God in prayer!*
> *O what peace we often forfeit, O what needless pain we bear,*
> *All because we do not carry, Everything to God in prayer!*
> *Have we trials and temptations? Is there trouble anywhere?*
> *We should never be discouraged, Take it to the Lord in prayer.* [2]

I spent three hours with Jesus that Monday morning. Oh, the beauties of homeschooling! I told the children we were having a "delayed opening" that day, because I needed to talk to the Lord for more than my usual time. I cried and cried, and I asked God about all of it. In Susan's email, she had written, "All the children miss you every time, every day... Aaron says 'hi'... We cannot wait to see you again."

What was my heart to do with the timing of these words? *Really*? It seemed torturous, or maybe – *divine*?

We accomplished a few things in homeschool, after my morning in prayer (and a morning of PBS[3] for the kids). Late that same afternoon, we had soccer. I asked Adam to take the kids by himself that night because, yes, I needed more time with the Lord. This time, however, I was longing only to sit in his presence, just to be still, because the morning weeping and wrestling had physically worn me out. I wasn't up for wrangling kids who were wrangling soccer balls.

It turned out that Adam was running late – so much for my plans! I took the kids to soccer myself, but planned to leave as soon as my husband arrived. I was *not* intending to stay. But I started talking to my friend Lindsey McRae about all the Africa happenings...

Lindsey was among the women (including Anne, Stephanie and Adrienne) who had been praying for me since "my" idea the previous Thursday. She had also emailed that she couldn't believe I was thinking of returning so soon, and she "yelled" in her email, "I WANT TO GO TOO!!!!!"

When I told her at soccer that we were not going to Africa, Lindsey said, "Oh no!" followed by, "Well, what if we just *all* went anyway (*meaning,* she and her husband Jay, along with me and Adam, along with anyone else who wanted to go)?"

"Hmmmm." I started thinking, and *that*, as many know, can be a dangerous activity in *this* brain.

Lord Almighty, God of Israel, you have revealed this to your servant… So your servant has found courage to pray this prayer to you.

2 Samuel 7: 27

Within the course of the next week, we were checking ticket prices and praying fervently. Several of us, including my mom, decided to fast for a day, as well. In God's interesting timing, some of our friends were also scheduled to share with our community group that weekend – they were, of course, missionaries to Kampala, Uganda.[4]

I sat down to pray on September 25, around 9:30 a.m., after dropping kids at tutorial and preschool. I wrote in my journal, "We are longing to hear You, to see You, to know You in this and to walk forward in obedience. Please guide us, Lord – do You want us to go? Holy Spirit, just as I have been praying for the last week, help me today to pay attention, to listen and to hear...

"We trust that You *WILL* speak and that we *WILL* hear... but...

(I was about to write, "*WHEN* will we hear?" Implying, *We kind of need to know something now* because of shots and passports.)

My brain was moving faster than my pen, so I never scribbled those next words on paper. God quickened my Spirit. Very quietly, and very clearly, the Lord whispered, "You *ALREADY HAVE* heard me, though, remember? In the hook-up line... You heard me..."

As I was formulating my fleshly objection to His still, small voice, again God repeated, "But do you not think I am in charge of hook-up lines too? I am in charge of all things. YOU HEARD ME. I work in all ways and in all places. There are no coincidences."

he weeper started weeping. I took some time just to bask in God's love, as well as to commit. "Yes, Lord, I heard you."

I *am* going... *back...* to Africa.

Then I heard the voice of the Lord saying, "Whom shall I send? And who will go for us?" And I said, "Here I am. Send me!"

Isaiah 6: 8

By the time fall arrived in 2012, I had been in a yearlong season of reading (and praying through) the book of Isaiah. The weeks of praying about another trip, and continuing to pray *over* and *about* and *for* Africa, were no different. During the months leading up to my third trip, however, God seemed to be highlighting one passage anew – Isaiah 35. This chapter, in the middle of this one book by this one major prophet, kept bubbling to the top.

He seemed to be showing me, over and over again, that He was going to use our Nashville group in the lives of these children. He made it apparent that he would work in *our* hearts even more so, through the children and through the people of Masindi. He showed me how he was going to use our group to bring literal nourishment to these needy kids, along with emotional healing and physical help, while delivering spiritual water to my own thirsty heart and redemptive new life in my own unfolding story.

God was impressing on us all that two adoptions, as unbelievably good as they were, were just the beginning of the story. Two orphans provided a bridge to Africa, so that God could write a much larger story, with *many* more orphans (on both sides of the ocean). Our first trip was not simply an avenue to bring us to Uganda, it also paved the way for many future trips – and many future "players." God used a dirt path (or two) to forge a multi-directional, invisible inter-continental freeway.

"A highway will be there... (Is. 35: 8)"

During our second trip, the story "burst into bloom" (Is. 35: 2a). We would "rejoice greatly and shout with joy" (Is. 35: 2b) upon our arrival. And quite literally, the orphans welcomed us "with singing" (Is. 35: 10b). But all of these things, literal and emotional, would only lay the groundwork for a

191

spiritual highway that God would continue to drive into the depths of *all* of our hearts. We understood, with increasing perspective, this route between two countries was not simply spanning human hearts and far-removed relationships, it was quite literally a "Cross-road" bridging Heaven and earth.

As I began to consider a third trip, within just one calendar year, I saw "the glory of the Lord, the splendor of our God" (Is. 35: 2, end) like never before. He shined light on the multi-faceted layers of His goodness and faithfulness. The complexity, the beauty, the impossibility of a Love so great as His, with a story "for such a time as this."

In our group, the breadth of talents and gifts is simply amazing to me! Amongst our eight families, I think every field or profession is covered: a pastor, a nurse practitioner, teachers and a social worker, one in church ministry and another in parachurch ministry, several savvy businessmen, an attorney, an accountant, and two "youth leaders:" one, the director of youth ministries at a church, and another, the headmaster of a Christian school.

But what was my specific role? What gifts and passions did *I* have that He could *possibly* use in the story He was writing?

I completely missed "the writing on the wall" – that God might be calling me to be physical hands for this story, that I might be a vessel by which he could tell His story – *on paper.*

For if you remain silent at this time… relief and deliverance will come from another place… And who knows but that you have come to your… position for such a time as this?

Esther 4: 14

I have had a passion for writing since I penned poetry in elementary school. My first real diary in middle school was not an accidental occurrence or a pre-teen whim; I poured my heart onto the pages that I filled. To this day, I have boxes upon boxes of journals.

And don't even get me started about how empowered and excited I felt to be perched behind my Grandy's ancient typewriter, the musky smell of his basement office was not only safe and familiar to me, but it was also inviting and welcoming. I spent hours alone there feeling self-important for sitting where my hero sat, and I came alive with each *click, click, spin.*[5]

During high school, God focused and further developed my love for writing. English and Yearbook were always my favorite classes, and these teachers were always among my favorites as well. And for Heaven's sake, they were smart a smart bunch: graduates of Middlebury, Duke, UC Berkeley, Columbia, Oberlin, University of Vermont. Most of them were young, filled with their own passions for literature, ideas, research, and for *life* – because it is life, after all, that we read, and about which we write.

My love for books, for reading and writing, and for language was truly set aflame in high school. I did not major in English at UNC, however, simply because I thought it was going to be too hard. I had already done four years of back breaking, nose-to-the-grind studying, and I was somewhat unintentionally giving up the workload (as implied by the less-than-stellar choices I intentionally *did* make). Still, though, my two favorite courses at Carolina: an English seminar where we critiqued film (through much writing and many theses), and my African American literature class with Dr. Reginald Hildebrand.[6]

Through many hard years of marriage, I could barely do anything, except survive. My prayer journals were certainly a lifeboat, but it wasn't until the year after Austin was born when I very clearly began to hear God's call to write. There was a "burning bush" involved – though the shrubs in my yard were never on fire, God kept hinting about his call on my life through scriptures highlighting his call on Moses in the Bible.

This theme became so frequent and so weird (popping up everywhere I turned), that I eventually challenged Him on it, much like Moses did. "Me? *Me*, God? Are you sure? Are you *actually* telling me this?"

I asked him for the proverbial "sign," just before driving to our women's retreat one weekend during the winter of 2007. If he couldn't give me a *real* burning bush, then I prayed at least he could give me a more obvious indicator of his direction. (I am good at asking God to make something more obvious, when it is already as plain as day.)

During one of the very first sessions at the retreat, God spoke. We were in a time of guided contemplative meditation, but musical lyrics played in the background – about Moses and about God's multiple provisions to the Israelites. At the same time, several scriptures from Exodus were projected onto the screen in the front of the meeting room.

I had almost begun to laugh out loud, but instead, I felt a lump in my throat as I prayed silently, "I get it, God. I get it. Point taken."

And then, though we had been instructed to remain *completely* silent, my friend Stacey, who was sitting next to me, whispered out of the clear blue, "Allison, you should write a book." (God is good at giving me beyond what I have asked for.)

I had told few people about God calling me to write – Stacey was not one of them. I knew beyond the shadow of a doubt that God was speaking to me through her.

Now Moses was tending the flock of Jethro, his father-in-law, the priest of Midian, and he led the flock to the far side of the wilderness and came to Horeb, the mountain of God. There the angel of the Lord appeared to him in flames of fire from within a bush. Moses saw that though the bush was on fire it did not burn up. So Moses thought, "I will go over and see this strange sight – why the bush does not burn up."

When the Lord saw that he had gone over to look, God called to him from within the bush, "Moses! Moses!"

And Moses said, "Here I am."

Exodus 3: 1-4

I wrestled a little with God the rest of the retreat weekend, but when I got home – *I started writing.* I had several ideas, and pursued them each, sometimes waffling back and forth. For almost 3 years, I worked on 3 different book ideas. To this day, there are still *three* partial manuscripts stored in the recesses of my first laptop.

Then, God began calling me to Africa; He broke my heart for a country I had never seen and a people I had never met. And I stopped writing. Almost cold. I remember telling some of my friends at the lake, in the summer of 2010,

> *I have nothing to write about anymore. Everything seems like a waste of time compared to doing something – doing anything – to help these children and these people. These are the books I would write, if I could (<u>The Hole in Our Gospel</u>, for example; I was reading it that summer), but I don't need to – they've already been written. Richard Stearns has already done a spectacular job![7]*

So instead of writing, I spent a couple more years reading – everything I could get my hands on about the needs and the stories in the places I had never been. I prayed, and I cried. And I prayed some more. Since I couldn't go, I immersed myself in the pages I read, while I continued to ask God, "What can I do?"

Then... I got to go to Africa – *twice*!! And now, God was calling me back a third time.

He did more than that, however. He started to shine a light on my personal involvement. He made it clear, but I was so oblivious at first that – it seemed to come out of the *clear blue*, my part to play in the story that He was writing.

Specifically, I was to start writing *that story*.

There are so many smaller stories that make up this one big story: how God is using temporary and circumstantial "gladness and joy" to breathe life into each of us, life that will ultimately "crown [many, many] heads with *everlasting* joy" (Is. 35: 10).

We could provide physical relief in present need; we could be His hands and feet. Our relationships and the many levels of fellowship would be emotional salve for us all; God lavishes his love through community for our redemption and healing. But every reality here is only a foreshadowing of that final day when "sorrow and sighing will flee away" forever (Is. 35: 10).

And God was calling *me*, specifically, to write about it all.

I was overwhelmed, but ecstatic. I was fully aware of my weaknesses and inexperience, but more so, I was aware of His power and provision. Finally, He had my full attention, and I didn't question for one second what He spoke over me. I wrote in my journal as God announced it:

"What you are going to do, Allison, is much like what Haregewoin Teferra did in Ethiopia (via author Melissa Fay Greene)[8] – You are going to tell the story of Susan and Isaac and Family Spirit."

I had not been praying about writing, or even *doing* any writing. I had not been praying about the first two trips or the work from the first two trips. I had not been praying about orphans or adoptions – in that moment, I was only praying, "Do you want us to go to Africa a third time at Christmas?"

I heard, "Yes." And no sooner than I accepted God's call to go again, there was an "and…"

"Dust off your laptop, *because you are doing this.*"

That is why, for Christ's sake, I delight in weaknesses, in insults, in hardships, in persecutions, in difficulties. For when I am weak, then I am strong.

2 Corinthians 12: 10

God brought to my mind exact conversations that I had with specific friends over the previous year. Comments I had made months before came rushing back to me....

> "I don't want to write any more. I want to tell the world about what is going on in Africa... (And I said this way before I ever went to Africa!)
>
> "I want to go around to churches and show videos and pictures of REAL CHILDREN...
>
> "I want hearts to break as mine is breaking... so I can raise money and do something!!
>
> "How can I sit still and write when there are kids starving, without clean water, medicines, or... parents!!!?? I WANT TO DO SOMETHING! Money is what they need, along with support, and help, and awareness – *not words on paper.*"

Such were the remarks flashing back through my mind, but God put my desires and my calling on a collision course, I believe. All of a sudden, and seemingly out of nowhere, it became so glaringly obvious to me.
I asked:

> *God, over the last couple of years, I have read at least five books that are narratives of real life stories, from places in America and China too (not just Africa). Why haven't I thought of this before? It has been almost a whole year since*

we first went to Africa... why haven't I thought of this sooner, *it seems so simple and so clear?*

To which God seemed to answer, "You haven't thought of it before, *because it is not your idea*! It is Mine! And the timing is Mine too."

But do not forget this one thing, dear friends: With the Lord, a day is like a thousand years, and a thousand years are like a day.

2 Peter 3: 8

Our God is WILD! He called me to write, and then He waited almost 5 years to tell the *why* and the *what*. He began to show me that stories are *important*, and He continued showing me this for the three years that I wrote about Family Spirit.

Yes, we need to feed and clothe these orphans. We need to give them fresh water, a place to sleep and to bathe. There are still so many physical needs. But if we address the whole person, then we address their story, too – because it is a reflection of the heart and the soul; their story is the picture of who God is making them to be.

My friend Angie (in our Africa group) has said so many times and in so many ways, "Our goal is not simply to deal with mouths and stomachs, minds and bodies... our goals is to LOVE. *PEOPLE*. Who have hearts and hurts. Who have their own passions and pains."

Nutrition matters, but when I look into those little faces, I do not see a place to put food – I see eyes longing to be truly seen. Water matters immensely too, but when I hold dirty hands, I do not see the need for a bath – I see arms reaching out for love. And medicine is crucial! It is quite literally, life and death, but if we heal only bodies, we are still missing the greatest wound of all – hearts that are broken.

We can address every physical need, but if we fail to address the heart, we have failed to address the story. And if we fail to see the story, we haven't truly seen the child. Story is what makes the invisible *visible*. It is what makes the heart real and the person tangible.

Jesus did many miracles in the Bible. He fed the 5000 (Mk. 6: 30-44). He met the thirsty woman at the well (Jn. 4: 1-26). He healed the invalid (Jn. 5: 1-15), and He even raised the dead (Jn. 11: 38-44). But He did more than perform miracles; He told stories.

He didn't just provide food, water, and medicine… He painted pictures of the people who needed these things. He told their stories. He saw them – not just their physical needs, but the emotional and spiritual needs of their hearts, too. And he heard them – not just their audible cries for help, but their souls calling out… the deepest cries of their hearts.

Why is *seeing* the heart so important? Because Jesus became the image of the invisible God so that we would *see* God's own heart for us (Col. 1: 15). In seeing God's heart, we know the heart of El Roi, *The God who Sees* (Gen. 16: 13).

Why is *hearing* their stories so important? Because Jesus became The Word, The *Logos*, so he could write Himself across the pages of scripture – His Love Story to Us, that we might read it and hear it. In God's communication of the Old and New Testaments, we understand that we have a God who hears *us,* also (Gen. 16: 11).

He not only wrote the biggest story of all time, The Bible, but He is writing still. He is inscribing us *all* into this story – His story. You and me, and orphans in Uganda. They have stories to tell, parts to play, just like you and I do, wherever God calls them.

In the beginning was the Word, and the Word was with God, and the Word was God.

John 1: 1

I told Stephanie (my prayer partner who is also in our Africa group), God was not simply blowing my mind. He was blowing my entire head off my shoulders. He had wowed and wooed me, indescribably so, *yet again*. Never before had so many things happened in a short 2-week period, except (oh, yeah) in Africa – twice.

Adam and I were discussing our trip with our Missions Director, Shane Bowen (the same conversation in which he recommended "Miraculous Movements" [9] to me, the book about Muslims around the world coming to Christ). In walked Sam Crenshaw. He and Adam began talking about a hiking adventure of some sort that one or both of them had been on. I held on to that one word and interposed, "You want a *real adventure*, Sam? Then you need to come with us to Africa."

It was almost as good as done the minute the words came out of my mouth. Sam and his roommate Randy Morrison were then seniors at The University of Tennessee. They raised support for the trip through our church.

Rachel Ladner, Lindsey McRae and I had all been in a women's Sunday school class together (2010) at West End Community Church, so we went in as 3 peas in a pod. We invited many different people, but Rachel just happened to be the only one who accepted the invitation. Her home church (growing up), Covenant Presbyterian, in Cleveland, Mississippi, generously funded her entire trip.

In under three months, God brought a team together for the third trip. Lindsey and Jay McRae were committed from the beginning, but God added Sam, Randy, and Rachel. Seven is the number of completion in the Bible, and this team certainly felt wonderfully right and complete!

The fall was another whirlwind of passports and planning, bank withdrawals and booking tickets. Same song, third verse – in terms of the preparations. Lindsey pretty much took care of our standard lodging reservations. And I went out a purchased a digital voice recorder. I knew this trip would be different for me, and I would start by sitting with Susan while she shared her story. (Sam would take this same recorder to interview Isaac for me on the next trip.)

Susan and Isaac had given their blessings to begin the journey of writing a book. Everyone in our Nashville group approved as well. I began typing the story even before the holidays arrived.

Our family didn't end up skipping Christmas, but I did forego many of the usual trappings and trimmings. I put out *only* our Advent Wreath and my treasured Nativities, including the ornately carved wooden crèche that I had purchased that summer in Jinja, Uganda.

I left all of our traditional Christmas ornaments in the attic, and I printed out pictures of the children on pearlescent paper, instead. I used a circle cutter and a hole-puncher to turn each photo into an ornament. My kids helped me cover the edges of the paper in glue and sprinkle glitter around the borders to frame each child. We hung them all over our tree with red organza ribbon, beautiful but simple forget-me-nots.

We left for Uganda the day after Christmas, and I took these ornaments in a jumbo-sized zip-top plastic bag. During our week in Masindi, between Christmas and New Year's, I delivered each embellished photo to the child whose picture was on it.

For to see your face is like seeing the face of God…

Genesis 33: 10 (partial)

Before we left, we held a shoe-drive: "Crocs for Christmas."[10] Because of the dirt on the ground, as plentiful as clouds in the blue Ugandan sky, we deemed that these resin-like shoes would prove the absolute best for covering children's bare feet. They are comfortable, can be easily washed, even with a small amount of rainwater, and they will not mold or become rancid. They are also lightweight, which made them perfect for long-distance travel.

We collected maybe 50 pairs, not nearly enough, but our shortage was propitious for the local economy in Masindi. Turns out, a tradesman in town sold a very similar type slide-on shoe. On our third trip, we also began filling a spreadsheet with the names and information about the kids at Family Spirit: shoe size included!

Once we obtained enough data, Rachel and Lindsey rode with Mustafa on his boda to purchase all of the additional shoes that we needed. Adam and Jay rode with Isaac to see his farmland and start discussions on what it would look like to till fields and grow crops. Sam and Randy played drums... and they played soccer.

As with our previous trips, we brought more deflated soccer balls to use, and then to leave. The guys were so filthy from playing *so hard* one day, that there were perfectly straight lines on their ankles when they removed their socks that evening. What looked like a suntan was really caked on dirt. Thanks to Randy's personal dedication to the sport, we used the first aid "insta-ice" pack for the first time. A nasty fall in a particularly competitive moment led to a lot of swelling on his leg.

We also bought huge cardboard boxes of baby formula on this trip. Baby Sam (Susan and Isaac's youngest) was nearing the window where he needed to stop nursing (to prevent transmission of HIV). So, we picked up as much canned formula as we could afford at the big grocery store in Kampala, and we carried it on to Masindi for Susan. She would be able to use any surplus formula to receive another infant if necessary. Family Spirit normally cannot accept infants in need, because they simply cannot afford the formula for feeding babies.

The last night we were there, we stayed past dusk. The crowd of children circled around me, when I sat on the concrete stoop to read from the *Jesus Storybook Bible*.[11] They were mesmerized as God's word came alive, and most of them listened intently. I'm not sure what they found more

202

intriguing: God's unique love for them... or the tears in my eyes, as I told them about a love so wondrous as this.

It would be hard to adequately summarize the flurry of activity on each trip, just as it would be on this trip. More than anything else – we tried to love kids. And in the loving, we got far more in return than we gave.

Well, in another story, it would be all over and that would've been… The End.

But not in this story.

God loved his children too much to let the story end there. Even though he knew he would suffer, God had a plan – a magnificent dream. One day, he would get his children back. One day, he would make the world their perfect home again. And one day, he would wipe away every tear from their eyes.

You see, no matter what, in spite of everything, God would love his children – with a Never Stopping, Never Giving Up, Unbreaking, Always and Forever Love. And though they would forget him, and run from him, deep in their hearts, God's children would miss him always, and long for him – lost children yearning for their home.

Jesus Storybook Bible[12]

The very next summer, 2013, another team of high school students returned: Sam Crenshaw, Bobby Freeman, Janie Omer and Ryan Doyle were among the leaders. Though I didn't get to go, I organized another charity drive for Family Spirit, along with many others who have come to love the kids. This time we asked our churches for sponsors: men, women, children and families who would purchase a *Jesus Storybook Bible*.

Our local bookstore ordered boxes upon boxes of Bibles and sold them to us at an extremely discounted rate.[13] We had enough donors to give one Bible to each child. There were over 200 front pages, dedicated to over

200 individual kids, by over 200 local families, who had each slid a photograph between the cover and the front page. So that each girl would have her own, and each boy would have his own.

I can't stop loving you.
You are my heart's treasure.
But I lost you.
Now I'm coming back for you.

I am like the sun that gently shines on you,
chasing away darkness and fear and death.
You'll be so happy –
you'll be like little calves running free
in an open field.

I am going to send my Messenger – The Promised One.
The One you have been waiting for.
The Rescuer.

He's coming. So, get ready!

Jesus Storybook Bible[14]

Diana Batarseh[15] spoke recently during a devotional time at my daughter's tutorial. There were children of all ages in the room, from screaming babies to roaming toddlers, along with the wide range of children who attend school there (Kindergarten through 8th grade). Also present: children like myself, almost 40. Nothing gets me like a good children's story, and my kids are always so pleased to see me stifling my tears in public among their peers.

Diana took *The Runaway Bunny* by Margaret Wise Brown[16] and added two words to the title for the purposes of her presentation, "Jesus and The

Runaway Bunny." And just like that: My life in a board book. (Especially the part about the circus act.)

There were many times, in my childhood, where I felt I was not enough. Or that I was too much. The enemy whispered, "Keep trying, doesn't matter anyway. You'll never measure up. Keep on running."

Or, on the other end, "Be quiet. No one will like the real you. Hide."

I weathered the adolescent years under the same lies, which seeped into friend groups and left me longing to win affection from boys, as well. I wanted to fit in, and I wanted to be loved.

The already shaky foundation on which I stood suffered a devastating blow in high school. God continued leveling me, so that he would have a place to build.[17]

And college. I thought I was running. Escaping. I thought I was making off with my freedom, but I was narrowly avoiding a total entrapment. All along, God knew. He had directed my paths. He had paved a highway that would lead me right to His Heart.

Every time I hid, his hands were present, though hidden from my sight. Only looking back are they visible.

Every time I ran, His Spirit was the wind that blew me where he wanted me to go. Though I was ever running, he was always running after me. Hindsight is 20/20.

Whatever I made *of* myself, I couldn't escape the fact that it was God who had made me. And all of my escaping was just God molding and shaping and forming me into the daughter I was made to be.

You see, Jesus is the tree that I came home to…
Because real freedom isn't in flying; it is in resting…
in the shadow of His wings…[18]
in the arms of Jesus…
the branch of the tree of Jessie…[19]
the Tree of Life. [20]

His Heart became my home. He was my Father all along. And he caught me in His arms and held me there in his embrace… so that He could direct all of my paths for the rest of my life… and so that He could use me in a group from Nashville to show children in Masindi that they, too, have a home in His heart and a Highway on His roadmap.

To humans belong the plans of the heart, but from the Lord comes the proper answer of the tongue… In their hearts, humans plan their course, but the Lord established their steps.

Proverbs 16: 1, 9

These orphans are not numbers or statistics. They are not invisible. They have lost parents and friends. They have lost homes, and they may have even lost heart. But they have not lost their true identity, because Jesus has not lost *them*. He is running after them even now.

He is running after these two also – I have saved their story for last.

Then Jesus told them this parable: "Suppose one of you has a hundred sheep and loses one of them. Doesn't he leave the ninety-nine in the open country and go after the lost sheep until he finds it? And when he finds it, he joyfully puts it on his shoulders and goes home. Then he calls his friends and neighbors together and says, 'Rejoice with me; I have found my lost sheep."

Luke 15: 3-6

Miriam and Sally

No one can tell these 9 year olds twins apart. I started asking who was who at the beginning of each trip. I learned if I could identify the clothes that each girl had on the first day, I could usually identify them the remainder of the trip. The children rarely change clothes during the length of time we are there.

But on my third trip to Masindi, one of the other children gave me the secret to discerning which twin was Miriam and which one was Sally. One has a small scar on her head. Although at this moment, I cannot remember which one that is!

When we arrived in December of 2012, on that third trip, the twins were not there. I figured they were with distant relatives, like many of the other children, since we were there at Christmastime. The children will often be requested at home during school breaks (which are not nearly as frequent as in America), so that relatives can have extra help for labor on the farm or in the home.

I assumed that to have been the whereabouts of the twins. I later discovered this was *not* the case. They returned the third day of our trip.

Isaac had taken them to their mother's home, so they could be with her in her final days of her battle with AIDS. He took them to her bedside, and they stayed for several days, through her funeral and burial. Isaac went to retrieve them one afternoon while we played with the other kids, and they returned in fancy dresses, very much out of place at Family Spirit, but with downcast faces… which always fit in.

How do you approach nine-year old sisters who have just come back from their mother's funeral? They were the same age as my own daughter. I did not know the twins as well as some of the other children, or as well as Hannah Whit knew them. But I got down on my knees and hugged them. I didn't have words to speak, just love to give and my silent recognition that a dark and painful story, too common in Africa, had made its way into the lives of two more children in Uganda.

I cried constantly on my first two trips to Africa. Sobbed rivers of tears uncontrollably, many behind sunglasses because it was just too embarrassing – my swollen eyes never recovered their normal appearance before the crying would start up again too soon. But I thought, by my third trip, that I was over most of the weeping. My eyes would be pricked with tears that, if I breathed deeply enough and paused just long enough, I could sometimes control.

Just when I thought I was finally growing scabs over all the raw pain I constantly encounter at Family Spirit, these fresh wounds bled out in front of me. Why? Why Lord, did these sweet girls have to be left without a mother? They spent the last three years living away from her, living at Family Spirit, waiting while she languished. And finally it happened.

Death is always near. Raised from age 6 to age 9, already as orphans, in full expectation of their certain future... until finally the future became the present, and she was gone, forever. In her wake, there were two more orphans in Africa.

I am an orphan on God's highway
But I'll share my troubles if you go my way
I have no mother, no father
No sister, no brother
I am an orphan girl

I have had friendships pure and golden
The ties of kinship have not known them
I know no mother, no father
No sister, no brother
I am an orphan girl

But when he calls me I will be able
To meet my family at God's table

I'll meet my mother, my father
My sister, my brother
No more an orphan girl

Blessed Savior make me willing
Walk beside me until I'm with them
Be my mother, my father
My sister, my brother
I am an orphan girl
I am an orphan girl

Orphan Girl by Gillian Welch[21]

All my life, I have wanted to be deeply known and unconditionally accepted. All my life, I have been that orphan girl spiritually, unaware that what I longed for, more than anything else, was a place to call home. Never did He leave me or forsake me – He did not leave me as an orphan; He came to me.

And along with many others in Nashville and beyond, I am being written into a story where He is coming after orphans in Uganda. Children longing for the attention of a Father, craving the affection of a Mother, needing the companionship of siblings and the warmth of a home. Lives so vastly different than mine on the outside, but so spiritually and emotionally similar on the inside.

He has rescued families in Nashville to enable us to return for them, time and again. And He is rescuing orphans at Family Spirit, to return them to the home he has for them – first and foremost, His Heart.

The name for the village "Masindi" originated from the word "Businde," meaning "the footmarks and the route of the Great King of Bunyoro." Since my third trip, there have been 6 trips to date (a total of 9). God Almighty is making *His* highway there: The King of Glory is forging a road to Masindi and crossing bridges to many hearts.

And a highway will be there… and those the Lord has rescued will return…

from Isaiah 35: 8 & 9

Chapter 10 | A Son : Nyakoojo Isaac

Praise be to the God and Father of our Lord Jesus Christ, the Father of compassion and the God of all comfort, who comforts us in all our troubles, so that we can comfort those in any trouble with the comfort we ourselves receive from God. For just as we share abundantly in the sufferings of Christ, so also our comfort abounds through Christ. If we are distressed, it is for your comfort and salvation; if we are comforted, it is for your comfort, which produces in you patient endurance of the same sufferings we suffer. And our hope for you is firm, because we know that just as you share in our sufferings, so also you share in our comfort.

2 Corinthians 1: 3-7

If there exists one passage of scripture that describes the mission of Family Spirit, it is found in these verses. And if there is one man behind that mission, that man is Isaac.[1]

Born Nyakoojo Rufunda Isaac, his mother gave birth to him in Masindi Hospital, on March 12, 1961. When I hear Anne's and Lindsey's accounts of this hospital in 2011, I can scarcely imagine what it was like exactly a half century before. His hospital birth in those days, however, could only point to the prosperity of his family. And *this* boy was good news to that family.

Susan told me, "He was the only boy, and a boy had not been expected." Family and church members also called him "special." He remained special as the only son; there was a sister before him and 3 after.

The literal translation of his African name "Nyakoojo" is "A boy!" His name is a joyful proclamation that his birth ushered in the promise of a son to a mother who had lost 5 sons previously to miscarriage. The word "nyakoojo" standing alone only states the obvious, but given as a name, as it was given to Isaac, it announces an impossible blessing, "Lord, you have given us a son!"

Considering the first name he was given, and the circumstances surrounding his birth, one cannot help but think of God's promise to give a son to Abraham, and His faithful fulfillment of that promise through Isaac, which means "laughter." How much more fitting that Isaac was given the same Christian name as Abraham's son, seeing all the children he would raise!

Taken together with "Rufunda," his father's family name, Isaac's entire name reads almost like an announcement of good news in times of trouble, "Nyakoojo Rufunda Isaac: A son has been given to the Rufunda family, and his name is Isaac!"

This God-given truth in Isaac's life would serve to be no different for the children at Family Spirit: good news in times of trouble, comfort in distress. It echoes the message of the Gospel itself – life in death. His mother's patient endurance, in both suffering and loss, brought her a son, and her son's own suffering would ultimately produce hope and comfort in the lives of hundreds of children.

The Spirit of the Sovereign Lord is on me, because the Lord has anointed me to proclaim good news to the poor. He has sent me to bind up the brokenhearted, to proclaim freedom for the captives and release from darkness for the prisoners, to proclaim the year of the Lord's favor and the day of vengeance of our God, to comfort all who mourn, and provide for those who grieve in Zion — to bestow on them a crown of beauty instead of ashes, the oil of joy instead of mourning, and a garment of praise instead of a spirit of despair. They will be called oaks of righteousness, a planting of the Lord for the display of his splendor.

Isaiah 61: 1-3

Isaac was one of five full siblings, but he had many half brothers and sisters. He told how his mother was one of "maybe four or five wives" of his father. Isaac's mother and her biological children lived on a "kibanja," a plot of land that a husband gives to each separate wife. All of the half-siblings enjoyed playing together, and the wives would often help one another with childcare.

Isaac's grandmother nursed him until he was three years old. They forged an obvious bond, and remained close throughout her life. His mother was too scared to breastfeed him, because so many people had told her that she had no chance of having a son. It seems her refusal to nurse Isaac stemmed from the fear that she would be unable to give him the love and nourishment he needed. She was in awe of her incredible gift and simultaneously afraid to fully embrace him in his earliest years.

Isaac's story, from the start, is likely as foreign to most Americans as it was to me. I struggled, immediately, to accept that a Christian family could assume the lifestyle of polygamy. Emotions gripped me over Isaac's home life: sadness for Isaac mixed with anger at a culture that oppresses women in this manner. What child wants to share their father with other families? What wife wants to share her husband? Yet, in Africa, this is often the norm.

Tim Keller writes in his book *Every Good Endeavor*,

> *All Christians live in cultures and work in vocational fields that operate by powerful master narratives that are sharply different from the Gospel's account of things. But these narratives work at such a deep level that their effects on us are hard to discern. An American who first moves to a foreign country is shocked to discover how many of her intuitions... are particularly American ones... By living in another culture, she gets a new vantage point from which she can be critical of herself, and as a result she will slowly change, dropping some attitudes and adopting others.*[2]

I'm certainly not saying, nor is Keller, that I should adopt a Ugandan worldview. What is suggested, I think, is to embrace a Gospel-worldview, both in America *and* in Uganda. (Even as a writer of this book, the story I tell would look very different if I were not a Christian.)

For me, the immersion into African culture has been an impetus for the critical examination of *both* cultures. It always behooves me as a Christian to challenge the ideas and values embraced by my country, city and community, lest I am being changed by these presuppositions without being aware of it. Both here and abroad - God has used my observations and experiences in Uganda to aid me in the scrutiny of my own beliefs and behaviors in *this* culture - the buckle of the Bible belt.

Being in a society so different from my own has made it clear that my operational worldview is often "American" or "Southern" – and not Christian. This fact became plain to me when I was quick to cringe at the heartbreak of polygamy in Isaac's childhood or respond internally in disbelief that Isaac's mother allowed his grandmother to nurse her infant. God was quick to convict me –

"Is the union of marriage honored and esteemed in America?" He asked me. Then, He was quick to remind me of the obvious – many men and women have multiple partners in *this* country. Broken homes are prevalent *here*, too.

"Do women in America believe the lies of the enemy?" God also challenged me. Of course we do. *I* do. I battle them daily.

The first lens through which I saw Isaac's story was an American one. God has gradually helped me adopt a Christian lens. Sin is sin, and it is as prevalent here as it is there. And Satan is the enemy, as real in Uganda as he is in America. The devil may show himself differently in other parts of the world, but he is fundamentally the same:

He speaks the same language across continents, near or far. "When he lies he speaks his native language, for he is a liar and the father of lies" (John 8: 44b).

He behaves the same in any corner of the world. "Your enemy the devil prowls around like a roaring lion, looking for someone to devour" (I Peter 5: 8b).

He is bent on destruction in every culture, and he starts unraveling *all* cultures by decimating the family. "The thief comes only to steal and kill and destroy" (Jn. 10: 10a)

If we claim to be without sin, we deceive ourselves and the truth is not in us.
I John 1: 8

Though polygamy is not a common cause of our suffering in America (at least not by the same face it takes in Africa), I am no less grieved over the men and women in this country who also settle for the lie – people who desire deeply intimate, committed relationships and who compromise instead for casual sex... people who ultimately long to feast on the meaning and purpose and relationship that only God can offer within marriage, but who are satisfied with the crumbs often served by our culture.

Are the sexual conquests in our country really any different? Are we not also defining for ourselves, in America, what marriage should look like (or eschewing marriage altogether)? Are our homes and families not also plagued by brokenness and shattered by compromise?

Polygamy is a historic and deeply imbedded practice in Africa, often condoned and many times accepted. However, American society is just as broken by the distortion of love that is given through the media's portrayal of marriage, the frequency of casual sex, and the prevalence of pornography. Polygamy even has a home here in America: "Open relationships," hailed in numerous places as "the new way to keep a marriage alive."[3] We simply have another name for it: "polyamory."

Christian homes and marriages are not immune to relational brokenness. Just as there are many Christians in the world, there is sadly much of the world in many Christians. This is as true in America as it is in Uganda.

Flee from sexual immorality. All other sins a person commits are outside the body, but whoever sins sexually sins against their own body. Do you not know that your bodies are temples of the Holy Spirit, who is in you, whom you have received from God? You are not your own; you were bought at a price. Therefore honor God with your bodies.

I Corinthians 6: 18-20

While I struggled with the rampant polygamy in Uganda, and how it touched Isaac's family as well, I struggled far longer, more deeply and more personally, with Isaac's sweet mother offering her baby boy to be nourished by someone else. There is certainly nothing morally wrong with another woman nurturing your child – we have our own breast milk banks here in America and the concept of a wet nurse is ancient and common in many cultures.

But, as a mother myself, it saddens me to think of Isaac's mother, paralyzed in fear. Likely, she desperately wanted to embrace and nourish Isaac, to give life to her miraculous and sweet gift. But, in fear, she made the choice to pass this blessing along to her own mother.

 "You will harm him."

"You don't have what it takes."

"If he fails to thrive or to survive, it will be your fault."

Are these the convoluted lies that Satan whispered to her?

Isn't it just like the enemy to drive choices out of fear and confusion? He convinced her to relinquish those precious first years to another woman, when I am sure she longed to be the one holding her son close to her heart. How common is our plight – to believe distortions instead of receiving perfect gifts from heaven!

God used Isaac's mother to remind me how often I, too, parent out of fear… how often I believe the subtle, but deeply deceptive and twisted lies of the enemy instead of standing firm in the truth. How often I, too, quickly and with good intentions throw away a blessing in motherhood instead of receiving it with arms wide open! How often I believe the lie that I do not have what it takes!!

But the Lord is faithful, and he will strengthen you and protect you from the evil one.

2 Thessalonians 3: 3

Isaac was raised in the church and memorized Bible passages as a young boy. He said, "I was lucky enough to go to a church school where we had daily prayers." He loved the prayer time, and he said that this time became a favorite hobby of his.

> "Growing up, every Sunday was Holy to our family. We used to go to church – and pray. [Period.] We could work in our garden on Saturdays, but on Sundays you prepared to go to church, and when you came home, you would wash your clothes [so that you were ready] for school on Monday."

Isaac was baptized when he was around 9 years old, but he was first required to complete a 6-month training course to learn more about the Bible and the Anglican Church. Three years later, he was confirmed in the church.

After his confirmation, he went through another 6-month training, where he learned still more about the Bible and about God. "That's when my Dad gave me my own Bible. I kept reading it – it was good that it was in the local language, but when I joined secondary school, that is when I got a Bible printed in English."

When Isaac was a child, he wanted to be a soldier. Idi Amin was leader of Uganda from around the time Isaac was 10 until he was almost 20. "Most of us, at our young age, we had no clue what was going on. We saw him as... a hero, a powerful man, a war general."

> "We later realized that maybe the regime was bad because essential commodities began to disappear. Salt, sugar and soap were scarce. These things were nowhere to be seen. Only strong supporters could have such things then – soldiers had the first priority. No one could talk about Idi Amin or his regime because you could be injured or harmed – neighbors would tell officials of such talk."

Isaac undoubtedly knows today that Amin's "regime killed many people, even in the open, by firing squad," but it seems likely that a glamorized (and propagandized) version of this horrific reality originally influenced his early childhood career aspirations.

As he grew and progressed in school, Isaac's father often urged him to become a teacher. For this reason, he joined a teacher college, but after taking the entrance exam, he had a change of heart. He decided he did not want to teach, regardless of his father's guidance and influence, and he did eventually join the police forces.

Even there, however, they directed his career by training him to become an instructor. Though Isaac's father had died by this time, he realized that his father was still "telling" him that he should be a teacher! Isaac served in the police force until 1995, when he was tested positive for HIV, "then they looked at me as if I was unfit to work in the Ugandan police force, and I was put on a forced retirement."

Isaac went back to Masindi and joined the Philly Lutaaya Initiative, which was made up of people living with HIV and AIDS. Like so many, Isaac respected the singer after whom the organization was named, because "he *told* people, 'I am sick'," instead of hiding. By his public announcement, Lutaaya also began to reduce the stigma and provide encouragement for others living with the disease.

Isaac gave a personal, first-hand account of the AIDS epidemic at that time:

> "By then, in the late 90's, many people had died, but very
> few people knew about HIV in the community of Masindi.
> We took people to the hospital, and they would die, leaving
> behind young ones. Both parents dying on the same day,
> even, with the child remaining.   We had to stay with those
> children, because the community would refuse them. They
> looked upon these children as 'cursed,' because there were
> many practicing witchcraft." (Children with HIV/AIDS are
> often maimed or killed by witch doctors. These assaults are
> believed to protect the community, or they are committed
> in a sacrificial exchange for the health or life of another
> member of the family.)

Children also came from outside Masindi looking for work. No one could trace the whereabouts of their parents or relatives. "Our work was to remain with the children. This is when we built [the group that would become Family Spirit]. The thought was, 'Since we are going to die also, why not start a charitable organization [to care for these children?]"

In 1999, the group of supporters totaled 19, including Isaac, but 7 died within the first few years because they had "no treatment" for the virus. The exorbitant costs prohibited anyone from *actually obtaining* the anti-retroviral medicines. Given Isaac's estimate of the treatment cost in Ugandan Shillings, I researched the exchange rate around the year 2000. It would have cost roughly $1000 - $2000 (American dollars) *each month,* depending on how you calculate for inflation.

It is no surprise that Isaac stammered in disbelief, "Even today, no one could afford this. It was only government officials who could afford this. Who could manage this? *No one* could manage this in the late 90's. Even today, no one could raise it."

This would be hard for most people in America, but totally impossible in Uganda. The irony is that people were fired because of their disease status, like Isaac, but they needed medicines they couldn't afford even *with* the job. HIV/AIDS was truly a death sentence. Those who became visibly sick were forced to slowly deteriorate in front of the watching world, in front of children and spouses, with absolutely no medical intervention. And it wasn't just a few people – it was happening *everywhere*.

By 2000, there were around 13 children under the care of the group of which Isaac was a part. He declared, "Someone needed to bring attention to these children, to start talking about them – those who couldn't care for themselves." So their group of like-minded, concerned adults came together for a meeting.

They began discussing names for the "home" and the ministry, and "Family Spirit won out" because they wished to engender the feelings of familial support, even though the children had come from many different parts of Uganda. Some had come from outside the country, even, and other children, Isaac admitted, "We did not know anything about them. . . where they were from, who they had left behind, why they were here in Masindi."

They desired to promote the loving relationships nurtured by a real family, "People living together and sharing the resources they have."

It reminds me so much of the family of believers in the early church also –

All the believers were together and had everything in common. They sold property and possessions to give to anyone who had need.

Acts 2: 44-45

Isaac lived through a decade of Idi Amin, followed by the first 2 decades of the AIDS epidemic. As if that weren't enough, then came Joseph Kony. In 2002, Family Spirit accepted the first group of children displaced by the LRA in Northern Uganda. An army truck arrived in Masindi, full of children.

"They told us they were leaving 32 children behind, but they would pick them up in 2 days. They left 4 bags of beans and some posho (ground corn), and they told us the balance of food would be [collateral] for the 13 children we already had… They convinced us, 'We're coming back.'"

Issac's account reminded me of a story my grandmother told me from the early 1900's. Her father was a dentist, and a man came into town needing dental work during the length of his stay. My great-grandfather, Dr. Hudson, performed the work. The man left him a yellow diamond as collateral, until he could come back to pay the balance in cash. He never returned, and the diamond has been in our family for four generations.

Clearly, Isaac's story is *strikingly* different. I was shocked that the army men left food as collateral – *for children*! In 2002! Isaac was shocked also, especially as no one ever returned for the children.

I cannot imagine the far greater shock and fear of the orphans.

I cannot imagine the horrors they had already endured.

I cannot imagine their confusion about their "temporary" living arrangements.

I cannot imagine their desperate sadness when they realized they were not going home; no one was coming back for them; there was no chance of reuniting with siblings, parents or relatives. And I simply cannot stomach that this was only a decade ago… and worse, that Kony is still at large today.

Isaac reported, "We *were* convinced [that they were coming back], but when [the men in the army truck] left, they did not come back. And we couldn't trace where the children had come from, except that they had come from the northern part of Uganda, which was over 200 km from Masindi (roughly 125 miles away, and at least double the driving time because of the road conditions).

"Most people were running *to* Masindi from another part of
Uganda. The only way to explain it is that these people [and
children] were refugees in their own country. And people
wanting to go north could not – roads were closed and
there were no busses traveling in that direction.

"Later, we were much affected with trying to find relatives
for the children, to see if they *could* be found. People were
shocked and in disbelief that we would [want to] go
anywhere near northern Uganda – because on those roads
there were a lot of ambushes. We were very scared, and
people would be very shocked when we returned, that we
had gone [in the first place] and had made it home [alive]."

When the food began running out, that is when the group (that supported
Family Spirit) "started looking up and down" for ways to help the children.
They did not have any resources, so they formed their first volunteer
board. These members were the first to assist Family Spirit in advocating
for the children. "We needed people who could contribute money, but we
let them know they were not responsible for other things."

Still, Isaac described his surprise at God's provision through certain people
stepping up in an unsolicited manner. He mentioned a businessman,
Bitamazire Keith, who convinced many people to join the board. He also
told me that one man on their board, Dr. Abiriga, offered free medical
services for any and all of the children, which he continued to give until
around 2009.

Free anti-retroviral medicines were finally made available to parts of
Uganda by 2000, and thankfully, in Masindi by 2002.

Then the King will say to those on his right, "Come, you who are blessed by my Father; take your inheritance, the kingdom prepared for you since the creation of the world. For I was hungry and you gave me something to eat, I was thirsty and you gave me something to drink, I was a stranger and you invited me in, I needed clothes and you clothed me, I was sick and you looked after me, I was in prison and you came to visit me..."

The King will reply, "Truly I tell you, whatever you did for one of the least of these brothers and sisters of mine, you did for me."

Matthew 25: 34-36, 40

Isaac has been surprised at how God has provided for his own life also. When Family Spirit was formed, he thought he might live for another six months. He certainly did not predict that he would be living over a decade later. "I did not expect that God would still have me alive," he confessed.

Assuming that he would die and leave all the children, he desired to raise awareness all the more "so that maybe some good Samaritan would come and take on the children." He wonders now, in awe, not only at how God has used him, but also at how God has blessed him...

> "I look at what the children have given me – they are the life in me. The love they give me is the comfort I have, and when I see children changing from a bad state to a better state, I feel at least I've contributed something to the world... So when I look at the children I have at Family Spirit, and they call *me* Dad, that gives me comfort.
>
> "They love me very much, despite the fact they know I am HIV positive. They *all* love me, but especially the ones who are 'living positively' also. They look at me as if – *they have hope.* I tell them, 'One day you will grow bigger than me,' so they get hope. I also get hope.

"Even my own relatives, apart from my mother, just hated me because of this status. I lost a job, because of my status. Because of my status, and because of talking about my status, I lost love from my people. But when I get love from the children, I feel that I must love them even more because they have given me that chance."

"Do you hear what these children are saying?" they asked him.

"Yes," replied Jesus, "have you never read, 'from the lips of children and infants you, Lord, have called forth your praise'?"

Matthew 21: 16

Most of the children have unimaginably abhorrent pasts. Because of their parents' offenses, the marriage may languish, but "a child suffers worse than the others," Isaac said. He described an all too common scenario: "When a man or woman commits an offense, the police will just come and arrest that person." Children are often left, overlooked, or placed in jail with the parent(s).

Isaac discussed the lopsided effects of children in divorce, home violence, and war, also. He lamented that children do not make the decisions to bring adversity upon the country, the family, or themselves, yet they are greatly wounded. "They are innocent victims!"

This is another way that Family Spirit supports the community of Masindi and beyond. Beyond orphans, they rescue children from domestic violence and from abandonment. In an unofficial capacity, they function very much like child and family protective services would in America.

He recalled a specific story of a certain child who was locked in the house by relatives. Isaac and others heard about him, and they went to investigate. After they found him, they took him to the hospital acute care.

He spent time in the hospital, and then he came to Family Spirit. "He was getting better. We had even requested for a school uniform…" Isaac trailed off. The relatives took him back home, even as the uniform was being made for him. He wasn't long in their care again, and he passed away.

Isaac longs to be able to continue to support such children, in urgent and perilous situations. His long-term vision is that some of the kids at Family Spirit would stay on or come back as adults. He prays that there will be "even 10%" who remain to take care of the responsibilities of educating and nurturing the future generations.

Already, there are young adults who have been released from Family Spirit into society, those who work in the community. Isaac beamed, "They love Family Spirit. At times, they come [back] and visit. They love [the children] very much. That shows me that the children can take over even when we [the adults] are not [living]."

As for the rest, he longs for them to "give love" and share the spirit of family in other parts of Uganda and "elsewhere in the world," whether that means casting a vision within their communities or starting more institutions just like Family Spirit. Most of all, he desires that these kids will one day train entire communities "to love children," so the need for orphan care would drastically abate.

He longs for support in their vision – he not only recognizes all the good that can be done at Family Spirit, but also he sees how their help can impact children far into the future. The privations are many: they are still not receiving the best level of nutrition possible (particularly those with HIV); they lack money for secondary and technical education; and there are still many farming and construction needs. Isaac prays for more people to support the long-term vision of Family Spirit, so that one day, they are self-sustaining.

He is also quick to clarify that institutional life is still not the same as having a loving, nuclear family. He longs for some of the children to be adopted, where appropriate, "so that some of them would have a chance of

225

having a home, whether inside Uganda or outside. A child living in a home will have a different life from a child raised in an institution."

Religion that our Father accepts as pure and faultless is this: to look after orphans and widows in their distress and to keep oneself from being polluted by the world.

James 1: 27

As with all stories, from the beginning of humankind, the enemy is present from the start. So, too, is God's redemption! He is "making a way in the wilderness (Is. 43: 19)" physically, spiritually, emotionally and relationally, too. Unlike Isaac's father who chose multiple wives, and unlike Susan's father who chose multiple mistresses, Isaac and Susan have chosen to honor each other alone, as long as they both shall live.

God's redemption is at work in their children too! Besides the many they are raising at Family Spirit, they are mother and father to their two biological children as well. Susan and Isaac stood up to the lies of the enemy over starting a family, when they had every real reason to live in fear.

As a woman with HIV, it is quite *literally* a possibility to harm your child by passing the disease along to them – in the birthing process and afterwards in the breast milk. But Isaac and Susan took every precaution advised by doctors, at every stage in pre- and post-natal development, and chose to believe God and wholly put their trust in Him.

She elected to give birth both times by caesarian section, to prevent the exchange of blood in the birth canal. Then she nursed her babies for the prescribed time – the doctors told her she could safely breastfeed her own infants until they were three months old, so she treasured the chance to give them this life. Though she lived with Satan's nagging fear, like many mothers, she walked in faith with her Redeemer.

Isaac is thankful, and you can read the gratitude across his face every time you are with him. He is quick to focus on his blessings: "I'm living HIV positive, living a normal life. I'm married to my wife. We have 2 children, and they are living negatively [without HIV]."

God's redemption is not only evident *in their own lives*, but also *through the ministry of their hearts and hands.* Susan and Isaac are building a spiritual legacy for those who will outlive them – for the many children they are raising, and for their biological children as well... not one, but two... *sons.*

Children are a heritage from the Lord, offspring a reward from him. Like arrows in the hands of a warrior are children born in one's youth. Blessed is the man whose quiver is full of them...

Psalm 127: 3-5

As for Isaac, like his name says, he has brought laughter into the lives of many children, and like "Abraham," he is the "father to many." What an incredible thread of redemption God has woven into Isaac's story, and subsequently into the lives of the multitude of children in his care. His father desired that he would be a teacher, while he wanted to be in the militia. In God's splendor and planning, now he is both: teaching kids at Family Spirit and battling for children of all ages through the work that he does.

I cannot help but think of the old children's song:

I may never march in the infantry
Ride in the cavalry,
Shoot the artillery,
I may never fly o'er the enemy,
But I'm in the Lord's army![4]

Like Abraham was father to the many after him, every type of son and daughter in the Bible, *with every story imaginable,* Isaac is quite literally fighting for masses of children. Armed with various tactics, he is going to war for a generation of children with a plethora of hopes and a vast diversity of needs: by protecting and providing, by giving and guiding, by instructing and interceding.

Isaac is a father to the "Jacobs," in whom God is creating a new nation and through whom God is raising up a new generation with a new name and a new identity. He is a father to the "Josephs," whom God will use to rescue the very people who oppress them. He is also the father to many "Joshuas," leaders and warriors, strong and courageous, so needed in a country and a world where fewer and fewer men are "stepping up."

Isaac is a father to the "Esthers," in who are in Uganda "for such a time as this," and to the "Marys," offering courage and life to their communities, listening to God's call and following bravely. Also to the "Ruths," strong and loyal servants, and the "Deborahs," who will lead in love.

Isaac is a father to priests like Ezra, heads of state and army like David and Solomon, influential landowners and farmers like Job, and tradesmen like Peter. He is a father to the rebels for the Lord like Miriam, prayer warriors like Hannah, and encouragers like Elizabeth.

And he is father to the "Daniels" who will exalt God in an orthodox and Biblical tradition, despite the culture in which they live that intermingles with wicked and evil customs, as commonly accepted as polygamy and as demonic as child-sacrifice. He is a father as well to the doctors like Luke, who will be incredibly important in the medical field – healing and researching cures – treating the sick and diseased in the name of Christ, "bringing light" into the darkness of AIDS.[5]

I pray Isaac is a father to many other types of disciples, who will follow Christ anywhere and everywhere into their God-given spheres of influence.

In the Bible, Abraham's and Isaac's stories, like so many after theirs, ended in fulfillment – through faith in Christ. This is Isaac's ultimate prayer for Family Spirit – that each narrative would find its highway home to a

Heavenly Father. That each story would be marked by The Savior.

Isaac cannot do this task alone. Family Spirit needs help, both physical and financial. Most importantly, I believe, the children need truth-tellers. Just like our own children, these kids need men and women who will be their spiritual parents. People who will speak words of life over their stories – who will pour healing over their pasts, while lighting passion and purpose over their futures.

"Look up at the sky and count the stars – if indeed you can count them." Then He said to him, "So shall your offspring be."

Genesis 15: 5

Most nights, I lay with each one of my children before bedtime. Usually Liam, then Austin, and finally Hannah Whit. There is rhythm and predictability to the routine.

Recently, I got up to leave Austin's room, but he wanted me to stay longer. I had tickled him, scratched his back, rubbed his head and smoothed his hair, said prayers with him and listened quietly to the details of a troubling part of his day, but it wasn't enough... he wanted me to stay longer. So – *I did.*

I got back into his bed and just held him. While I lay there, I thought of all the children longing to be held – *anytime* during the day. Kids at Family Spirit will go all day, many days in a row, without touch. No one will hug them, kiss them, put an arm around their shoulders or hands on their faces. Certainly no one will tuck them in at night. They won't get undivided attention; they will likely get very little attention at all.

The next morning, Austin came into the den as he often does. It was still early, and I was sitting in my prayer spot, a small club chair, in the dim light. It didn't matter that I had a Bible in my lap, with a pen and a journal. Didn't matter that books or notebooks were spread out in front of me at my feet on the ottoman, and hot coffee was right next to me on the table with low-lit lamp. It didn't matter, quite frankly, that I was in the middle of something (*with Jesus*). It never does.

I heard Austin's heavy footsteps hitting the floor, my early riser. He marched right into the den, swung himself right over the arm of my chair. He landed awkwardly in my lap, for he is getting too big to sit in the same small chair with me. This didn't faze him (it never does). He curled his legs up, put his head on my chest, and again I held him, like bookends to his night.

Our God is a nurturer. We were created to nurture and to be nurtured, but scores of kids will never get the nurture they need. So, do we give up? No! We rise up! Not just in Masindi, but in ministry wherever we are. We step onto the mission field, the battlefield, wherever that is, and we play the part God is calling us to play.

Our God is also the director of the largest, grandest, most amazing love story ever written – not just in Masindi, but in all the world. He has written parts for us to play – only I can fulfill my part, and only you can fulfill yours. This is true for the children at Family Spirit, too. They have parts to play, big plans and bold callings. They need people reminding them of this, as often as possible.

No one will listen to their dreams at night. No one will pray God's word over their futures or battle *for them* in prayer. No one will tell them they are "kind, smart or important."[6] No one will be waiting for them in the morning.

But we can help. Despite obstacles. Despite limitations. Despite being on opposite ends of the world.

"Take heart," Jesus said, "I have overcome the world" (Jn. 16: 33).

This is the Good News of the Gospel. It is a message needed in Masindi - it is a message needed everywhere.

Onward Christian soldiers, marching as to war,
With the Cross of Jesus going on before.
Christ the royal Master, leads against the foe;
Forward into battle see His banners go!

Onward then, ye people, join our happy throng,
Blend with ours your voices in the triumph song.
Glory, laud and honor unto Christ the King,
This through countless ages men and angels sing.[7]

God is looking for a few good men and women to step up and fight. It might be in Masindi, but most likely it will be in your own corner of the world. God is leading you down a path right now – this book is not just about the many people who have parts to play in Uganda or in Africa... it is about your part to play as well, wherever you are.

Look at all the pathways God has paved in this story, all the intersections He continues to provide. He is paving and providing in your story at well. There is nothing spectacular about me or about any of the people in this book. God is beckoning – we are simply walking the byways. We are ordinary people with an extraordinary God!

He may not be calling you to Masindi. But He is calling you home. If you have chosen your own path, look for *His* road in your life. No matter how far you have stayed from it, in His kindness, He is leading you back. No matter how safe you have played it, in His power, He is raising you up.

He has for you unimaginable promises and unbelievable adventure. He longs to fill you with life that overflows. Not just eternally, but now, too.

...it will be for those who walk on that Way.

Isaiah 35: 8

Epilogue | The Future of Family Spirit and The Masindi Project

As of the publishing of this book in November 2015, *147*[1] has come alongside our group to help feed kids in Masindi. Janie Omer, originally in our small group of families, is now assisting *147* as they assist Family Spirit.

It remains the heart of our group, *The Masindi Project*, to do whatever is necessary to love Family Spirit *for life.* Ultimately, we desire for them to be in a position where their ministry to orphans in Uganda is self-sustaining. The bottom line is this - ***to show God's Father-love to the fatherless*** by embracing them with opens arms and overflowing hearts... until their bellies, *and their lives*, are overflowing as well.

We have been able to send many teams through various avenues: Christ Presbyterian Church, West End Community Church and several trips that have been privately funded. *147* began sending teams as well, in 2013.

Our group has continued to send one collective check every month, by international money transfer, to our trusted friend in Masindi – Mustafa. He has bought food for us, and he has delivered it to Family Spirit for over 3 years now. Mustafa has been an aid to us, and an advocate for the children, from day one. He is hardworking and self-sacrificing. Along with updates on the kids, he sends us pictures of our receipts via text, and saves a paper file to hand off to us every time a team arrives.

Starting in 2012, Mustafa bought beans and posho, which is a corn-based porridge. In the beginning, that was simply all we could afford. Posho has a low nutritional value, and it is lacking in many essential vitamins and minerals, fat and protein. However, it is an affordable staple in the Ugandan diet, and just the introduction of a regular and consistent caloric intake made a marked physical difference in kids' growth rates and weight gain over the first 2 years!

We witnessed pronounced signs of physical development not seen before, and now Family Spirit is able to supplement the weekly meal offerings with several additional foods. Through the grassroots efforts of many generous donors, the nutritional needs of the orphans are being met in greater capacities. Our efforts are full of promise thus far, yet still incomplete... **Will you join with our families as we band together with Family Spirit in Uganda?**

God grew a few families quickly into 8 families, and He has added greatly to our numbers since. Many more families and individuals, singles and students, have gone and have given. God is truly forming an entire community to stand hand in hand around His children at Family Spirit... imagine what we could do if you linked arms with us!

Our long terms goals include educational provision in the form of child sponsorship, along with building projects, facilities upgrades and medical assistance when needed. We still feel, however, that all charitable endeavors are ancillary until the children are eating 3 meals a day, every day - highly nutritious foods, all month long. **Our immediate and urgent goal is to feed the children without gaps and without shortage**. **To do this, we need donors who will commit to monthly giving.**

This will allow us a predictable yearly budget with ample funds to boost the nutritional value of the food we are able to provide to the kids. We aim to increase our pledges to Family Spirit that we may promptly expand the feeding program to include: eggs, chicken, silverfish, seasonal fruits and vegetables, and milk/formula for the infants and toddlers.

Family Spirit is not alone anymore... neither are we. As we have given, God has certainly given back, "**pressed down, shaken together, and pouring over**" (Luke 6: 38) – tightening the cords of love between our hearts and the hearts of the precious kids in Masindi; deepening our love for each other and our relationships with the One who first loved us. God's highway is there.

➤➤

His roads are multi-faceted, and His purposes are many-splendored. Beyond nutrition, education, and medicine, and far beyond physical needs, hearts are finding healing and stories are finding hope - in Jesus. He has filled my own heart and furthered my own story, and He has given me the same deep longing for the children.

I desire for Jesus to so greatly impact their hearts that they use their stories to greatly impact their world. Through orphans in Masindi, God has helped me find my voice. And, through God, I aim to help them find *their voices* as well.

Our stories are not static, and they are not one-dimensional. I am honored for you to read in this epilogue, one major update and many more voices...

Mustafa

There is an update on Mustafa, the magnanimous man from Masindi: He has given his life to Jesus Christ.

He continues to wear the biggest smile you have ever seen, but there is Spirit behind it now. He still loves sitting in prayer circles with our teams, but he no longer does so as an observer – he is an active participant! His contributions during prayer "reflect his new reality," as Pastor Ryan Doyle said, and he recently gave his testimony at a village church, the Bigando Miracle Center.

Mustafa and Ryan are going through a Charles Spurgeon devotional together (thanks to modern technology). He has the Gospel of Matthew on CD and enjoys listening to worship music recorded by Ryan.

As for that baptism, it hasn't happened yet. I [still] hope to be there when it does...

Adrienne Freeman

Our journey to Masindi was a long one. The Lord had begun to do some serious work in my heart during 2011. His work resulted in lots of tears and hard conversations about God's heart for the poor, the orphaned, and the oppressed.

Africa has been on my heart since I was a kid. My parents spent a couple months in Kenya when I was little, and I spent a summer in West Africa before college. But somehow, I had never before seen things through this lens, *His lens*. He was breaking my heart for the people there. After coming home many times to find me in a puddle of tears, one particular night Bobby walked in and said "Let's go."

I think I looked shocked and said, "Are you serious?" *He was.*

I started making calls the next day, and within a matter of weeks, we had dates on the calendar. We began preparing for a two-week trip to Uganda and Ethiopia. In the interim, the Morrows came back from Uganda after adopting a baby girl from a village called Masindi.

I vividly remember Anne filling me in about their trip at church one morning and telling me that the kids at Family Spirit were hungry (Family Spirit is where Ali Rose had been dropped off as an infant). I waited for her to finish her sentence. I was waiting for her to say they were hungry to learn, or hungry for attention, but they were just hungry. *For food.*

They were not getting 3 meals a day, and some days they were not getting any meals at all. How could they learn, grow or have any hope for a vibrant future when they were starving?

The Lord paved the way and our two-week trip was quickly extended to three weeks. We headed to Masindi for the last 5 days of our stay. The Lord provided for every detail, including donors who wanted to buy food for Family Spirit while we were there.

Janie Omer, 'American Mom' to Mustafa

In the fall of 2011, when I was first asked about a mission trip to Uganda, I was beyond excited. I had never been on a mission trip out of the country before (I had never been out of the country before, period), and the idea of Africa just made my heart swell. Then, I realized that I was not only going to get to go on a mission trip to Uganda... I was actually going to be planning and leading said mission trip!

In the blink of an eye, and literally that fast, I thought, "Okay, Lord, this is nuts! I not only know nothing at all about Uganda, but also, I know nothing at all about planning, organizing, and executing a mission trip – in the US, much less half way around the world!"

Needless to say, after a lot of prayer, and a lot of the "this is too, too, too, too, big for me" moments, I decided to start asking questions. I was leading the trip along with my buddy, Ryan. He had been to Uganda several times, and he gave me some brochures and pamphlets of places to stay, along with possible places to serve while we were there. That was all I had!

So, I asked questions of people who had been there before – basic things like: What airline did you use? Did you use a travel agent? What about transportation once you got there? Will we feel safe? What do you wear? And have you ever been scared for your life there?!?! Just simple, every day, logistical type questions.

Then, I began – to plan, make notes, book reservations, and pray! We prayed that 12 people would sign up for that trip. Logistically, we thought that would be the most we could handle for the "pilot" trip. We put the word out there, and we prayed some more, "Lord, please send us the exact people that You want to go."

We had 25 people sign up for that first trip in 2012!

Now, 25 people on a domestic mission trip would be a lot, but 25 people on an international mission trip to Uganda, led by a newbie – it felt like 75 people! But, God was so faithful. All the logistics fell into place: flights, hotel reservations, ground transportation, places to serve, etc.

We prepared! We got ready (*as ready as we possibly could*) to go to Masindi, Uganda and serve an orphanage and school there, "Family Spirit Children's Centre." That is where my buddy Ryan had been before, so that was a natural place to start our trip.

We arranged a daily VBS for about 200 children. We prepared to sing, to play and to teach kids about Jesus. We planned as much as we could. But, as is always the case when the Lord takes you out of your comfort zone, WE WERE NEVER GOING TO BE PREPARED FOR WHAT WAS ABOUT TO HAPPEN TO OUR HEARTS!

Forty-eight hours after departure from Nashville, which included 24 hours of flying, 5-6 hours on a bus, layovers at airports and no real sleep... we arrived at Family Spirit Children's Centre, Masindi, Uganda, and I would never be the same.

Our arrival was met with laughter, joy and welcoming hearts – they were so glad that 25 of us were descending on their home for a week or so. They bombarded us with hugs and squeezes and a joy that felt different from anything I had ever felt before.

They immediately asked us to take our seats so that they could give us a proper greeting – they wanted to sing and perform for us. So we sat. In the dirt and in the little patches of grass, we sat. I sat and cried.

These children were the least of these. Their clothes were tattered and torn, and their hearts were fragile. So very fragile, yet so FULL of JOY!!! I sat and watched as a little boy kept taking something out of his pocket. He pinched off some of the food and put some in his own mouth, while also giving away to others and sharing. The craziest thing was, the food (whatever it was) wasn't getting any smaller. I believe that the Lord kept providing, so that he could share *and* have plenty for himself also.

Before we left home, we had a huge desire to adopt a couple of boys into our family – either domestically or from abroad. My husband prayed, "Lord, if our boys are there, please help Janie find them." We had been praying by name for them – Michael and James. (I had tried to change James to Josiah, but my children wouldn't let me).

So, I inched closer to this little boy who was giving away his food, and I asked his name. He said, "My name is Joseph."

I said, "I'm sorry, what did you say your name is?"

"My name is Joseph."

Could this be too good to be true? Could this be one of the boys for whom I had prayed for over a year? Then, he proceeded, "And, that is my brother, Micah."

What? Are you kidding me? The very first two boys that I actually met at Family Spirit are Micah and Joseph. Sounds really close to Michael and Josiah (the name I wanted to sub in for James)!

I just knew that these boys were "our" boys that we had prayed for by name – they were to be Omers. I could not wait to tell my husband.

Now, six trips later, Joseph and Micah are still my boys, although they do not live in the US with us. After much digging and asking, I realized that these boys would never live stateside with us, but they would always be our boys who lived in Uganda. They have parents – their parents just can't take care of them, so they live full time at Family Spirit and go to school there.

The love affair of my heart with all the children at Family Spirit resembles
the love that I have for Joseph and Micah. At first, there was a little group
of about 4-5 children, mostly boys that I bonded with and loved on. I
promised to come back the next year.

Year by year, the number has grown by about 20. Now, I can't keep up
with the number any more. I think about ALL of them, all of the time. I am
so deeply wrapped up in each of them... and their stories and their
hearts. I am so thankful that it seems like I have known them all of their
lives, and I will know them for the rest of mine.

I love that the Lord has called me to serve at Family Spirit. I love that even
when I am not there, I feel a deep connection to each and every one of
them. God is continuing to do great and mighty things at Family Spirit,
both spiritually and physically.

The children are no longer starving and hungry all the time. They are fed
daily – lots of yummy foods that are also wholesome and nutritious. They
don't have to wear tattered and torn clothing anymore. They have school
uniforms and play clothes, and they are able to stay clean on a daily
basis. Their daily needs are being met, and they are loved and safe.

The one thing that hasn't changed (and it continues to bless me more than
almost anything I have ever experienced) is their JOY! The joy that they
had on that very first day (back when they didn't have a clue when their
next meal would be) is the same joy that they have today, having all of their
basic daily needs met. You see, their joy is not of this world – it is the joy of
Jesus! He is the source of their joy – not what they have or don't have.

I am so thankful that the Lord has allowed me to go to Masindi many, many
times, to "taste and see that He is good" (Ps. 34: 8). God is good all the
time, and all the time God is good! I am thankful that these children, who
are the least of these, will go out this very next year into their community
and serve. They understand that "to whom much is given, much is

required" (I Cor. 4: 2). They are ready; they are willing; and they are excited for a season of serving.

Praise God alone who has given us this gift of Family Spirit – and each of those precious "babies" that I love with my whole heart!

Angie Gage

After 25 years of praying for an opportunity to go to Africa, to love the people I felt connected to in my heart, God answered my prayer. I helped to lead a group of students on a mission trip to Uganda. At that time Family Spirit was a name that represented something beautiful but unknown.

When I arrived in Masindi, I felt a strange sense of connection to the place and to the people. Even the things around me felt familiar. Immediately after arriving at Family Spirit, and hearing the voices of the children singing to welcome us, I felt a strong bond of love.

It wasn't even 10 minutes before I had little hands in mine and little arms around my legs, hugging me. I will never forget the beautiful brown eyes looking at me, nor the glowing faces and the big genuine smiles all around me. I was sure from the beginning, my being at Family Spirit was more about the gifts I was going to receive than what I had anticipated giving.

I was very shocked to see that there was real poverty in the world and children who literally go to bed hungry night after night. Despite the obvious signs of malnutrition, there was evidence of true joy and life bubbling out of these kids through their songs, their laughter, their play and their great capacity to give and receive love.

As my heart was so deeply touched, my mind kept wondering how we could help these kids and families on a more long-term basis. I began to ask God to use our team to provide a plan that would help sustain them physically, nourish them emotionally, and encourage them spiritually. I knew that so many programs end up hurting and not helping long term, so I wasn't interested in quick-fix solutions.

After talking with Isaac and Susan, and hearing their hearts, their dreams, their plans and their hopes, I knew we had to pray earnestly and take action to help. We wanted to give dignity and honor to them.

I wish I could see the families and children in Masindi daily, but I believe I'm giving in a way that honors God. I firmly believe God hears and answers all of our team prayers for his will to be done and his amazing children to be cared for. It is a gift to be on this journey with amazing friends here in the U.S. – and to work as one body, following Christ in His mission to love people!

Stephanie Edwards

Nearly five years ago was the first time I heard of Family Spirit. I had been praying with my prayer partner, Allison, among other things: for children, for adoption, and for the people of Africa.

One of Allison's closest friends, Anne Morrow, was traveling to Africa with another one of their friends, Tara. Tara and her husband, Drew, were adopting two boys from Uganda, and Anne made the trip to Jinja with them.

Several months after Anne got back from Uganda, the Lord called her and her husband, Nate, to adopt a child as well. Their daughter, Ali Rose, would be in my prayers long before I really knew all the details of Family Spirit, and long before I knew Ali Rose's sweet family, The Morrow Crew.

In the beginning, I only knew Anne because she was in a long-term Bible study group with Allison. Now, however, we are all involved together with Family Spirit... and we are just three of the eight total families. In His goodness, God has woven together all of our circumstances and lives, in one way or another, in support of Family Spirit.

Allison has long had a heart for adoption, for Uganda and for Family Spirit. She dearly loves Susan and Isaac, who are both pouring their lives out to care for these orphans in Masindi. Allison loves the orphans too! Many of these children have lost both of their parents to AIDS, while some have parents who have simply abandoned them.

Allison's passion for Family Spirit was, and is, infectious. Her passion called me to stop and let the Spirit move in my heart for these precious children. As the Lord adopts us as His own children, His desire for us is that we adopt others. That adoption may not be a legal adoption, or a change of guardianship, but we are nonetheless all called to care for these children and share His love for them in whatever way we can.

Susan and Issac are true examples of this calling. Psalm 68: 5-6, "A father to the fatherless, a defender of widows, is God in his Holy dwelling. The Lord sets the lonely in families...."

Sometimes I think it is just so hard for us to wrap our minds around children consistently not having enough food to eat, places to sleep, etc. The Lord calls us to take a closer look *and to act* - whether by going, giving, praying, spreading the word... whatever He whispers to your heart. It is amazing what happens when we let the Lord take a little bit of our time, money and passion. He knows how to use it much better than we do. He can use the $10, $25, $50, or whatever amount of money we will give each month, for such amazing good in the lives of these kids.

As Jim and I have yet to travel to Uganda, I have gotten to know Susan, Isaac and these precious kids through the passion, pictures and stories of the seven other families in our group. The Edwards' biggest contribution has been prayer. We wait expectantly for the Lord and for our next steps in the journey with these incredible people from Masindi.

Lindsey McRae

Orphans have been on my heart since I was in high school, maybe longer. You see, when I was in high school, my sisters and I became orphans. We lost both of our parents to cancer just a few years apart.

As I grew older I have always felt a passion for children without parents, and I have been intrigued by families that adopt. My sisters and I were fortunate that we lived in America – we had good friends and family that took us in and provided for us. I've often thought about other children around the world that were not as fortunate – the ones in third world countries without anyone to help them. In high school, I even wrote my senior research paper on orphans and orphanages.

Fast forward to 2012. I was talking to my good friend, Allison Hodges, about a trip to Africa. She had hoped to go, but it looked like the trip had fallen through. I looked at her and said, "What if *we* just go?!"

It was a crazy whim of an idea that God put in my head right in that moment. That idea ended up sending our two families, along with a few other friends, around the world to Masindi, Uganda that Christmas. We spent ten days at Family Spirit.

One of the things that first stood out to my husband, Jay, and I when we first were touring the orphanage was the "bedrooms" where the boys slept. They would sleep with two, three, sometimes four boys in one bed smaller than an American twin bed. And the beds were dirty, smelly, and covered in bugs. Such a drastically different scene than the cozy beds each of our two boys slept in at home, and it hit us hard. With tears in our eyes we continued to tour the orphanage and our eyes were opened to true poverty. Children sick with HIV or AIDS, not knowing when their next meal would be.

During our time there, we sat with the children, played, gave them treats, painted their nails, sang, read the Bible to them, and mostly just loved them. It was a joy to be with the kids. They were genuinely happy and it was contagious. They had such a pure joy in their hearts even in the midst of unbearable living conditions and little food. It was truly an eye opener for this American girl who struggles with the idol of comfort and materialism.

I knew that Family Spirit would forever hold a place in my heart when we left. The children's faces are imprinted in my mind. Jay and I are honored to walk alongside the other families that are committed to helping feed these sweet children – and helping in any other way that we can.

Rachel Ladner

God put the children of Africa on my heart long ago, and I always knew I wanted to get there to hold and love them. However, I never knew exactly how that was going to happen until God put Allison in my life.

I was sitting in front of Allison at church (West End Community Church in Nashville) and saw in the bulletin that she and a small group of people were traveling to Africa in December. I immediately knew that God was opening this door for me, and I did not hesitate. Through His grace, and the generosity of my family and hometown church (Covenant Presbyterian in Cleveland, Mississippi), everything fell into place very quickly, and I watched a lifelong dream come to fruition.

Below is an excerpt from my journal, written during our trip:

12/29/12

We arrived in Africa on the night of December 27 after nearly 30 hours of travel. From Entebbe, we drove to Kampala, where we stayed at the Adonai Guesthouse. Yesterday, we exchanged money and bought items for the children at the Nakumat (grocery). From Kampala, we drove to Masindi; this is where we will stay and visit the children at Family Spirit.

A small group of us went yesterday (Allison, Lindsey, Sam, Randy and myself) for a quick hello, to let the children know that we had arrived. It was getting close to dinner, so we only stayed about 15 minutes. In the very short period of time, my heart was broken and renewed all at once. These children have nothing, and they need so much love.

There was a little boy named Joel, who walked right up to me and wanted to be held. You could tell he had just been crying and desired to be comforted. He held on to me so tightly and would not let me put him down. *He just wanted to be held*! What a moment!

In the midst of this trip, I am going through my own personal and health struggles; previously, I have been totally consumed by them. Wondering constantly where is God? What have I done to deserve this? What is wrong with me? I have completely lost my way.

However, in that moment with Joel, a small child I had never seen before, I felt a true love that could only come from God; I felt needed; and I felt real human connection, maybe for the first time. This is life! This is feeling!

I know these children will break my heart – my jaded, icy heart. That is what I want, and I know that is what I need. To feel pain, sorrow, grief, happiness, joy and the indescribable power of God's love for these children – *and for me*.

Sitting on the porch outside of my room at the Masindi Hotel, I am emotional. Look at what I have. Even here, I have so much more than these children and the people of Masindi.

They have so many unmet needs, and so many of them live in dire circumstances, yet they step outside to wave as you walk past. They offer you food and water when you enter their homes. What a beautiful expression of God's great love and the ability to find contentment in any circumstance.

Being here has enabled me to remove my mask and recognize the troubles of a fallen world. I am able to accept that there is hope and healing to come – not only in Africa, but in my life as well.

Sam Crenshaw

My trip to Africa in 2012-2013 was by no means an accident. I walked into church one day praying that the Lord would give me an opportunity to go on an "adventure." As I poked my head into the prayer room, the Hodges were praying about a trip to Africa.

They asked if I wanted to go, and I said, "Yes," right then and there.

My heart, even now, is so overwhelmed when I think of God's goodness... when I think of the wonder that He shared with me on that trip. One memory that really stands out to me was loving on two sweet sisters named Grace and Peace. Both had been living at Family Spirit for a couple of years, and they were so wonderfully precious and sweet.

As I got to know them a little better each day, they opened up and started to feel more and more comfortable around me. It was so amazing to see the love that God has for "the least of these." Orphans, kids without earthly parents – what a strange concept to most of us! Yet these two girls had their heavenly Father, and their joy was greater than any I had ever experienced.

Every hug, every smile, every question about Jesus just melted my heart. It was so wonderful to experience the love of Christ through two sweet girls, 2000 miles away. I will never forget them, and am so glad to have experienced such a rich taste of the love of God.

<u>Sandra Edwards</u>

About three years ago, I began a spiritual journey. I had a huge gaping hole in my heart...

I was born Jewish, but in my later years, I married a Christian man. I allowed myself to fall away from attending Temple, and I just became complacent. I met a wonderful man, Carter Crenshaw, who also happened to be a pastor.

He met me on one of my "down" days, and he offered to talk to me. He also invited me to attend his church, West End Community Church. I took him up on his invitation. I loved the people, the music, and the sermons – I was overwhelmed with a mixture of emotions, and I cried every Sunday that I attended church there.

I never felt this same pull to God at The Temple as a Jewish woman. I also had never before experienced such loving people and such meaningful worship. I was thirsty for more from West End Community Church and from its loving congregation.

In my desire for more, I became a member of a small group early in my spiritual journey. I learned to share and pray with these wonderful people. Through the group, God was growing my faith, but then I had an "Ah-ha" moment...

I had a medical emergency requiring me to have surgery on my spine. I was petrified! Would this surgery render me crippled? Would it leave me unable to be the active wife, mother, grandmother and person that I had always been?

I was laying on the gurney. Nurses were prepping me for surgery. Just as they were rolling me back, I had a very warm feeling come over me. Then – I SAW JESUS! He was looking down on me, and He reassured me that He would be guiding the surgeon's hands. He told me that everything would be alright.

He encouraged me, "Go to sleep. You will be 'as good as new' when you wake up."

When I did wake up, I *was* "as good as new." I cried to my husband, "I saw Jesus! He reassured me that I would be OK. I know what being a Christian is all about now." That is when I realized who Jesus was and the part He would play in my life and in my spiritual journey.

I later went to a Women's Christmas dinner at West End Community Church, followed shortly thereafter by a church Women's Retreat. On that retreat, I met the sweetest, most precious, God-focused, Jesus-loving, people-centered women – Allison Hodges and Adrienne Freeman. These ladies did a presentation on Uganda and on Family Spirit orphanage.

I wanted to experience what Allison and Adrienne had experienced with those needy children in Masindi. I had so much love to give, and my cup was so overflowing with my newfound faith. I wanted to go to Family Spirit and share!

After the women's retreat, I knew I wanted to go to Uganda. I knew I wanted to drink up all of the life I could by being a Christian. I went to Bible Study, and my husband and I went to a Discovery class so that we could become members of the church. I had a strong desire to be baptized, and in my mind, this would complete my spiritual circle of life.

Then – I did go to Uganda! The very next summer after the women's retreat! Little did I know then that those adorable bald-headed children, dressed in tattered clothing, would give me more love than I could have ever imagined. The children of Family Spirit love their lives, their God, and their country. They don't care that they do not have shoes or toys. One doesn't miss what one has never had!

West End Community Church has given me new life by offering me Jesus Christ. Their pastor and their women's ministry have nurtured me in my faith. Then, my "Ah-ha moment" led me to become not only a church member, but also a Christian. I was baptized, and I went on that summer mission trip to Uganda.

Jesus is my Wonderful Savior! He walks with me every hour and every day of my life. I study more and more about Him in the Bible. I definitely feel my spiritual journey has come full circle and that huge, gaping hole in my heart is filled. I am at peace!

Margaret Gaw, Sophomore at Harpeth Hall School in Nashville[2]

written 8/19/14 (before her Freshman year of high school)

The world of Masindi, Uganda is a haven to me. Nobody is inside the mud shacks that line the dirt roads, because the sun is out and the day is beautiful. Everyone waves, "Kiki (what's up?)" as I walk by.
The children at the orphanage run and surround me with a joy I have never seen before. I must be holding 20 hands. We play the day away until the red, rich sun sets under the vast, African sky. The next day is the same, and the next, and the next. This world is so simple, love-filled, and joyful.

This world is filled with pain as well. Children who are fourteen years old look eight years old because of malnourishment. Women walk miles and miles for a cup of water. After primary school, boys wander the streets because there are no funds for secondary school. Sick parents die because there is no medical treatment available.

Why are these people so joyful, welcoming, and giving when there is so much pain, suffering, and loss? I have learned that the people of Masindi, Uganda, and specifically Family Spirit, commit themselves to Christ Jesus, and their hope and love are manifested from His Word.

written 11/15/15 (a year & half after her trip, during her Sophomore year)

It's been about a year and a half since my trip to Uganda and being in Masindi and working at Family Spirit are memories from the past. However, the love and joy I experienced at Family Spirit is the same love and joy on which I base my faith today.

Family Spirit gave me a cornerstone for my faith, because the people showed me the love, joy, and righteousness that God provides to *His* people. In my materialistic and performance-based world, it is difficult to cultivate the spiritual mindset like Family Spirit. But if I ever need to re-center my life back on "the things unseen," I pick up my journal from my trip to Uganda – I can read the love of Christ Jesus in each line of my story during my time at Family Spirit.

Therefore we do not lose heart. Though outwardly we are wasting away, yet inwardly are we being renewed day by day. For our light and momentary troubles are achieving for us an eternal glory that far outweighs them all. So we fix our eyes not on what is seen, but on what is unseen, since what is seen is temporary, but what is unseen is eternal.

2 Corinthians 4: 16-18

My Mom, Ann Gober

God spoke to me about caring for Adam and Allison's kids, rather than traveling *with them* to Africa. There weren't many well-defined details. It was more of a knowing in my soul, but I believe with all my heart – that *knowing* was from God.

Each time Allison came home from visiting Africa, my heart would swell with desire to go with her on the next trip. And I knew there would always be a next trip! The stories she told me drew me in.

Stories of the countryside, and the animals, and the red dirt- but mostly the stories she told me of the people, *and especially* the children. I wanted to see their faces with my own eyes and experience their touch with my own hands. Wanted it then, and still want it now. And so I began to pray, asking God to make it clear to me if I should travel with Allison the next time she would go.

Before my husband and I took our summer trip to Maine (the summer of 2013), Allison allowed me the privilege of taking her book with me, the book that you hold now in your hands, about Susan and Isaac and all the sweet children.

There were only a handful of chapters then, but she asked me to read it... to begin to proof those first words and thoughts. Through her words, once again, I was drawn to Africa in my mind. I could picture the images and the people she described so clearly that I could almost touch them. Her writing carried me to that distant place. It brought tears to my eyes and placed in my heart an even stronger desire to go.

I wondered, "Is this proofing assignment something God is using to say that *He also* desires *for me* to go?" So, I prayed some more – for more clarity, more certainty, more signs.

Back at home after Maine, people in my small group at church would mention Africa, and I would think, "Is that You, God?"

Programs on television would mention missionaries in Africa, and I would think, "So, you're telling me to go, God?"

But my questions always had more questions, because the answers didn't feel settled in my heart. And so I prayed – *even more.*
Then fall Bible study started at my church, and we studied Jonah. God told Jonah to go to Ninevah, but he didn't want to. I thought surely there was a message here for me – *God wanted me to go to Africa.* The only difference between me and Jonah was that I *WANTED* to go!

I was not going to end up in the belly of a fish! I would listen to God and go! Still, it didn't feel settled in my heart.

Early in our Bible study, there was a reference in our guide book to "future generations." I circled it, as well as the explanation that our personal stories should encourage others to follow hard after God.

The reference to future generations brought to my mind Adam and Allison's children – my sweet grandchildren. How would I influence them for God? How would I love them and care for them - *for God*? How would my life reflect my own seeking after and loving God?

That's when I recognized the first seed that God was planting in my heart to stay at home with my grandchildren (whether that meant one, or two, or all three of them), to care for them while Allison and Adam went to Africa without me.

Other insights and scriptures floated up to the top of my prayers throughout my study of Jonah. In John 21, when Jesus tells Peter to "feed my lambs," "tend my sheep," and "feed my sheep," I thought of *their* little lambs.

And in Isaiah 30: 15b it says, "in quietness and trust shall be your strength." I didn't feel that God was telling me _not_ to go to Africa - just not _now_. While I certainly want to offer something of myself to those in Africa, I felt God *asking* me to offer something of myself to Hannah Whit, Austin, and Liam.

"Go and wash in the Jordan seven times" (II Kings 5: 10-11)," was God telling me, "Go and care for them again, and maybe again, and again."

"You can go to Africa, but just not yet," God whispered to me.

All of these things (mentions of Africa, missionaries and TV, Bible study lessons) rolled over and over in my heart, somewhat confusing. But as I considered the idea of waiting to go to Africa, a gladness took root in my heart. I was glad to stay behind, glad that I could take care of my grandkids, whom I love so much. After all, no babysitter knows them as well as their grandparents, nor loves them like we do.

Finally, two more scriptures sealed the deal for me - Ps. 46: 10, "Be still and know that I am God," and I Cor. 14: 33, "For God is not a God of confusion, but of peace."

I felt God leaning into my heart and just telling me, "I've got this!" He was telling me to be still, to trust, and to know His peace. He doesn't desire to confuse me about where I should go to glorify Him. He wanted me to know that I can glorify Him at home with my own family, just as much as in Africa, and just maybe – He plans to use the time with my sweet grandkids to equip me even better for my journey to Africa one day.

So there you have it – nothing dramatic, or eloquent, or angels swooping down from the heavens... but a gentle knowing and a peace that passes all understanding. My part to play, thus far, has been caring for my grandchildren.

My Daughter, Hannah Whit Hodges

My trip to Africa was an amazing experience. I remember so much need and poverty, but I also remember happy faces and open hands. In Masindi, braids were almost always in my hair, and a smile was almost always on my face.

I also made a very close friend named Calla. Though older than me, she was just as playful as I was. Many tears were shed at our parting, but I know God caught all of them in beautiful bottles.

I still miss Calla and Family Spirit, but I know one day I will return.

Notes | A Bibliography

Unless otherwise noted, scriptural references are taken from the Holy Bible, New International Version (NIV). (Grand Rapids, MI: Zondervan, 2011).

Names of orphans have been changed, and the names of adults have been changed occasionally, where necessary.

INTRODUCTION
1. Larry Bolden, *The Battle for Your Heart* and *The Battle for Your Domain*, The Wellspring Group: www.wellspringgroup.org
   I am glad that I get to mention "The Battle" in my very first note, as my life has been shaped and molded by this journey. This book would likely not be in your hands without the influence of Larry Bolden and so many others at Wellspring. Though I have not used any direct quotes from the Battle material, of which I am aware, there are undoubtedly themes throughout. The 4 Biblical Realities of Wellspring that will appear in this book are: 1) God has chosen you for his Larger Story. 2) God has given you a part to play in that Story, and if you do not find the way, no one will. 3) Evil is hunting you, to take you out of the Story. 4) The Fellowship desires to protect you and propel you into your part.
2. Scotty Smith, from one of his prayers at West End Community Church, www.westendcc.org
3. Oswald Chambers, "Building For Eternity, May 7." *My Utmost For His Highest.* An Updated Edition in Today's Language. James Reimann. (Grand Rapids, MI: Discovery House Publishers, 1992.)

PROLOGUE
1. Dustin Swinehardt, from a series of talks he gave at Young Life Family Camp, Windy Gap, N.C. May, 2014.
2. Ernest Hemingway, *Green Hills of Africa.* (New York: Charles Scribner's Sons, 1935), 192.
3. Kakira Sugar Plantation, Uganda. www.kakirasugar.com

4. C.S. Lewis, *The Last Battle*. (New York: Macmillan Publishing Co., Inc., 1956), 101.

CHAPTER 1
1. I attended high school at Providence Day School, Charlotte, N.C., and was blessed by incredible teachers and thinkers there!
2. During my days at UNC-CH, I attended church at Chapel of the Cross Episcopal Church in Chapel Hill, N.C.
3. C.S. Lewis, *The Magician's Nephew*. (New York: Macmillan Publishing Co., Inc., 1956), 135 - 138.
4. The Covenant Counseling and Education Center, Birmingham, AL. www.covenantcounsel.com

CHAPTER 2
1. Most of the information written in this chapter comes from Susan's own memories. It has been corroborated many places. For more reading on the LRA, and the efforts in place to stop them, please visit: www.lracrisistracker.com.
   Please also visit www.invisiblechildren.com
2. One of best articles I read on the Night Commuters can be found at: http://www.nbcnews.com/id/9006024/ns/dateline_nbc/t/childre n-war-uganda/#.Vhaf4bQboII. (The mention of a woman named Angelina in this article is purely coincidental. It is not the same woman.)
3. Brennan Manning, *The Ragamuffin Gospel*. (Colorado Springs: Multnomah Books, 1990), 25.
4. I highly recommend the book by Sara Hagerty, *Every Bitter Thing is Sweet*. (Grand Rapids: Zondervan, 2014). Though I had not read Sara's book when I wrote these words, I have since. Now every time I see the words, I think of her book. I reference it here, because it is a wonderful and worthy read.

CHAPTER 3
1. Christian Leadership Concepts (or "CLC") was started by one of Adam's good friends, Hal Hadden. For more information: www.christianleadershipconcepts.org

2. Erin ("Sheff") and Jeff Brovet – Sheff is a friend of mine from college, and got to Africa with her husband via an incredible story: Early in their marriage, they spent a vacation in Africa. They went sightseeing and went on safari, but part of their trip was serving for a few days with some of their friends at an orphanage in South Africa. While they were there, they connected with an orphan named William.

   When they returned to the States, they could not get this little boy out of their minds or off of their hearts. They wrestled for many weeks about what this could mean and what God might be telling them. They finally decided they would pursue the adoption of William – they assumed this must be what God wanted.

   They soon found out, however, that adoption was not a possibility, because adoption was closed at that time for US citizens. They were shocked – if adoption was not the answer, then what was God still trying to tell them? They prayed again for some period of weeks, wondering if maybe they should just go and serve in the children's home.

   In the continuing silence from God, Jeff ultimately asked the Lord for a dream one night. He woke up the next morning – *no dream*. After breakfast, however, he and Sheff stepped out of the house together to walk in their neighborhood for exercise. While they walked, Sheff started, "I have to tell you about the most amazing dream I had last night…"

   In the dream, young William was adult William – dressed in a beautiful suit; he was smiling; he was well. They took this as an amazing sign from God to "sell everything and go" to South Africa, and to serve God there for one year.

   God provided in unbelievable ways once they committed, and ultimately, one year turned into almost three in South Africa. By spending this time in South Africa, they discovered they were able to adopt *as South African citizens* – and they did adopt – a little girl named Bongi.

3. Melissa Fay Greene, *There Is No Me Without You.* (New York: Bloomsbury USA, 2006).

4. Karin Evans, *Lost Daughters of China: Adopted Girls, Their Journey to America, and the Search for a Missing Past.* (New York: Jeremy P. Tarcher/Putnam, 2000).
5. Abraham Nhial and DiAnn Mills, *Lost Boy No More: A True Story of Survival and Salvation.* (Nashville: Broadman and Holman Publishers, 2004).
6. Stephanie Nolen, *28 Stories of AIDS in Africa.* (New York: Walker and Company, 2007).
7. Francis Chan, *Crazy Love: Overwhelmed by A Relentless God.* (Colorado Springs: David C. Cook, 2013).
8. David Platt, *Radical: Taking Back Your Faith From the American Dream.* (Colorado Springs: Multnomah Books, 2010).
9. Tim Keller, *Generous Justice: How God's Grace Makes Us Just.* (New York: Penguin Group, 2010).
10. Richard Stearns, *The Hole in Our Gospel: What Does God Expect of Us? The Answer That Changed My Life and Might Just Change The World.* (Nashville: Thomas Nelson, 2009).
11. "American Idol Gives Back." *American Idol.* Fox. April 2007, 2008, 2010. Television.
12. Ellie's Run is held every May in Nashville. For more information: www.elliesrun.org
13. Visit my website: www.untilitoverflows.com/hallelujah-tees/ All proceeds benefit the feeding program at Family Spirit, other Christian ministries, Missions, and adoptions.
14. Katie Davis is now Katie Davis Majors. She can be found at: www.amazima.org/about-us/katies-story/ and in her book with Beth Clark, *Kisses from Katie: A Story of Relentless Love and Redemption.* (New York: Howard Books, 2011).
15. Randy Pope of Perimeter Presbyterian Church in Atlanta wrote this 3-year plan for discipleship, copyrighted in 1996. For more information: www.perimeter.org
16. Ibid. Chapter 9, 189-217.

CHAPTER 4

1. You can find Mandy Gallagher at www.pressinginformore.com. She and her husband Mike wrote the Foreword of this book, as well.

2. "The rapid test is an immunoassay [lab test] used for screening, and it produces quick results, in 30 minutes or less." www.cdc.gov/hiv/basics/testing.html

3. Carter Crenshaw, head pastor at West End Community Church: www.westendcc.org

4. Oswald Chambers, "Gracious Uncertainty, April 29." *My Utmost For His Highest.* An Updated Edition in Today's Language. James Reimann. (Grand Rapids, MI: Discovery House Publishers, 1992).

CHAPTER 5

1. Robbie Brenner, Gary Safady, Craig Chapman, Deborah Giarratana (Producers), and Marc Forster (Director). (2011). *Machine Gun Preacher* [Motion Picture]. USA: MGP Productions, LLC.

2. Ibid.

3. Sally Lloyd-Jones, *Jesus Storybook Bible: Every Story Whispers His Name.* Illustrated by Jago. (Grand Rapids, MI: Zondervan, 2007), 179.

4. Andrew Adamson, Douglas Gresham, K.C. Hodenfield, Mark Johnson, David Minkowski, Perry Moore, Philip Steuer, Matthew Stillman (Producers), and Andrew Adamson (Director). (2005). *The Chronicles of Narnia: The Lion, The Witch, and The Wardrobe* [Motion Picture]. Walt Disney Pictures and Walden Media.

5. C.S. Lewis, *The Chronicles of Narnia.* 1976, 7-volume box set. (New York: Macmillan Publishing Co., Inc., 1956).

6. C.S. Lewis, *The Lion, The Witch and The Wardrobe.* (New York: Macmillan Publishing Co., Inc., 1956), 64.
   The whole quote reads,

   > "Safe?" said Mr. Beaver. "Don't you hear what Mrs. Beaver tells you? Who said anything about safe? 'Course he isn't safe. But he's good. He's the King, I tell you."

7. Flannery O'Connor, *Mystery and Manners: Occasional Prose.* Selected and Edited by Sally and Robert Fitzgerald. (New York: Farrar, Straud & Giroux, 1969). eBook Kindle edition (Sept. 2012), location 701.

8. C.S. Lewis, *The Magician's Nephew.* (New York: Macmillan Publishing Co., Inc., 1956), 90.
9. Eric Metaxas, *Bonhoeffer: Pastor, Martyr, Prophet, Spy.* (Nashville: Thomas Nelson, 2010), 69.
10. Westminster Presbyterian Church, 3900 West End Avenue, Nashville, TN.

CHAPTER 6
1. www.christpres.org
2. Esther 4: 14
3. Merriam-Webster's Collegiate Dictionary, Eleventh Edition. (Springfield, MA: Merriam-Webster, Inc., 2012). 598.
4. Scotty Smith, April 6 of *Everyday Prayers: 365 Days to a Gospel-Centered Faith.* (Grand Rapids, MI: Baker Books, 2011), 110.

CHAPTER 7
1. Thank you doesn't really seem to express my gratitude to our Summer 2012 senders, but "Thank You" anyway... for the eternal and powerful work of which you are a crucial part: Ann and Mac Gober, Susan and Denny Ragland, Pam and Larry Hodges, Catherine Hodges (1923-2014), Beth and Beaver Garza, Melissa and Kurt Koehn, Stacey Peterson, Janet and Gary Greene, Vanessa and David Schweihs, Rhonda and Scott Sims, Stephanie and Jim Edwards, Margie and Jackson Moore, Lindsey and Jay McRae, Kathy and Scott Brown, Brenda and James Adair, Debbi and Paul King, Cindy and Steve Kessleman, Claire and Grant Jordan, Poppy and Brian Driskell, Beth and Mike Jones, Lindsey and Michael Purifoy, Elizabeth Robinson, Betsy and Joe Thomas, Katharine and Matthew Breaux, Jennie and Ben Brewer, Anna and Justin Gilmore, Ted and Jeanne Melcher, Judy and Ed Dorris, Zac and Alli Campbell, Lindsley and John Long, and my church, West End Community Church

2. God has given Bob Goff a gigantic heart for Uganda, as well. For more on Bob Goff (and more on loving God and living large), please read one of my favorite books, *Love Does: Discover a Secretly Incredible Life in an Ordinary World.* (Nashville: Thomas Nelson, 2012).

3. These objections may sound familiar, as with those who disagree with or play devil's advocate to David Platt's book *Radical*, Richard Stearnes' *A Hole in Our Gospel*, or Francis Chan's book *Crazy Love.* Ibid. I also recommend reading *Anything* by Jennie Allen. (Nashville: W Publishing, 2011).

4. Paul Miller, *A Praying Life: Connecting with God in a Distracting World.* (Colorado Springs: NavPress, 2009), 37.

5. www.visitingorphans.org

6. A *huge* thank you to Susanna Singleton for conducting a taped interview with Mustafa for me on a subsequent trip.

7. Mzungu means "white person."

8. Steve Holy, (2001). Good Morning Beautiful. [Co-Written by Zack Lyle and Todd Cerney.] On *Blue Moon.* Curb Records.

9. Beyoncé, (2008). Single Ladies (Put a Ring On It). [Co-Written with Terius "The-Dream" Nash, Thaddis "Kuk" Harrell, and Christopher "Tricky" Stewart]. On *I am... Sasha Fierce.* Sony BMG.

10. Jerry Trousdale, *Miraculous Movements: How Hundreds of Thousands of Muslims Are Falling in Love with Jesus.* (Nashville: Thomas Nelson, 2012). 52-53. An inspiring read for those with hearts for Muslim friends – "Discover the sometimes humorous, often sobering, but encouraging true stories of how Muslim leaders and entire communities are embracing Christ" (from the back cover of the book).

11. John Newton, *Amazing Grace.* (1779).

12. Brooke and Steven Edging:
    www.facebook.com/missionsedge/ and
    www.theedgings.blogspot.com and
    www.missionsedge.com
13. www.ekisa.org
14. www.twomenandatruck.com
15. *We Fall Down.* [Written by Kyle David Matthews].

CHAPTER 8
1. Ibid, 29.
2. Eugene H. Peterson. *The Message: The Bible in Contemporary Language.* (Colorado Springs: NavPress, 2002.)

CHAPTER 9
1. *O: Cirque Du Soleil.* Dir. Franco Dragon. Guy Laliberté, Founder and Creative Guide. Performed at the Bellagio Las Vegas, 2012.
2. Joseph M. Scriven, *What a Friend We Have in Jesus.* (1855). Music by Charles C. Converse.
3. Public Broadcasting Service. Television.
4. Brooke and Steven Edging. Ibid.
5. My Grandy was a Lt. Col. in the Air Force, attended law school, passed the bar exam, took accounting classes, sat for his CPA exam, worked a lifelong career with the Tennessee Valley Authority... and all of this from nothing, as a child of the Great Depression.
    From his paper route as a very young child, he worked hard and knew the value of a dollar. He taught me the importance of saving. When my brother and I were little, he took us to Baskin-Robbins for ice cream. He later told us it killed him to spend so much on an ice cream cone! But he did just about anything and everything for both of us: from vacations and trips, to helping with our first car, education and college.

Grandy also sowed Crimson blood in our family line. He took my dad to football games growing up, during Bear Bryant's reign at The University of Alabama – despite the fact that my dad attended college at The University of Tennessee, he remains a die-hard Bama fan to this day... as do I.

Grandy taught me what a gentleman looked like – he taught me that a man should walk on the street-side of the sidewalk, should help me up and down stairs and in and out of cars, and should hold my door every time. Be he taught me far more than that – he was my hero.

I introduced him to everyone who was anyone to me, and when Adam asked my dad to marry me in 1999, he made a separate appointment with Grandy, to ask for my hand. When I walked down the aisle toward Adam in 2000, my dad was on my left, and Grandy was on my right.

I have memories of Grandy too numerous to count, and I miss him every day. He bought me my first laptop in 2007, and he always encouraged me in my studies, my pursuits and my dreams – including my decision to start writing.

6. I'm not sure Dr. Hildebrand knows how much of an impact he had on my life. I looked him up, however, while finishing this book, and it appears he is still at UNC. I plan to send him a copy of the book, along with a thank you!
http://history.unc.edu/people/faculty/reginald-f-hildebrand/

7. Ibid.

8. Ibid.

9. Ibid.

10. Crocs Corporation www.crocs.com We made a formal request to "Crocs" to donate, but we were unsuccessful. However, church and community members generously donated the gently used shoes.

11. Ibid.

12. Ibid, 35-36.

13. Logos Bookstore, owned by Ken Najar. 4012 Hillsboro Pike #6, Nashville, TN 37215

14. Ibid, 174.

15. Diana Beach Batarseh. www.askmewhooo.com

16. Margaret Wise Brown, *Runaway Bunny*. Illustrated by Clement Hurd. (New York: Harper Collins, 1942).

17. There is a wonderful C.S. Lewis quote that also summarizes what God has done in my life: "Imagine yourself as a living house. God comes in to rebuild that house. At first, perhaps, you can understand what he is doing. He is getting the drains right and stopping the leaks in the roof and so on; you knew that those jobs needed doing and so you are not surprised. But presently he starts knocking the house about in a way that hurts abominably and does not seem to make any sense. What on earth is He up to? The explanation is that He is building quite a different house than the one you thought of – throwing out a new wing here, putting on an extra floor there, running up towers, making courtyards. You thought you were being made into a decent little cottage: but He is building a palace. He intends to come and live in it Himself." From *Mere Christianity*. (San Francisco: Harper Collins Edition, 2001), 205.

18. Psalm 36: 7

19. Isaiah 11: 1

20. Rev. 2: 7, 22: 2, 22: 14

21. Gillian Welch. (1996.) Orphan Girl. On *Revival*. Almo Sounds.

CHAPTER 10

1. This chapter would not have been possible without Sam Crenshaw. He interviewed Isaac for me in 2013, which helped immensely for 2 reasons: I was not on the trip; also,

it was more appropriate for a man to do the interview. Sam, I am forever indebted to you!

2. Timothy Keller with Katherine Leary Alsdorf. *Every Good Endeavor: Connecting Your Work to God's Work.* (New York: Dutton, 2012). 181-182.

3. Sadly, there are articles everywhere such as: Sachar Kidron, "Is an Open Marriage the Secret to Keeping Love Alive?" *Haaretz.* Haaretz Daily Newspaper Ltd., July 26, 2015. Web. http://www.haaretz.com/israel-news/.premium-1.667407 Bella DePaulo, Ph.D., "Keeping Marriage Alive with Affairs, Asexuality, Polyamory, and Living Apart." *Psychology Today.* Sussex Publishers LLC, June 2, 2011. Web. https://www.psychologytoday.com/blog/living-single/201106/keeping-marriage-alive-affairs-asexuality-polyamory-and-living-apart Gabrielle Robin, " It's not about the sex': The case for open relationships." Salon. Salon Media Group, Inc., Mar. 7, 2015. Web. http://www.salon.com/2015/03/08/it's_not_about_the_sex_the_case_for_open_relationships_partner/

4. *I'm in the Lord's Army.* Anonymous. Sung to the tune of the old folk song, *The Old Gray Mare.* (Unknown author.)

5. Though all of these people are highlighted in any good study Bible, I highly recommend these books by Ann Spangler for further study:
Ann Spangler and Robert D. Wolgemuth. *Men of the Bible.* (Grand Rapids: Zondervan, 2002).
Ann Spangler and Jean E. Syswerda. *Women of the Bible.* (Grand Rapids: Zondervan, 2007).

6. A saying I adore, from the book I adore by Kathryn Stockett. *The Help.* (New York: Penguin Group, 2009).

7. Sabine Baring-Gould. *Onward Christian Soldiers.* (1865.) Music by Arthur S. Sullivan.

EPILOGUE

1. *147 Million Orphans*, an organization founded and run by Gwen Oatsvall and Suzanne Mayernick, Co-CEO's. www.147millionorphans.com

2. Harpeth Hall School, 3801 Hobbs Road, Nashville, TN 37215

Acknowledgements

There are so many people to thank that I cannot possibly thank them all here (including the many friends and supporters of Family Spirit). God has woven so many people into this story, and He continues to write more in still.

Yet I have to start somewhere, so I will start with those who first planted seeds deep in my heart, even as they were sowing seeds on the mission field, many in Africa.

To Angela Stem Mills, I cannot even begin to thank you appropriately here, but I have a feeling I will be able to aptly express myself in Heaven. Would you have ever guessed God could have used you in the salvation story of someone like me? I thank my God every time I remember you...

Thank you to all who have labored on the continent of Africa – your stories, ministries and lives have been extremely impactful to me in countless ways. Thank you to the Brovets, from Raleigh, N.C., who labored in South Africa, and to the Elders who lived and worked there more recently. To the Crowders, who serve in South Sudan and Kenya with *SIM*. I love you, Beverly. To Emily Huff with *Share International*.

Thank you to Quincee Gideon, battling the brokenness of the children in Africa with *The Nameless Project*. She is another gal living large and loving big in Uganda.

Thank you to Brooke and Steven Edging from West End Community Church, for being our permanent hands and feet in Uganda.

Thank you to Richard Stearns and Bono (and U2), whom I have never met. For your witness and your powerful words and for your actions of comfort and hope. God has crowned you with glory and honor for such a time as this. Your ministries have so powerfully touched millions, of whom I am just *one*. Thank you for your words (and your lyrics), for fighting the good fight. You have engendered passionate resolve, purpose and courage in my own heart. You can find Richard at *Compassion International* and in his unbelievable books, *The Hole in our Gospel, He Walks Among Us,* and *Unfinished.* And you can find U2, *well,* just about anywhere.

Thank you to Katie Davis Majors, whom I first met during *Amazima's* infancy at a fundraiser that Adam and I co-hosted with Anne and Nate Morrow. Thank you, Katie, for sparking something within all of us. I pray one day the story in Masindi will look something like the story in Jinja. And I pray for even more people to link arms with Uganda... Africa... the World, until all of our smaller stories overlap in His Greater Story.

Thank you to the Maddux family at our church for adopting your precious boys from Jinja. For bringing Anne and Mandy into your story, that the Morrows and the Gallaghers would also eventually feel called to Africa to adopt. Thank you to the Doyles for following calls to adopt from Masindi (and from Jinja).

Thank you to the journey girls for being there when it all started with Anne. To Lindsey Purifoy, Misty Trone, Jennie Brewer, Rachel White, Beth Garza, Betsy Thomas, Karen Logan. And thank you to the core group of our women's Sunday school class for the exact same thing. To Lindsey McRae, Stephanie Edwards, Rachel Ladner, Elizabeth Robinson... for continuing to be such wonderful friends every day. Love you all so much.

In addition to the Morrows and Doyles mentioned above, thank you to the rest of our Masindi Fellowship group for sending and for going. For praying without ceasing. To the Freemans, the Gages, the Omers, the McRaes, and the Edwards. I love doing life with you all; I love being a part of this story with you.

Thank you Stephanie, my dear prayer partner. We have only just begun to taste the miracles that are wrought from the hand of our Father in heaven who hears our every plea. Thank you for walking with me through many years and through supplication of every kind. I love you, sister.

267

To Rachel Ladner, Randy Morrison, Sam Crenshaw. For making us laugh harder than we ever have. For your continued support financially. For your prayers and friendship. To Sam, for your continued service. I knew in the prayer room at West End you had caught the bug, like I, before ever stepping foot in the red dirt....

And thank you to the McRaes for going on this trip also; Lindsey, you are the reason it happened!

Thank you to the high school students and other members of Christ Presbyterian Church and of our church, West End Community Church, for helping us love the people of Uganda. For playing your hearts out in the mud and for sweating and laboring for the Gospel with us. Thank you again to Susanna Singleton for recording Mustafa's story, and again to Sam for interviewing Isaac!!!

Thank you to Candice Ashburn Moore for incorporating our smaller mission into your greater ministry, for a time, and to Bob Goff for many things... among them speaking out for the least and the lost, prisoner and judge, orphan and widow... but thank you most of all for stepping out of your tree house office to help us ALL. You can find Candice at *Her Passion Minsitries / Passion Partners*. You can find Bob in his book *Love Does* (His phone number is in the back).

Thank you to Mustafa, Joel, and of course to Susan and Isaac for the calling you so tirelessly follow. Your sacrifice and obedience to do His will are beyond comparison – we are all so grateful for the thankless job you do. Thank you for your many prayers, your perseverance and your longsuffering. God is using you to "work all things into good." He is weaving your own redemption into ours and into the lives of so many little ones.

Thank you to George of Paraa Lodge – here is to many more lion sightings. Thank you for calling Aslan for me on your cell phone. Thank you to everyone at Masindi Hotel, and to Tom at Adonai House in Kampala for graciously hosting us so many times.

Thank you to Beth Roberts for your tireless help with the beautiful website, www.untilitoverflows.com. Thank you for playing your crucial part in this story. I cannot believe what has happened in one year (since November 2014)... it started with you.

Thank you to my Covenant cheerleaders: Heather Schnoor, Ginger Hyatt, Nicole Boylan, Christina Holling and Jamie Morrison. And to my other cheerleaders: Beth Jones, Catha Skinner, Carole Peterson, Libby Glisson, Marie Foresman, Lori Morrison, Lana Myers, Kristi McDougal, Lindsley Long, Emarie Irvine, Reba Sloan, Beth Miller, Kathy Collins, Kimberly Cook, Julia Lammert, Kimberly Naranjo, Julie Thompson, Kate Griffin, Cindy Lee, Tammy Fisher, Rebekah Conley, Alli Campbell, Boyd Long, Abney Harper, MC Phillips, Claire Parker and my summer women's Bible Study (2015) with Lindsey Doyle! Thank you to Stacey Peterson from the very beginning... Finally, to Emma and Kate!

To Larry Bolden, and to ALL of my battle team members past and present: Lindsey Purifoy, Judy Dorris, Lori Hooven, Betty Ashton Mayo, Rachel White, Karen Logan, Amy Robbins and Laura Armistead. This book is a product of your prayers. You have given me courage and offered me protection. Thank you for bringing me before God and standing beside me "to run the race that is set before me."

Especially to Laura Armistead, thank you. Thank you for giving up weeks of your life to edit this book. I cannot believe how God provided for me in and through YOU! Thank you for playing your irreplaceable part in His Larger Story. This book simply would not have happened without you. Besides your wisdom and expertise, thank you for listening to my fears, understanding my tears, and *literally* for fighting the battle with me. I consider you the General – thank you for giving me orders and keeping me on track. Thank you for your beautiful green editorial boxes and for your perfect suggestions! I could not have made it to the end without you – I will never stop thanking God.... And I will never forget seeing my cover page for the first time.

Thank you, Mom and Dad. I am not sure my marriage would have endured hell without knowing that you both had already been through it – *and survived.* I couldn't have gone to Africa (three times) or written a word without your help (with the kids and beyond). Thank you for providing childcare for our kids and money for (our other) kids in Masindi. Dad, your relationship with Jesus inspires me each and every day. Thank you for making me feel "radiant." Mom, your life is a living testimony to God's hope, mercy and grace. You are beautiful inside and out. Thank you for encouraging me, holding my hand, holding my heart... I love you both. And to Doc – one day soon we will make the trip together! Love you!

Thank you to my sweet Hannah Whit; we will go back again soon! *Be joyful in hope; patient in affliction; faithful in prayer* (Rom. 12: 12).

Thank you to my strong and sensitive Austin; I know you are ready! *...the Lord said to me, "Do not say, 'I am too young.' You must go to everyone I send you to and say whatever I command you"* (Jer. 1: 7).

Thank you to my lion-hearted Liam; God is just opening your eyes. *Be strong and courageous. Do not be afraid; do not be discouraged, for the Lord your God will be with you wherever you go* (Joshua 1: 9).

To my hero husband, thank you. "Zero to hero," is how you put it. I can scarcely find words. I love that I can say, "Miracles never cease," and mean it literally. *Many, O Lord my God, are the wonders you have done, the things you planned for us. None can compare with you; were I to speak and tell of your deeds, they would be too many to declare* (Ps. 40: 5). Thank you for fighting for my heart, providing and protecting. Thank you for breathing life into my love for Masindi and supporting Family Spirit with me. You are always in the top of your field, continually number one to our kids, and you are forever the champion of my heart. You believed in me when I didn't believe in myself. I look forward to reading your first book, too...

And to my Jesus. *There is no one else but You.* I love you.

Bonus Material | A 14-Day Devotional

Day One

Liam "Fierce Protector & Guardian of Will" Hodges has only 2 inner natures –One is a still sea. The other is a howling hurricane. There are few in-betweens. This child does not do gentle rains, steady downpours, nor even thunder and lightening. He is sunny skies and a gentle breeze, or he is an island overtaken by a gale force tempest. 0 to 60 faster than a Ferrari.

A few weeks ago, the seas were stirring like a cyclone – he was sobbing and screaming in the den. But much to my surprise, he went to his room to calm down: The. First. Time. I. Asked. Him.

I've grown, perhaps, in parental consistency. He's grown in his ability to self-regulate. But more than that, Jesus' love has taken root in his heart, and I've been seeing foliage and fruit.

I heard Liam that day, as he continued to moan and carry-on from his room. After five minutes or so, however, Hannah Whit came tearing out of her own room down the hall to the den, where I was holding my breath – and my tongue. She said, "Mommy! I just overheard Liam praying about his behavior, and then he said, 'Jesus, will you take my day, and clean it up... And make it shiny?'"

Jesus calms the storms that rage within us. He turns our hurricanes into safe harbors and brings rest to the squalls in our souls and circumstances.

{Matthew 11: 25-26, 28-30 ESV}

At that time, Jesus declared, "Thank you, Father, Lord of heaven and earth, that you have hidden these things from the wise and understanding and revealed them to little children; yes, Father, for such was your gracious will... Come to me, all who labor and are heavy laden, and I will give you rest. Take my yoke upon you, and learn from me, for I am gentle and lowly in heart, and you will find rest for your souls. For my yoke is easy, and my burden is light."

When Adam and I dropped our girl off for her very first week of overnight camp, I could tell she was nervous. I held back my own tears (and that is no small feat), so I wouldn't send us both into an emotional tailspin. Adam was apparently doing the same thing. He was reassuring and stoic until we got back in the car together, at which point he confessed he got choked up making that top bunk for her, baby pictures flashing through his mind.

How did this happen? What were we thinking? How did we get here? If we are honest, aren't those the questions that send us off on every great adventure? Sam asks Frodo in Tolkien's classic, "I wonder what sort of a tale we've fallen into?"

And in Lewis' *Narnia*, when Lucy discovered snow in the back of the wardrobe, she "felt a little frightened, but she felt very inquisitive and excited as well."

In the spirit of life's adventures, I asked Adam to give me a scripture that best describes God's gallant heart. After all, the man has an affinity for adventure and an impressive resume of exploits which includes (but is not limited to) 11 "fourteeners," a Mt. Ranier summit, and staring straight up any vertical wall of ice with highly questionable charisma.

Adam offers the story of Zacchaeus. Here are his three reasons:
(1) Any true adventure summons us to look not only outward, but also inward. Zacchaeus is drawn not only to the beauty of Jesus, but also to the beauty of his own brokenness.
(2) A true adventure captivates us and propels us to do something radical. Physically Zacchaeus climbs the tree to behold Christ. Spiritually, he gives up his wealth and his theft to FOLLOW Christ.
(3) A true adventure gives us single-minded focus. Zacchaeus overcame the physical limitations of his shorter stature and found a way to see. Spiritually as well, he could "see" the truth, hope, and life that Jesus offered so clearly that he could ignore the lies and silence the naysayers.

{Luke 19: 1-10 NIV}

<u>Day Three</u>

I spent a few months steeping in Isaiah 30. Just when I thought I had mined it all, God ground out another gold nugget for me. Like this one:

"You said, 'No…'"

{Isaiah 30: 16 NIV}

How often do I flat out tell God, "NO!" Big ways, little ways, many ways. I'm not *trying* to say No; I don't WANT to say No. But I'm just so good at it that sometimes "NO" comes as second nature... Sin nature. Like Jonah.

Of course, this would one of Liam's favorite stories in the *Jesus Storybook Bible*. Of course, that story pushes that "No-Nugget" further into my heart. God tells Jonah (*He doesn't ask*), "GO!" and here's what happens, in a God-tell nutshell:

- •Jonah runs. God relents.
- •Jonah's request. God's rescue.
- •Jonah repents. God repeats.
- •Jonah rages. God responds.

(Then God, quite literally, has the last word.)

One morning, I was in the kitchen calling Liam for breakfast. And calling. And calling. Where did I finally find him? Outside. On top of my car. Why? Because he's Liam. Who knows why? (I've never found him there before, and I haven't found him there since.)

But it made me wonder, where will I be when GOD calls ME? And will I come when he calls? Will I go where He tells me to go? Will I say YES?

I've been sensing God is up to something, though I don't know what exactly, but I am listening and waiting. And I find it convicting, and a little funny, and a little sad, that He has to remind me FIRST, "Don't say, 'No,' when I tell you... "

Though I don't know where God will call me or what He will tell me, I am praying (now) for the preemptive obedience and forward-faith to give Him an affirmative. When God says "GO," I don't want to say "NO."

Day Four

We were reaching for a new habit, family devotion time, and this prayer from Prophet Austin: "Dear God, When Mommy thanked you for Aslan (our dog), and for your creation, like the beach, it reminded me when Aslan (the Lion) was walking on the beach in the movie and the waves seemed to bow down to him, to grab at him. Lord, just like little pieces of sand in our toes, you grow little faith to big faith, you take little seeds and make mighty oaks."

This is the kid who told us, when he was 5 or 6, that he wanted to go to "pastor school." We told him indeed, maybe God was calling him to be a pastor, but he had to graduate high school first.

He clarified, "No, I'm talking about the 'pastor school' I can go to right now – the one the pastor teaches on Sunday morning before church... (slight misunderstanding about being able to attend adult Sunday school as a Kindergartner)"

{Hebrews 11:1 NKJV}

Now faith is the substance of things hoped for, the evidence of things not seen. For by it the elders obtained a good testimony.

What a great translation of this bedrock verse! I long for a life filled with solid SUBSTANCE: physical proof of the invisible Spirit who has wooed and captivated my heart (like Noah building a mammoth boat with a faith that "loosened the great deep and opened the windows of heaven!" Heb. 11: 7 and Gen. 7:11... Any coincidence with the reversal of numbers there? Doubt it.)

I want a life where God takes seeds, small as granules of sand, and produces mighty multitudes: waves of overflowing EVIDENCE of His existence (like Sarah laughing at the good pleasure of the Lord's love AND leaving a legacy of laughter in the life of Isaac; Heb. 11: 11, Gen. 21: 3, 6)!

"And what more shall I say?" I long for a GOOD TESTIMONY to the lion-like power and presence of Jesus that is born from surrender to my Savior (like "Gideon and Barak and Samson and Jephthah, also of David and Samuel and the prophets" (Heb. 11: 32).

<u>Day Five</u>

One Sunday, the amazing Randy Pope (from Perimeter Presbyterian in Atlanta) preached at West End. His topic: Romans 6. I had listened to that particular sermon previously, but I was thrilled to hear it again because it is one of my all-time favorites on daily living and the reality of our pervasive struggle with sin - or I will speak for myself, "...*MY* pervasive struggle with sin."

So, I spent a couple of weeks reflecting on Romans 6 during my quiet time, so powerful is the message, and so well-communicated by Randy (Go to: https://www.perimeter.org/pages/worship/randy-pope-recommends/ and click on the music note icon for the MP3, "How to be Filled with the Spirit.")

It is not only a future promise for the believer in Christ- it is a present reality, an everyday TRUTH on which we can stand. This post is for you, but it is especially for me – I'm raising this passage as an Ebenezer ("a memorial of God's great help and deliverance," NIV Life Application Study Bible note).

My Bible also says, "During tough times, we may need to remember the crucial turning points in our past to help us through the present. Memorials can help us remember God's past victories and gain confidence and strength for the present."

Then Samuel took a stone and set it up between Mizpah and Shen. He named it Ebenezer, saying, "Thus far the Lord has helped us."

{1 Samuel 7: 12 NIV}

The Lord rescued the Israelites from death at the hands of the Philistines. And He has rescued us from death itself through Jesus. Death has no hold eternally, for those in Christ - nor does sin, darkness or evil have any rule, reign or mastery over us. "Here I raise my Ebenezer, here by Thy great help I've come... Come Thou fount of every blessing."

My Ebenezer is this: Jesus Christ. He was raised on a cross and then raised from the dead. "Thus far, I have come" by his birth, by his life, by his blood... through his sacrifice, in his death and through his resurrection... through the gifts of His Holy Spirit and His Word.

Day Six

Then Samuel took a stone and set it up between Mizpah and Shen. He named it Ebenezer, saying, "Thus far the Lord has helped us."

{1 Samuel 7: 12 NIV}

Sometimes it is good to sit on a particular verse or in a particular passage for more than just one day! Day Six builds upon Day Five...

In my 5th grade girls' Sunday School class, we carried one analogy through the parables of Jesus –

Our nothingness (we are spiritually bankrupt apart from Christ)
and
HIS EVERYTHING
(He is **'I AM:'** omnipotent, omniscient, almighty, perfectly just, full of love.)

For example, we start with an empty thirst (physically, emotionally, etc.), and He gives us streams of living water (John 7: 37-39).

We bring nothing but hunger (empty stomachs and spiritual longings of all kinds), and He is the Bread of Life (John 6:35).

We carry death (2 Cor. 4: 10); He offers resurrected life (John 11).

We have nothing/are nothing/bring nothing to the table... without Christ who says, "Only one thing is needed..." (Luke 10: 42). And it is a person.
And it is Jesus. And He is everything. He was raised on a cross as the ultimate Ebenezer (stone of help and deliverance).

"So this is what the sovereign Lord says: 'See, I lay a stone in Zion, a tested stone, precious cornerstone for a sure foundation; the one who relies on it will never be stricken with panic' (Isaiah 28: 16)."

"And I, when I am lifted up from the earth, will draw all people to myself" (John 12: 32).

<u>Day Seven</u>

I am still speechless over a recent gift I received from my Dad - a necklace, along with a card, that arrived in the mail.

Why is it that gifts can be so powerful, words even more powerful, and maybe most powerful of all when they are given by a father? I think it is because our fathers have probably the most unique opportunity and ability to channel the immeasurable love and truth of our Heavenly Father. I feel so loved and so "RADIANT" (the word engraved on the necklace), and I cannot stop welling up with tears...

Because my Dad presented a mirror to me of my Abba in Heaven, who is the ultimate giver of every good gift (James 1: 17), and who not only speaks words of love, hope, encouragement, truth, and beauty, but who also IS THE WORD, made flesh (John 1: 1).

Thank you seems to fall short, but I am thankful (and still speechless).

{Psalm 34: 5a NIV}

Those who look to Him are radiant...

<u>Day Eight</u>

I once texted a friend, "One day I'm up; one day I'm down."

Shows me that my faith is often more tied to my circumstances than it is to MY GOD.

Sometimes I feel like I'm straddling Heaven and earth- one foot in the Word, one foot in the world. Sometimes, try as I might, I cannot make the two ends meet.

The reality is that I do nothing; He did it all.

I can pray my confusion, "Lord, I do believe; help me overcome my unbelief" (Mark 9: 24).

Jesus mediates the mystery of this condition, so the Father looks on me with love, not disappointment. I have a Savior who bridged Heaven and earth- He has made near those who were once far away (Eph. 2: 13).

This is the Good News of the Gospel: He has done what I could not. He is doing what I cannot. My circumstances may change, but my God does not.

{Isaiah 54: 10 NIV}

"Though the mountains be shaken and the hills be removed, yet my unfailing love for you will not be shaken, nor my covenant of peace be removed," says the Lord, who has compassion on you.

<u>Day Nine</u>

I was once told that I will not have a large impact on orphans in Africa until I have a large platform. True bad news. Check out my numbers- just a tiny drop in the vast ocean of social media.

Like Paul says, "I am less than the least of all the Lord's people," (Eph. 3: 8).

I am a nobody in the eyes of our culture, as are those sweet orphans, I might add. Marginalized, relatively unimportant to the masses. Nameless nobodies in a world where success is defined by money, influence and fame. The world tells us that it is a numbers game.

I won't deny the reality of my circumstances, but I'm not trusting in them either (...she says, as she preaches to herself).

"Some trust in chariots and some in horses, but we trust in the name of the Lord our God" (Ps. 20: 7).

Have you ever faced a giant like Goliath or an impenetrable and fortified city like Jericho? Remember with me, and take heart, "Do not be afraid or discouraged because of this vast army. For the battle is not yours, but God's" (2 Chron. 20: 15b).

You are not forgotten, nor am I, and never will He leave His children as orphans. (John 14: 18).

Since my earthly platform is tiny, like granules of shifting sand between my toes, I'll trust in the solid rock underneath my feet. That Rock Is Christ (1 Cor. 10: 4).

{Deuteronomy 9: 3a & Deuteronomy 31: 8 NIV}

Be assured today that the Lord your God is the one who goes across ahead of you...

The Lord himself goes before you and will be with you; he will never leave you nor forsake you. Do not be afraid; do not be discouraged.

<u>Day Ten</u>

If you feel confused, know this: Jesus is clarity. He says, "Wait. It will become clear" (Is. 30: 18, 21).

If you feel sad, know this: Jesus is joy. He says, "Wait... weeping may stay for the night, but rejoicing comes in the morning" (Ps. 30: 5b).

If you feel hopeless, know this: Jesus is hope. He says, "Wait. I am your portion. I am good to those whose hope is in me" (Lam. 3: 21-26).

If you feel helpless or anxious, know this: Jesus is power and peace. He says, "NO NEED TO WAIT- HELP IS ALREADY HERE" (Ps. 33: 20, Ps. 118: 7, Heb. 13: 6).

What a friend we have in Jesus!! What a friend He has left us, to live in our hearts...

{John 14: 26-27 AMP}

But the Helper [Comforter, Advocate, Intercessor - Counselor, Strengthener, Standby], the Holy Spirit, whom the Father will send in my name [in my place to act on my behalf], He will teach you all things. And He will help you remember everything that I have told you. Peace I leave with you; my [perfect] peace I give to you; not as the world gives do I give to you. Do not let your heart be troubled, nor let it be afraid. [Let my perfect peace calm you in every circumstance and give you courage and strength for every challenge.]

<u>Day Eleven</u>

I have felt God calling me to do something that seems monumentally impossible. It always amazes me how well he loves me through my friends. God's timing is always perfect and His encouragement through His body is powerful! This was written by my friend Christina Holling:

You are His **poiema** (Greek – "a work of God"). You are His **masterpiece**!

At our elementary school cross-country meet, there was a little girl who got trampled near the starting line. (It's always interesting that it's human nature to start with intensity, and then we become exhausted and run without that intensity we had at the beginning.)

The little girl was hurt, heartbroken and embarrassed. My natural instinct as a mother was to run out on the course and hold her. She didn't want to run anymore, but I didn't want her to not finish, even if she walked and was the last one across the finish line. So I held her sweet little hand and walked the course with her while she settled down, and then I looked at her and asked, "You wanna start running again?"

She did, and I cheered her on and met her at the finish line grabbing her in celebration!

I tell you this because I want you to have that encouragement in your life, too. I pray that when you get trampled on the course, that you know what it feels like to have God running out, holding you tight, and walking hand in hand towards the finish line. He's going to meet you at the end and pick you up, hug you tight, and twirl you around...I can see it now. Continue to show those kids in Africa how amazing they are. They are God's masterpiece!

{Ephesians 1: 17-19 ESV}

I pray... that the God of our Lord Jesus Christ, the Father of glory, may give you the Spirit of wisdom and of revelation in the knowledge of him, having the eyes of your hearts enlightened, that you may know what is the hope to which he has called you, what are the riches of his glorious inheritance in the saints, and what is the immeasurable greatness of his power toward us who believe, according to the working of his great might...

Day Twelve

Have you ever found yourself thinking, "Wait. What just happened?"

Or, "Hold on. Things are not going according to [my] plans."

When our circumstances don't line up with our intentions and desires, we have two options:

(A) a host of negative behaviors stemming from a host of negative emotions

(B) contentment that comes from surrendering negative emotions and trusting in God despite circumstances.

My youngest child is choosing option B more and more- it is not only miraculous, but it is also contagious. God has plenty to teach me through observing and parenting my children, but as I watch my youngest joyfully surrender, God continues to challenge me to take a second look at *my own* contentment.

"...I have learned to be content whatever the circumstances. I know what it is to be in need, and I know what it is to have plenty. I have learned the secret of being content in any and every situation, whether well fed or hungry, whether living in plenty or in want. I can do all things through him who gives me strength" (Phil. 4: 11-13).

God continues to remind me [and convict me]- in every circumstance and in every way- "I've got this. No, really. I've got... IT... ALL. You can trust me with EVERYTHING."

{Proverbs 16: 9 NIV}

In their hearts, humans plan their course, but the Lord establishes their steps.

Day Thirteen

Are you in a place where it appears you have exhausted all your options?

Think you've done everything there is to do?

 Feel like your back is up against the wall?

Stand firm then...

My sweet friend Beth Jones always has encouraging nuggets of truth to speak over me: "Stand firm then," she told me when I thought I was at the end of my rope.

In Christ, we are never passive. Even our silent, still waiting can be an active choice to stand firm.

And of course, we should also, "Pray in the Spirit on all occasions with all kinds of prayers. With this in mind, be alert and always keep on praying for all the Lord's people" (Eph. 6: 18).

Simply put – "Pray without ceasing" (1 Thess. 5: 17).

Our very real enemy is never passive, nor should we be. There may be days when we are not advancing, but retreating is not an option, "for we are not unaware of [Satan's] schemes" (2 Cor. 2: 11).

STAND FIRM.

{Ephesians 6: 10-20 NIV}

"...and after you have done everything, to stand. Stand firm then..." (v. 13-14)

<u>Day Fourteen</u>

One rainy day, not too long ago, the metal drain system funneling water off the back of my house was so loud, I could hear it inside the house - with the back door closed!! I started thanking God that we didn't have a bedroom near this end of the house, when He reminded me that this is His analogy for a quarrelsome wife!

I'm not going to give anybody a lecture about nagging today, but I did think about this...

What if we were just as steadfast with our encouragement (as my drain was at dripping) and just as generous with words of life (as God is with the rain He sends)?

If it sounds this cacophonous to whine and to complain, to provoke and to pester... Then what does it look like to speak gracious words that comfort and cheer, refresh and restore?

Do everything without grumbling or arguing...

And what is the end result?

...That you will shine like stars in the sky (NIV)
...holding out and offering to everyone the Word of Life (AMP).

{Philippians 2: 14-16}

Words that give life do not rain on others' parades; they shine like stars in the sky! Not only that, our words of encouragement ultimately reflect *His* words of life and light- "the true light that gives light to everyone" (Jn. 1: 9).

Speak words often as a way to lavish love; be intentional about encouragement; send a letter or an email of thanksgiving and gratitude; call out God's glory in the lives of the people around you - look for the good and say it out loud.

And if you ARE a wife... do all of these things multiple times each day for a certain someone who needs to hear them around the clock!!

284

About The Author

I spent the first half of my life running. And searching. Running from one thing; searching for the next. Searching for things and people and experiences that promised to fill the gaping hole in my heart… things and people and experiences that over-promised and under-delivered. Then I found Jesus. Rather, He found me. Found me, though He knew where I was all along.

God boldly promises, and *over*-delivers…
"Immeasurably more than all that you can ask or imagine." **[Eph. 3:20]**

God was offering me life – overflowing life.

I came to Jesus like the walking dead. A whitewashed tomb. That looked fine on the outside, mostly pulled together – but was empty and cold on the inside. FULL – but only "full of the bones of the dead." [Matt. 23:27]

Who wants to be pulled together, anyway? Don't we want to be bursting with life at the seams?

His invitation, "Sleeper awake. Rise from the dead! And I will shine on you! Your dawn has come. Your life will be filled with my light. You are a new creation… the old has gone, the new has come!" [Eph. 5:14, 2 Cor. 5: 17]

When I came to Him, I was looking for a clean slate and a fresh start. But He offers far more than a second chance at life – He offers *a wholly new life*. I came to Him full of desire for more. And He gave me more than I could have desired. A life overflowing with…
Meaning. Purpose. Hope. Love. Healing. Intimacy. Romance. Adventure. Beauty.

I sensed my heart's deepest desires were FAR from changing. They were actually about to be met…. Realized… Fulfilled! To the fullest! In and through the person of Jesus. The giver of hope… of every good and perfect gift… of all good things.

I haven't stopped asking… And He hasn't stopped giving.

Jesus answered, "Everyone who drinks this water will be thirsty again, but whoever drinks the water I give them will never thirst. Indeed, the water I give them will become in them a spring of water welling up to eternal life…" [Jn. 4:14-15, 26]
[*continually flowing, bubbling over, gushing fountains of endless life*]

"Sir, give me this water…"
                    Then Jesus declared, *"I – the one speaking to you – I am he."*

You can find Allison at
www.untilitoverflows.com *& Instagram @untilitoverflows*
where she continues to post stories and photos from Masindi
and
where she writes other musings about
her walk with…
her love for…
her all in all –
Jesus